MORRISON

CREATIVITY, INC.

CREATIVITY, INC.

OVERCOMING THE UNSEEN FORCES THAT STAND IN THE WAY OF TRUE INSPIRATION

ED CATMULL

with Amy Wallace

RANDOM HOUSE
NEW YORK

Published by Random House, an imprint and division of Random House LLC,
a Penguin Random House Company, New York.

RANDOM HOUSE and the HOUSE colophon are registered trademarks
of Random House LLC.

A hardcover edition has been published in the United States by Random House,
an imprint and division of Random House LLC.

ISBN 978-0-553-84122-0
eBook ISBN 978-0-679-64450-7

Printed in the United States of America on acid-free paper

www.atrandom.com

89

Book design by Diane Hobbing

For Steve

CONTENTS

INTRODUCTION: LOST AND FOUND

Every morning, as I walk into Pixar Animation Studios—past the twenty-foot-high sculpture of Luxo Jr., our friendly desk lamp mascot, through the double doors and into a spectacular glass-ceilinged atrium where a man-sized Buzz Lightyear and Woody, made entirely of Lego bricks, stand at attention, up the stairs past sketches and paintings of the characters that have populated our fourteen films—I am struck by the unique culture that defines this place. Although I've made this walk thousands of times, it never gets old.

Built on the site of a former cannery, Pixar's fifteen-acre campus, just over the Bay Bridge from San Francisco, was designed, inside and out, by Steve Jobs. (Its name, in fact, is The Steve Jobs Building.) It has well-thought-out patterns of entry and egress that encourage people to mingle, meet, and communicate. Outside, there is a soccer field, a volleyball court, a swimming pool, and a six-hundred-seat amphitheater. Sometimes visitors misunderstand the place, thinking it's fancy for fancy's sake. What they miss is that the unifying idea for this building isn't luxury but community. Steve wanted the building to support our work by enhancing our ability to collaborate.

The animators who work here are free to—no, encouraged to—decorate their work spaces in whatever style they wish. They spend their days inside pink dollhouses whose ceilings are hung with miniature chandeliers, tiki huts made of real bamboo, and castles whose meticulously painted, fifteen-foot-high styrofoam turrets appear to be carved from stone. Annual company traditions include "Pixarpalooza," where our in-house rock bands battle for dominance, shredding their hearts out on stages we erect on our front lawn.

The point is, we value self-expression here. This tends to make a big impression on visitors, who often tell me that the experience of walking into Pixar leaves them feeling a little wistful, like something is missing in their work lives—a palpable energy, a feeling of collaboration and unfettered creativity, a sense, not to be corny, of possibility. I respond by telling them that the feeling they are picking up on—call it exuberance or irreverence, even whimsy—is integral to our success.

But it's not what makes Pixar special.

What makes Pixar special is that we acknowledge we will always have problems, many of them hidden from our view; that we work hard to uncover these problems, even if doing so means making ourselves uncomfortable; and that, when we come across a problem, we marshal all of our energies to solve it. This, more than any elaborate party or turreted workstation, is why I love coming to work in the morning. It is what motivates me and gives me a definite sense of mission.

There was a time, however, when my purpose here felt a lot less clear to me. And it might surprise you when I tell you when.

On November 22, 1995, *Toy Story* debuted in America's theaters and became the largest Thanksgiving opening in history. Critics heralded it as "inventive" (*Time*), "brilliant" and "exultantly witty" (*The New York Times*), and "visionary" (*Chicago Sun-Times*). To find a movie worthy of comparison, wrote *The Washington Post,* one had to go back to 1939, to *The Wizard of Oz.*

The making of *Toy Story*—the first feature film to be animated entirely on a computer—had required every ounce of our tenacity, artistry, technical wizardry, and endurance. The hundred or so men and women who produced it had weathered countless ups and downs as well as the ever-present, hair-raising knowledge that our survival depended on this 80-minute experiment. For five straight years, we'd fought to do *Toy Story* our way. We'd resisted the advice of Disney executives who believed that since they'd had such success with musicals, we too should fill our movie with songs. We'd rebooted the story completely, more than once, to make sure it rang true. We'd worked nights, weekends, and holidays—mostly without complaint. Despite being novice filmmakers at a fledgling studio in dire financial straits, we had put our faith in a simple idea: If we made something that *we* wanted to see, others would want to see it, too. For so long, it felt like we had been pushing that rock up the hill, trying to do the impossible. There were plenty of moments when the future of Pixar was in doubt. Now, we were suddenly being held up as an example of what could happen when artists trusted their guts.

Toy Story went on to become the top-grossing film of the year and would earn $358 million worldwide. But it wasn't just the numbers that made us proud; money, after all, is just one measure of a thriving company and usually not the most meaningful one. No, what I found gratifying was what we'd created. Review after review focused on the film's moving plotline and its rich, three-dimensional characters—only briefly mentioning, almost as an aside, that it had been made on a computer. While there was much innovation that enabled our work, we had not let the technology overwhelm our real purpose: making a great film.

On a personal level, *Toy Story* represented the fulfillment of a goal I had pursued for more than two decades and had dreamed about since I was a boy. Growing up in the 1950s, I had yearned to be a Disney animator but had no idea how to go about it. Instinctively, I realize now, I embraced computer graphics—then a new field—as a means of pursuing that dream. If I couldn't animate by hand, there had to be another way. In graduate school, I'd quietly set a goal of making the first computer-animated feature film, and I'd worked tirelessly for twenty years to accomplish it.

Now, the goal that had been a driving force in my life had been reached, and there was an enormous sense of relief and exhilaration—at least at first. In the wake of *Toy Story*'s release, we took the company public, raising the kind of money that would ensure our future as an independent production house, and began work on two new feature-length projects, *A Bug's Life* and *Toy Story 2*. Everything was going our way, and yet I felt adrift. In fulfilling a goal, I had lost some essential framework. *Is this really what I want to do?* I began asking myself. The doubts surprised and confused me, and I kept them to myself. I had served as Pixar's president for most of the company's existence. I loved the place and everything that it stood for. Still, I couldn't deny that achieving the goal that had defined my professional life had left me without one. *Is this all there is?* I wondered. *Is it time for a new challenge?*

It wasn't that I thought Pixar had "arrived" or that my work was done. I knew there were major obstacles in front of us. The company was growing quickly, with lots of shareholders to please, and we were racing to put two new films into production. There was, in short, plenty to occupy my working hours. But my internal sense of purpose—the thing that had led me to sleep on the floor of the computer lab in graduate school just to get more hours on the mainframe, that kept me awake at night, as a kid, solving puzzles in my head, that fueled my every workday—had gone missing. I'd spent two decades building a train and laying its track. Now, the thought of merely driving it struck me as a far less interesting task. *Was making one film after another enough to engage me?* I wondered. *What would be my organizing principle now?*

It would take a full year for the answer to emerge.

From the start, my professional life seemed destined to have one foot in Silicon Valley and the other in Hollywood. I first got into the film business in 1979 when, flush from the success of *Star Wars,* George Lucas hired me to help him bring high technology into the film industry. But he wasn't based in Los Angeles. Instead, he'd founded his company, Lucasfilm, at the north end of the San Francisco Bay. Our offices were located in San Rafael, about an hour's drive from Palo Alto, the heart of Silicon Valley—a moniker that was just gaining traction then, as the semiconductor and computer industries took off. That proximity gave me a front-row seat from which to observe the many emerging hardware and software companies—not to mention the growing venture capital industry—that, in the course of a few years, would come to dominate Silicon Valley from its perch on Sand Hill Road.

I couldn't have arrived at a more dynamic and volatile time. I watched as many startups burned bright with success—and then flamed out. My mandate at Lucasfilm—to merge moviemaking with technology—meant that I rubbed shoulders with the leaders of places like Sun Microsystems and Silicon Graphics and Cray Computer, several of whom I came to know well. I was first and foremost a scientist then, not a manager, so I watched these guys closely, hoping to learn from the trajectories their companies followed. Gradually, a pattern began to emerge: Someone had a creative idea, obtained funding, brought on a lot of smart people, and developed and sold a product that got a boatload of attention. That initial success begat more success, luring the best engineers and attracting customers who had interesting and high-profile problems to solve. As these companies grew, much was written about their paradigm-shifting approaches, and when their CEOs inevitably landed on the cover of *Fortune* magazine, they were heralded as "Titans of the New." I especially remember the confidence. The leaders of these companies radiated supreme confidence. Surely, they could only have reached this apex by being very, very good.

But then those companies did something stupid—not just stupid-in-retrospect, but obvious-at-the-time stupid. I wanted to understand why. *What was causing smart people to make decisions that sent their companies off the rails?* I didn't doubt that they believed they were doing the right thing, but something was blinding them—and keeping them from seeing the problems that threatened to upend them. As a result, their companies expanded like bubbles, then burst. What interested me was not that companies rose and fell or that the landscape continually shifted as technology changed but that the leaders of these companies seemed so focused on the competition that they never developed any deep introspection about other destructive forces that were at work.

Over the years, as Pixar struggled to find its way—first selling hardware, then software, then making animated short films and advertisements—I asked myself: If Pixar is ever successful, will we do something stupid, too? Can paying careful attention to the missteps of others help us be more alert to our own? Or is there something about becoming a leader that makes you blind to the things that threaten the well-being of your enterprise? Clearly, something was causing a dangerous disconnect at many smart, creative companies. What, exactly, was a mystery—and one I was determined to figure out.

In the difficult year after *Toy Story*'s debut, I came to realize that trying to solve this mystery would be my next challenge. My desire to protect Pixar from the forces that ruin so many businesses gave me renewed focus. I began to see my role as a leader more clearly. I would devote myself to learning how to build not just a successful company but a sustainable creative culture. As I turned my attention from solving technical problems to engaging with the philosophy of sound management, I was excited once again—and sure that our second act could be as exhilarating as our first.

It has always been my goal to create a culture at Pixar that will outlast its founding leaders—Steve, John Lasseter, and me. But it is also my goal to share our underlying philosophies with other leaders and, frankly, with anyone who wrestles with the competing—but necessarily complementary—forces of art and commerce. What you're holding in your hands, then, is an attempt to put down on paper my best ideas about how we built the culture that is the bedrock of this place.

This book isn't just for Pixar people, entertainment executives, or animators. It is for anyone who wants to work in an environment that fosters creativity and problem solving. My belief is that good leadership can help creative people stay on the path to excellence no matter what business they're in. My aim at Pixar—and at Disney Animation, which my longtime partner John Lasseter and I have also led since the Walt Disney Company acquired Pixar in 2006—has been to enable our people to do their best work. We start from the presumption that our people are talented and want to contribute. We accept that, without meaning to, our company is stifling that talent in myriad unseen ways. Finally, we try to identify those impediments and fix them.

I've spent nearly forty years thinking about how to help smart, ambitious people work effectively with one another. The way I see it, my job as a manager is to create a fertile environment, keep it healthy, and watch for the things that undermine it. I believe, to my core, that everybody has the potential to be creative—whatever form that creativity takes—and that to encourage such development is a noble thing. More interesting to me, though, are the blocks that get in the way, often without us noticing, and hinder the creativity that resides within any thriving company.

The thesis of this book is that there are many blocks to creativity, but there are active steps we can take to protect the creative process. In the coming pages, I will discuss many of the steps we follow at Pixar, but the most compelling mechanisms to me are those that deal with uncertainty, instability, lack of candor, and the things we cannot see. I believe the best managers acknowledge and make room for what they do not know—not just because humility is a virtue but because until one adopts that mindset, the most striking breakthroughs cannot occur. I believe that managers must loosen the controls, not tighten them. They must accept risk; they must trust the people they work with and strive to clear the path for them; and always, they must pay attention to and engage with anything that creates fear. Moreover, successful leaders embrace the reality that their models may be wrong or incomplete. Only when we admit what we don't know can we ever hope to learn it.

This book is organized into four sections—Getting Started, Protecting the New, Building and Sustaining, and Testing What We Know. It is no memoir, but in order to understand the mistakes we made, the lessons we learned, and the ways we learned from them, it necessarily delves at times into my own history and that of Pixar. I have much to say about enabling groups to create something meaningful together and then protecting them from the destructive forces that loom even in the strongest companies. My hope is that by relating my search for the sources of confusion and delusion within Pixar and Disney Animation, I can help others avoid the pitfalls that impede and sometimes ruin businesses of all kinds. The key for me—what has kept me motivated in the nineteen years since *Toy Story* debuted—has been the realization that identifying these destructive forces isn't merely a philosophical exercise. It is a crucial, central mission. In the wake of our earliest success, Pixar needed its leaders to sit up and pay attention. And that need for vigilance never goes away. This book, then, is about the ongoing work of paying attention—of leading by being self-aware, as managers and as companies. It is an expression of the ideas that I believe make the best in us possible.

PART I

GETTING STARTED

CHAPTER 1

ANIMATED

For thirteen years we had a table in the large conference room at Pixar that we call West One. Though it was beautiful, I grew to hate this table. It was long and skinny, like one of those things you'd see in a comedy sketch about an old wealthy couple that sits down for dinner—one person at either end, a candelabra in the middle—and has to shout to make conversation. The table had been chosen by a designer Steve Jobs liked, and it was elegant, all right—but it impeded our work.

We'd hold regular meetings about our movies around that table—thirty of us facing off in two long lines, often with more people seated along the walls—and everyone was so spread out that it was difficult to communicate. For those unlucky enough to be seated at the far ends, ideas didn't flow because it was nearly impossible to make eye contact without craning your neck. More-over, because it was important that the director and producer of the film in question be able to hear what everyone was saying, they had to be placed at the center of the table. So did Pixar's creative leaders: John Lasseter, Pixar's creative officer, and me, and a handful of our most experienced directors, producers, and writers. To ensure that these people were always seated together, someone began making place cards. We might as well have been at a formal dinner party.

When it comes to creative inspiration, job titles and hierarchy are meaningless. That's what I believe. But unwittingly, we were allowing this table—and the resulting place card ritual—to send a different message. The closer you were seated to the middle of the table, it implied, the more important—the more central—you must be. And the farther away, the less likely you were to speak up—your distance from the heart of the conversation made participating feel intrusive. If the table was crowded, as it often was, still more people would sit in chairs around the edges of the room, creating yet a third tier of participants (those at the center of the table, those at the ends, and those not at the table at all). Without intending to, we'd created an obstacle that discouraged people from jumping in.

Over the course of a decade, we held countless meetings around this table in this way—completely unaware of how doing so undermined our own core principles. Why were we blind to this? Because the seating arrangements and place cards were designed for the convenience of the leaders, including me. Sincerely believing that we were in an inclusive meeting, we saw nothing amiss because *we* didn't feel excluded. Those not sitting at the center of the table, meanwhile, saw quite clearly how it established a pecking order but presumed that we—the leaders—had intended that outcome. Who were they, then, to complain?

It wasn't until we happened to have a meeting in a smaller room with a square table that John and I realized what was wrong. Sitting around that table, the interplay was better, the exchange of ideas more free-flowing, the eye contact automatic. Every person there, no matter their job title, felt free to speak up. This was not only what we wanted, it was a fundamental Pixar belief: Unhindered communication was key, no matter what your position. At our long, skinny table, comfortable in our middle seats, we had utterly failed to recognize that we were behaving contrary to that basic tenet. Over time, we'd fallen into a trap. Even though we were conscious that a room's dynamics are critical to any good discussion, even though we believed that we were constantly on the lookout for problems, our vantage point blinded us to what was right before our eyes.

Emboldened by this new insight, I went to our facilities department. "Please," I said, "I don't care how you do it, but get that table out of there." I wanted something that could be arranged into a more intimate square, so people could address each other directly and not feel like they didn't matter. A few days later, as a critical meeting on an upcoming movie approached, our new table was installed, solving the problem.

Still, interestingly, there were remnants of that problem that did not immediately vanish just because we'd solved it. For example, the next time I walked into West One, I saw the brand-new table, arranged—as requested—in a more intimate square that made it possible for more people to interact at once. But the table was adorned with the same old place cards! While we'd fixed the key problem that had made place cards seem necessary, the cards themselves had become a tradition that would continue until we specifically dismantled it. This wasn't as troubling an issue as the table itself, but it was something we had to address because cards implied hierarchy, and that was precisely what we were trying to avoid. When Andrew Stanton, one of our directors, entered the meeting room that morning, he grabbed several place cards and began randomly moving them around, narrating as he went. "We don't need these anymore!" he said in a way that everyone in the room grasped. Only then did we succeed in eliminating this ancillary problem.

This is the nature of management. Decisions are made, usually for good reasons, which in turn prompt other decisions. So when problems arise—and they always do—disentangling them is not as simple as correcting the original error. Often, finding a solution is a multi-step endeavor. There is the problem you know you are trying to solve—think of that as an oak tree—and then there are all the other problems—think of these as saplings—that sprouted from the acorns that fell around it. And these problems remain after you cut the oak tree down.

Even after all these years, I'm often surprised to find problems that have existed right in front of me, in plain sight. For me, the key to solving these problems is finding ways to see what's working and what isn't, which sounds a lot simpler than it is. Pixar today is managed according to this principle, but in a way I've been searching all my life for better ways of seeing. It began decades before Pixar even existed.

When I was a kid, I used to plunk myself down on the living room floor of my family's modest Salt Lake City home a few minutes before 7 P.M. every Sunday and wait for Walt Disney. Specifically, I'd wait for him to appear on our black-and-white RCA with its tiny 12-inch screen. Even from a dozen feet away—the accepted wisdom at the time was that viewers should put one foot between them and the TV for every inch of screen—I was transfixed by what I saw.

Each week, Walt Disney himself opened the broadcast of *The Wonderful World of Disney*. Standing before me in suit and tie, like a kindly neighbor, he would demystify the Disney magic. He'd explain the use of synchronized sound in *Steamboat Willie* or talk about the importance of music in *Fantasia*. He always went out of his way to give credit to his forebears, the men—and, at this point, they were all men—who'd done the pioneering work upon which he was building his empire. He'd introduce the television audience to trailblazers such as Max Fleischer, of Koko the Clown and Betty Boop fame, and Winsor McCay, who made *Gertie the Dinosaur*— the first animated film to feature a character that expressed emotion—in 1914. He'd gather a group of his animators, colorists, and storyboard artists to explain how they made Mickey Mouse and Donald Duck come to life. Each week, Disney created a made-up world, used cutting-edge technology to enable it, and then told us how he'd done it.

Walt Disney was one of my two boyhood idols. The other was Albert Einstein. To me, even at a young age, they represented the two poles of creativity. Disney was all about inventing the new. He brought things into being—both artistically and technologically—that did not exist before. Einstein, by contrast, was a master of explaining that which already was. I read every Einstein biography I could get my hands on as well as a little book he wrote on his theory of relativity. I loved how the concepts he developed forced people to change their approach to physics and matter, to view the universe from a different perspective. Wild-haired and iconic, Einstein dared to bend the implications of what we thought we knew. He solved the biggest puzzles of all and, in doing so, changed our understanding of reality.

Both Einstein and Disney inspired me, but Disney affected me more because of his weekly visits to my family's living room. "When you wish upon a star, makes no difference who you are," his TV show's theme song would announce as a baritone-voiced narrator promised: "Each week, as you enter this timeless land, one of these many worlds will open to you . . . ." Then the narrator would tick them off: Frontierland ("tall tales and true from the legendary past"), Tomorrowland ("the promise of things to come"), Adventureland ("the wonder world of nature's own realm"), and Fantasyland ("the happiest kingdom of them all"). I loved the idea that animation could take me places I'd never been. But the land I most wanted to learn about was the one occupied by the innovators at Disney who made these animated films.

Between 1950 and 1955, Disney made three movies we consider classics today: *Cinderella, Peter Pan,* and *Lady and the Tramp.* More than half a century later, we all remember the glass slipper, the Island of Lost Boys, and that scene where the cocker spaniel and the mutt slurp spaghetti. But few grasp how technically sophisticated these movies were. Disney's animators were at the forefront of applied technology; instead of merely using existing methods, they were inventing ones of their own. They had to develop the tools to perfect sound and color, to use blue screen matting and multi-plane cameras and xerography. Every time some technological breakthrough occurred, Walt Disney incorporated it and then talked about it on his show in a way that highlighted the relationship between technology and art. I was too young to realize such a synergy was groundbreaking. To me, it just made sense that they belonged together.

Watching Disney one Sunday evening in April of 1956, I experienced something that would define my professional life. What exactly it was is difficult to describe except to say that I felt something fall into place inside my head. That night's episode was called "Where Do the Stories Come From?" and Disney kicked it off by praising his animators' knack for turning everyday occurrences into cartoons. That night, though, it wasn't Disney's explanation that pulled me in but what was happening on the screen as he spoke. An artist was drawing Donald Duck, giving him a jaunty costume and a bouquet of flowers and a box of candy with which to woo Daisy. Then, as the artist's pencil moved around the page, Donald came to life, putting up his dukes to square off with the pencil lead, then raising his chin to allow the artist to give him a bow tie.

The definition of superb animation is that each character on the screen makes you believe it is a thinking being. Whether it's a T-Rex or a slinky dog or a desk lamp, if viewers sense not just movement but intention—or, put another way, emotion—then the animator has done his or her job. It's not just lines on paper anymore; it's a living, feeling entity. This is what I experienced that night, for the first time, as I watched Donald leap off the page. The transformation from a static line drawing to a fully dimensional, animated image was sleight of hand, nothing more, but the mystery of how it was done—not just the technical process but the way the art was imbued with such emotion—was the most interesting problem I'd ever considered. I wanted to climb through the TV screen and be part of this world.

The mid-1950s and early 1960s were, of course, a time of great prosperity and industry in the United States. Growing up in Utah in a tight-knit Mormon community, my four younger brothers and sisters and I felt that anything was possible. Because the adults we knew had all lived through the Depression, World War II, and then the Korean War, this period felt to them like the calm after a thunderstorm.

I remember the optimistic energy—an eagerness to move forward that was enabled and supported by a wealth of emerging technologies. It was boom time in America, with manufacturing and home construction at an all-time high. Banks were offering loans and credit, which meant more and more people could own a new TV, house, or Cadillac. There were amazing new appliances like disposals that ate your garbage and machines that washed your dishes, although I certainly did my share of cleaning them by hand. The first organ transplants were performed in 1954; the first polio vaccine came a year later; in 1956, the term *artificial intelligence* entered the lexicon. The future, it seemed, was already here.

Then, when I was twelve, the Soviets launched the first artificial satellite—Sputnik 1—into earth's orbit. This was huge news, not just in the scientific and political realms but in my sixth grade classroom at school, where the morning routine was interrupted by a visit from the principal, whose grim expression told us that our lives had changed forever. Since we'd been taught that the Communists were the enemy and that nuclear war could be waged at the touch of a button, the fact that they'd beaten us into space seemed pretty scary—proof that they had the upper hand.

The United States government's response to being bested was

to create something called ARPA, or the Advanced Research Projects Agency. Though it was housed within the Defense Department, its mission was ostensibly peaceful: to support scientific researchers in America's universities in the hopes of preventing what it termed "technological surprise." By sponsoring our best minds, the architects of ARPA believed, we'd come up with better answers. Looking back, I still admire that enlightened reaction to a serious threat: We'll just have to get smarter. ARPA would have a profound effect on America, leading directly to the computer revolution and the Internet, among countless other innovations. There was a sense that big things were happening in America, with much more to come. Life was full of possibility.

Still, while my family was middle-class, our outlook was shaped by my father's upbringing. Not that he talked about it much. Earl Catmull, the son of an Idaho dirt farmer, was one of fourteen kids, five of whom had died as infants. His mother, raised by Mormon pioneers who made a meager living panning for gold in the Snake River in Idaho, didn't attend school until she was eleven. My father was the first in his family ever to go to college, paying his own way by working several jobs. During my childhood, he taught math during the school year and built houses during the summers. He built our house from the ground up. While he never explicitly said that education was paramount, my siblings and I all knew we were expected to study hard and go to college.

I was a quiet, focused student in high school. An art teacher once told my parents I would often become so lost in my work that I wouldn't hear the bell ring at the end of class; I'd be sitting there, at my desk, staring at an object—a vase, say, or a chair. Something about the act of committing that object to paper was completely engrossing—the way it necessitated seeing only what was there and shutting out the distraction of my ideas about chairs or vases and what they were *supposed* to look like. At home, I sent away for Jon Gnagy's *Learn to Draw* art kits—which were advertised in the back of comic books—and the 1948 classic *Animation,* written and drawn by Preston Blair, the animator of the dancing hippos in Disney's *Fantasia*. I bought a platen—the flat metal plate artists use to press paper against ink—and even built a plywood animation stand with a light under it. I made flipbooks—one was of a man whose legs turned into a unicycle—while nursing my first crush, Tinker Bell, who had won my heart in *Peter Pan*.

Nevertheless, it soon became clear to me that I would never be talented enough to join Disney Animation's vaunted ranks. What's more, I had no idea how one actually became an animator. There was no school for it that I knew of. As I finished high school, I realized I had a far better understanding of how one *became* a scientist. The route seemed easier to discern. Throughout my life, people have always smiled when I told them I switched from art to physics because it seems, to them, like such an incongruous leap. But my decision to pursue physics, and not art, would lead me, indirectly, to my true calling.

Four years later, in 1969, I graduated from the University of Utah with two degrees, one in physics and the other in the emerging field of computer science. Applying to graduate school, my intention was to learn how to design computer languages. But soon after I matriculated, also at the U of U, I met a man who would encourage me to change course: one of the pioneers of interactive computer graphics, Ivan Sutherland.

The field of computer graphics—in essence, the making of digital pictures out of numbers, or data, that can be manipulated by a machine—was in its infancy then, but Professor Sutherland was already a legend. Early in his career, he had devised something called Sketchpad, an ingenious computer program that allowed figures to be drawn, copied, moved, rotated, or resized, all while retaining their basic properties. In 1968, he'd co-created what is widely believed to be the first virtual reality head-mounted display system. (The device was named The Sword of Damocles, after the

Greek myth, because it was so heavy that in order to be worn by the person using it, it had to be suspended from a mechanical arm bolted to the ceiling.) Sutherland and Dave Evans, who was chair of the university's computer science department, were magnets for bright students with diverse interests, and they led us with a light touch. Basically, they welcomed us to the program, gave us workspace and access to computers, and then let us pursue whatever turned us on. The result was a collaborative, supportive community so inspiring that I would later seek to replicate it at Pixar.

One of my classmates, Jim Clark, would go on to found Silicon Graphics and Netscape. Another, John Warnock, would co-found Adobe, known for Photoshop and the PDF file format, among other things. Still another, Alan Kay, would lead on a number of fronts, from object-oriented programming to "windowing" graphical user interfaces. In many respects, my fellow students were the most inspirational part of my university experience; this collegial, collaborative atmosphere was vital not just to my enjoyment of the program but also to the quality of the work that I did.

This tension between the individual's personal creative contribution and the leverage of the group is a dynamic that exists in all creative environments, but this would be my first taste of it. On one end of the spectrum, I noticed, we had the genius who seemed to do amazing work on his or her own; on the other end, we had the group that excelled precisely because of its multiplicity of views. How, then, should we balance these two extremes, I wondered. I didn't yet have a good mental model that would help me answer that, but I was developing a fierce desire to find one.

Much of the research being done at the U of U's computer science department was funded by ARPA. As I've said, ARPA had been created in response to Sputnik, and one of its key organizing principles was that collaboration could lead to excellence. In fact, one of ARPA's proudest achievements was linking universities with something they called "ARPANET," which would eventually evolve into the Internet. The first four nodes on the ARPANET were at the Stanford Research Institute, UCLA, UC Santa Barbara, and the U of U, so I had a ringside seat from which to observe this grand experiment, and what I saw influenced me profoundly. ARPA's mandate—to support smart people in a variety of areas—was carried out based on the unwavering presumption that researchers would try to do the right thing and, in ARPA's view, overmanaging them was counterproductive. ARPA's administrators did not hover over the shoulders of those of us working on the projects they funded, nor did they demand that our work have direct military applications. They simply trusted us to innovate.

This kind of trust gave me the freedom to tackle all sorts of complex problems, and I did so with gusto. Not only did I often sleep on the floor of the computer rooms to maximize time on the computer, but so did many of my fellow graduate students. We were young, driven by the sense that we were inventing the field from scratch—and that was exciting beyond words. For the first time, I saw a way to simultaneously create art *and* develop a technical understanding of how to create a new kind of imagery. Making pictures with a computer spoke to both sides of my brain. To be sure, the pictures that could be rendered on a computer were very crude in 1969, but the act of inventing new algorithms and seeing better pictures as a result was thrilling to me. In its own way, my childhood dream was reasserting itself.

At the age of twenty-six, I set a new goal: to develop a way to animate, not with a pencil but with a computer, and to make the images compelling and beautiful enough to use in the movies. Perhaps, I thought, I could become an animator after all.

In the spring of 1972, I spent ten weeks making my first short animated film—a digitized model of my left hand. My process combined old and new; again, like everyone in this fast-changing field, I was helping to invent the language. First I plunged my hand into a tub of plaster of Paris (forgetting, unfortunately, to coat it in

Vaseline first, which meant I had to yank out every tiny hair on the back of my hand to get it free); then, once I had the mold, I filled it with more plaster to make a model of my hand; then, I took that model and covered it with 350 tiny interlocking triangles and polygons to create what looked like a net of black lines on its "skin." You may not think that a curved surface could be built out of such flat, angular elements, but when you make them small enough, you can get pretty close.

I'd chosen this project because I was interested in rendering complex objects and curved surfaces—and I was looking for a challenge. At that time, computers weren't great at showing flat objects, let alone curved ones. The mathematics of curved surfaces was not well developed, and computers had limited memory capability. At the U of U's computer graphics department, where every one of us yearned to make computer-generated images look as if they were photographs of real objects, we had three driving goals: speed, realism, and the ability to depict curved surfaces. My film sought to address the latter two.

The human hand doesn't have a single flat plane. And unlike a simpler curved surface—a ball, for example—it has many parts that act in opposition to one another, with a seemingly infinite number of resulting movements. The hand is an incredibly complex "object" to try to capture and translate into arrays of numbers. Given that most computer animation at the time consisted of rendering simple polygonal objects (cubes, pyramids), I had my work cut out for me.

Once I had drawn the triangles and polygons on my model, I measured the coordinates of each of their corners, then entered that data into a 3D animation program I'd written. That enabled me to display the many triangles and polygons that made up my virtual hand on a monitor. In its first incarnation, sharp edges could be seen at the seams where the polygons joined together. But later, thanks to "smooth shading"—a technique, developed by another graduate student, that diminished the appearance of those edges—the hand became more lifelike. The real challenge, though, was making it move.

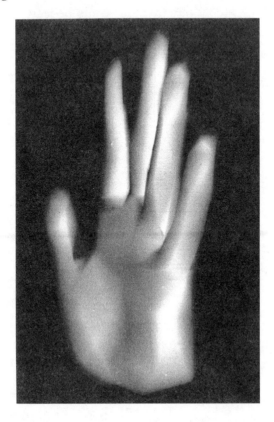

Hand, which debuted at a computer science conference in 1973, caused a bit of a stir because no one had ever seen anything like it before. In it, my hand, which appears at first to be covered in a white net of polygons, begins to open and close, as if trying to make a fist. Then my hand's surface becomes smoother, more like the real thing. There is a moment when my hand points directly at the viewer as if to say, "Yes, I'm talking to *you*." Then, the camera goes *inside* the hand and takes a look around, aiming its lens inside the palm and up into each finger, a tricky bit of perspective that I liked because it could be depicted only via computer. Those four minutes of film had taken me more than sixty thousand minutes to complete.

Together with a digitized film that my friend Fred Parke made of his wife's face around the same time, *Hand* represented the state-of-the-art in computer animation for years after it was made. Snippets of both Fred's and my films would be featured in the 1976 movie *Futureworld*, which—though mostly forgotten by moviegoers today—is still remembered by aficionados as the first full-length feature to use computer-generated animation.

Professor Sutherland used to say that he loved his graduate students at Utah because we didn't know what was impossible. Neither, apparently, did he: He was among the first to believe that Hollywood movie execs would care a fig about what was happening in academia. To that end, he sought to create a formal exchange program with Disney, wherein the studio would send one of its animators to Utah to learn about new technologies in computer rendering, and the university would send a student to Disney Animation to learn more about how to tell stories.

In the spring of 1973, he sent me to Burbank to try to sell this idea to the Disney executives. It was a thrill for me to drive through the red brick gates and onto the Disney lot on my way to the original Animation Building, built in 1940 with a "Double H" floor plan personally supervised by Walt himself to ensure that as many rooms as possible had windows to let in natural light. While I'd studied this place—or what I could glimpse of it on our 12-inch RCA—walking into it was a little like stepping into the Parthenon for the first time. There, I met Frank Thomas and Ollie Johnston, two of Walt's "Nine Old Men," the group of legendary animators who had created so many of the characters in the Disney movies I loved, from *Pinocchio* to *Peter Pan*. At one point I was taken into the archives where all the original paper drawings from all the animated films were kept, with rack after rack after rack of the images that had fueled my imagination. I'd entered the Promised Land.

One thing was immediately clear. The people I met at Disney— one of whom, I swear, was named Donald Duckwall—had zero interest in Sutherland's exchange program. The technically adventuresome Walt Disney was long gone. My enthusiastic descriptions were met with blank stares. To them, computers and animation simply didn't mix. How did they know this? Because the one time they had turned to computers for help—to render images of millions of bubbles in their 1971 live-action movie *Bedknobs and Broomsticks*—the computers had apparently let them down. The state of the technology at the time was so poor, particularly for curved images, that bubbles were beyond the computers' reach. Unfortunately, this didn't help my cause. "Well," more than one Disney executive told me that day, "until computer animation can do bubbles, then it will not have arrived."

Instead, they tried to tempt me into taking a job with what is now called Disney Imagineering, the division that designs the theme parks. It may sound odd, given how large Walt Disney had always loomed in my life, but I turned the offer down without hesitation. The theme park job felt like a diversion that would lead me down a path I didn't want to be on. I didn't want to design rides for a living. I wanted to animate with a computer.

Just as Walt Disney and the pioneers of hand-drawn animation had done decades before, those of us who sought to make pictures with computers were trying to create something new. When one of my colleagues at the U of U invented something, the rest of us would immediately piggyback on it, pushing that new idea forward. There were setbacks, too, of course. But the overriding feeling was one of progress, of moving steadily toward a distant goal.

Long before I'd heard about Disney's bubble problem, what kept me and many of my fellow graduate students up at night was the need to continue to hone our methods for creating smoothly curved surfaces with the computer—as well as to figure out how to add richness and complexity to the images we were creating. My dissertation, "A Subdivision Algorithm for Computer Display of Curved Surfaces," offered a solution to that problem.

Much of what I spent every waking moment thinking about then was extremely technical and difficult to explain, but I'll give it a try. The idea behind what I called "subdivision surfaces" was that instead of setting out to depict the whole surface of a shiny, red bottle, for example, we could divide that surface into many smaller pieces. It was easier to figure out how to color and display each tiny piece—which we could then put together to create our shiny, red bottle. (As I've noted, computer memory capacity was quite small in those days, so we put a lot of energy into developing tricks to overcome that limitation. This was one of those tricks.) But what if you wanted that shiny, red bottle to be zebra-striped? In my dissertation, I figured out a way that I could take a zebra-print or wood-grain pattern, say, and wrap it around any object.

"Texture mapping," as I called it, was like having stretchable wrapping paper that you could apply to a curved surface so that it fit snugly. The first texture map I made involved projecting an image of Mickey Mouse onto an undulating surface.

I also used Winnie the Pooh and Tigger to illustrate my points. I may not have been ready to work at Disney, but their characters were still the touchstones I referenced.

At the U of U, we were inventing a new language. One of us would contribute a verb, another a noun, then a third person would figure out ways to string the elements together to actually say something. My invention of something called the "Z-buffer" was a good example of this, in that it built on others' work. The Z-buffer was designed to address the problem of what happens when one computer-animated object is hidden, or partially hidden, behind another one. Even though the data that describes every aspect of the hidden object is in the computer's memory (meaning that you could see it, if need be), the desired spatial relationships mean that it should not be fully seen. The challenge was to figure out a way to tell the computer to meet that goal. For example, if a sphere were in front of a cube, partially blocking it, the sphere's surface should be visible on the screen, as should the parts of the cube that are not blocked by the sphere. The Z-buffer accomplished that by assigning a depth to every object in three-dimensional space, then telling the computer to match each of the screen's pixels to whatever object was the closest. Computer memory was so limited—as I've said—that this wasn't a practical solution, but I had found a new way of solving the problem. Although it sounds simple, it is anything but. Today, there is a Z-buffer in every game and PC chip manufactured on earth.

After receiving my Ph.D. in 1974, I left Utah with a nice little list of innovations under my belt, but I was keenly aware that I'd only done all this in the service of a larger mutual goal. Like my classmates, the work I'd championed had taken hold largely because of the protective, eclectic, intensely challenging environment I'd been in. The leaders of my department understood that to create a fertile laboratory, they had to assemble different kinds of thinkers and then encourage their autonomy. They had to offer feedback when needed but also had to be willing to stand back and give us room. I felt instinctively that this kind of environment was rare and worth reaching for. I knew that the most valuable thing I was taking away from the U of U was the model my teachers had provided for how to lead and inspire other creative thinkers. The question for me, then, was how to get myself into another environment like this—or how to build one of my own.

I walked away from Utah with a clearer sense of my goal, and I was prepared to devote my life to it: making the first computer-animated film. But getting to that point would not be easy. There were, I guessed, at least another ten years of development needed to figure out how to model and animate characters and render them in complex environments before we could even begin to conceive of making a short—let alone a feature—film. I also didn't yet know that my self-assigned mission was about much more than technology. To pull it off, we'd have to be creative not only technically but also in the ways that we worked together.

Back then, no other company or university shared my goal of making a computer-generated film; in fact, each time I expressed that goal in job interviews at universities, it seemed to cast a pall over the room. "But we want you to teach *computer science*," my interviewers would say. What I was proposing to do looked, to most academics, like a pipe dream, an expensive fantasy.

Then, in November 1974, I received a mysterious call from a woman who said she worked at something called the New York Institute of Technology. She said she was the secretary to the institute's president, and she was calling to book my airplane ticket. I didn't know what she was talking about, and I told her so. What was the name of the institute again? I asked. Why did she want me to fly to New York? There was an awkward silence. "I'm sorry," she said. "Someone else was supposed to call you before I did."

And with that, she hung up. The next phone call I received would change my life.

CHAPTER 2

PIXAR IS BORN

What does it mean to manage well?

As a young man, I certainly had no idea, but I was about to begin figuring it out by taking a series of jobs—working for three iconoclastic men with very different styles—that would provide me with a crash course in leadership. In the next decade, I would learn much about what managers should and shouldn't do, about vision and delusion, about confidence and arrogance, about what encourages creativity and what snuffs it out. As I gained experience, I was asking questions that intrigued me even as they confused me. Even now, forty years later, I've never stopped questioning.

I want to start with my first boss, Alex Schure—the man whose secretary called me out of the blue that day in 1974 to book me an airplane ticket and then, realizing her mistake, slammed down the receiver. When the phone rang again, a few minutes later, an unfamiliar voice—this time, a man who said he worked for Alex—filled me in: Alex was starting a research lab on Long Island's North Shore whose mission was to bring computers into the animation process. Money was not a problem, he assured me—Alex was a multimillionaire. What they needed was someone to run the place. Was I interested in talking?

Within weeks I was moving into my new office at the New York Institute of Technology.

Alex, a former college chancellor, had zero expertise in the field of computer science. At the time, that wasn't unusual, but Alex himself certainly was. He naïvely thought that computers would soon replace people, and leading that charge was what excited him. (We knew this was a misconception, if a common one at that point, but we were grateful for his eagerness to fund our work.) He had a bizarre way of speaking that mixed bluster, non sequiturs, and even snippets of rhyming verse into a sort of Mad Hatter–ish patois—or "word salad," as one of my colleagues called it. ("Our vision will speed up time," he would say, "eventually deleting it.") Those of us who worked with him often had trouble understanding what he meant. Alex had a secret ambition—well, not so secret. He said almost every day that he didn't want to be the next Walt Disney, which only made us all think that he did. When I arrived, he was in the process of directing a hand-drawn animated movie called *Tubby the Tuba*. Really, the thing never had a chance—no one at NYIT had the training or the story sensibility to make a film, and when it was finally released, it vanished without a trace.

Deluded though he may have been about his own skills, Alex was a visionary. He was incredibly prescient about the role computers would someday play in animation, and he was willing to spend a lot of his own money to push that vision forward. His unwavering commitment to what many labeled a pipe dream—the melding of technology and this hand-drawn art form—enabled much groundbreaking work to be done.

Once Alex brought me in, he left it to me to assemble a team. I have to give that to him: He had total confidence in the people he hired. This was something I admired and, later, sought to do myself. One of the first people I interviewed was Alvy Ray Smith, a charismatic Texan with a Ph.D. in computer science and a spar-kling resume that included teaching stints at New York University and UC Berkeley and a gig at Xerox PARC, the distinguished R&D lab in Palo Alto. I had conflicting feelings when I met Alvy because, frankly, he seemed more qualified to lead the lab than I was. I can still remember the uneasiness in my gut, that instinctual twinge spurred by a potential threat: This, I thought, could be the guy who takes my job one day. I hired him anyway.

Some might have seen hiring Alvy as a confident move. The truth is, as a twenty-nine-year-old who'd been focused on research for four years and had never had an assistant, let alone hired and managed a staff, I was feeling anything but confident. I could see, however, that NYIT was a place where I could explore what I'd set out to do as a graduate student. To ensure that it succeeded, I needed to attract the sharpest minds; to attract the sharpest minds, I needed to put my own insecurities away. The lesson of ARPA had lodged in my brain: When faced with a challenge, get smarter.

So we did. Alvy would become one of my closest friends and most trusted collaborators. And ever since, I've made a policy of trying to hire people who are smarter than I am. The obvious pay-offs of exceptional people are that they innovate, excel, and gener-ally make your company—and, by extension, you—look good. But there is another, less obvious, payoff that only occurred to me in retrospect. The act of hiring Alvy changed me as a manager: By ignoring my fear, I learned that the fear was groundless. Over the years, I have met people who took what seemed the safer path and were the lesser for it. By hiring Alvy, I had taken a risk, and that risk yielded the highest reward—a brilliant, committed teammate. I had wondered in graduate school how I could ever replicate the singular environment of the U of U. Now, suddenly, I saw the way. Always take a chance on better, even if it seems threatening.

At NYIT, we focused on a single goal: pushing the boundaries of what computers could do in animation and graphics. And as word of our mission spread, we began to attract the top people in the field. The bigger my staff became, the more urgent it was that I figure out how to manage them. I created a flat organizational structure, much like I'd experienced in academia, largely because I naïvely thought that if I put together a hierarchical structure—assigning a bunch of managers to report to me—I would have to spend too much time managing and not enough time on my own work. This structure—in which I entrusted everybody to drive their own projects forward, at their own pace—had its limits, but the fact is, giving a ton of freedom to highly self-motivated people enabled us to make some significant technological leaps in a short time. Together, we did groundbreaking work, much of which was aimed at figuring out how to integrate the computer with hand-drawn animation.

In 1977, for example, I wrote a 2D animation program called Tween, which performed what's known as "automatic in-betweening"—filling in frames of motion between key shots, an otherwise expensive and labor-intensive process. Another technical challenge that occupied us was the need for something called "motion blur." With animation in general and computer animation in particular, the images created are in perfect focus. That may sound like a good thing, but in fact, human beings react negatively to it. When moving objects are in perfect focus, theatergoers experience an unpleasant, strobe-like sensation, which they describe as "jerky." When watching live-action movies, we don't perceive this problem because traditional film cameras capture a slight blur in the direction an object is moving. The blur keeps our brains from noticing the sharp edges, and our brains regard this blur as natural. Without motion blur, our brains think something is wrong. So the question for us was how to simulate the blur for animation. If the human eye couldn't accept computer animation, the field would have no future.

Among the handful of companies that were trying to solve these problems, most embraced a culture of strictly enforced, even CIA-like secrecy. We were in a race, after all, to be the first to make a computer-animated feature film, so many who were pursuing this technology held their discoveries close to their vests. After talking about it, however, Alvy and I decided to do the opposite—to share our work with the outside world. My view was that we were all so far from achieving our goal that to hoard ideas only impeded our ability to get to the finish line. Instead, NYIT engaged with the computer graphics community, publishing everything we discovered, participating in committees to review papers written by all manner of researchers, and taking active roles at all the major academic conferences. The benefit of this transparency was not immediately felt (and, notably, when we decided upon it, we weren't even counting on a payoff; it just seemed like the right thing to do). But the relationships and connections we formed, over time, proved far more valuable than we could have imagined, fueling our technical innovation and our understanding of creativity in general.

For all the good work we were doing, however, I found myself in a quandary at NYIT. Thanks to Alex, we were fortunate to have the funds to buy the equipment and hire the people necessary to innovate in the world of computer animation, but we didn't have anyone who knew anything about filmmaking. As we developed the ability to tell a story with a computer, we still didn't have storytellers among us, and we were the poorer for it. So aware were Alvy and I of this limitation that we began making quiet overtures to Disney and other studios, trying to gauge their interest in investing in our tools. If we found an interested suitor, Alvy and I were prepared to leave NYIT and move our team to Los Angeles to partner with proven filmmakers and storytellers. But it was not to be. One by one, they demurred. It's hard to imagine now, but in 1976, the idea of incorporating high technology into Hollywood filmmaking wasn't just a low priority; it wasn't even on the radar. But one man was about to change that, with a movie called *Star Wars*.

On May 25, 1977, *Star Wars* opened in theaters across America. The film's mastery of visual effects—and its record-shattering popularity at the box office—would change the industry forever. And thirty-two-year-old writer-director George Lucas was only getting started. His company, Lucasfilm, and its ascendant Industrial Light & Magic studio had already taken the lead developing new tools in visual effects and sound design. Now, while no one else in the movie industry evinced even the slightest desire to invest in such things, George resolved in July 1979 to launch a computer division. Thanks to Luke Skywalker, he had the resources to do it right.

To run this division, he wanted someone who not only knew computers; he wanted someone who loved film and believed that the two could not only coexist but enhance one another. Eventually, that led George to me. One of his key people, Richard Edlund, who was a pioneer of special effects, came to see me one afternoon in my office at NYIT wearing a belt with an enormous buckle that read, in huge letters, "Star Wars." This was worrisome, given that I was trying to keep his visit a secret from Alex Schure. Somehow, though, Alex didn't catch on. George's emissary was apparently pleased with what I showed him, because a few weeks after he left, I was on my way to Lucasfilm in California for a formal interview.

My first meeting there was with a man named Bob Gindy, who ran George's personal construction projects—not exactly the qualifications you'd expect for a guy spearheading the search for a new computer executive. The first thing he asked me was, "Who else should Lucasfilm be considering for this job?" Meaning, the job I was there to interview for. Without hesitation, I rattled off the names of several people who were doing impressive work in a variety of technical areas. My willingness to do this reflected my worldview, forged in academia, that any hard problem should have many good minds simultaneously trying to solve it. Not to acknowledge that seemed silly. Only later would I learn that the guys at Lucasfilm had already interviewed all the people I listed and had asked them, in turn, to make similar recommendations—and not one of them had suggested any other names! To be sure, working for George Lucas was a plum job that you'd have to be crazy not to want. But to go mute, as my rivals did, when asked to evaluate the field signaled not just intense competitiveness but also lack of confidence. Soon I'd landed an interview with George himself.

On my way to meet him, I remember feeling nervous in a way I rarely had before. Even before *Star Wars*, George had proved himself as a successful writer-director-producer with *American Graffiti*. I was a computer guy with an expensive dream. Still, when I arrived at the shooting stage in Los Angeles where he was working, he and I seemed pretty similar: Skinny and bearded, in our early thirties, we both wore glasses, worked with a blinders-on intensity, and had a tendency to talk only when we had something to say. But what struck me immediately was George's relentless practicality. He wasn't some hobbyist trying to bring technology into filmmaking for the heck of it. His interest in computers began and ended with their potential to add value to the filmmaking process—be it through digital optical printing, digital audio, digital non-linear editing, or computer graphics. I was certain that they could, and I told him so.

In the intervening years, George has said that he hired me because of my honesty, my "clarity of vision," and my steadfast belief in what computers could do. Not long after we met, he offered me the job.

By the time I moved into the two-story building in San Anselmo that would serve as the temporary headquarters of Lucasfilm's new computer division, I had given myself an assignment: to rethink how I managed people. What George wanted to create was a far more ambitious enterprise than the one I oversaw at NYIT, with a higher profile, a bigger budget, and, given his ambitions in Hollywood, the promise of much greater impact. I wanted to make sure that I was enabling my team to make the most of that. At NYIT, I'd created a flat structure much like I'd seen at the U of U, giving my colleagues a lot of running room and little oversight, and I'd been relatively pleased with the results. But now I had to admit that our team there behaved a lot like a collection of grad students—independent thinkers with individual projects—rather than a team with a common goal. A research lab is not a university, and the structure didn't scale well. At Lucasfilm, then, I decided to hire managers to run the graphics, video, and audio groups; they would then report to me. I knew I had to put some sort of hierarchy in place, but I also worried that hierarchy would lead to problems. So I edged in slowly, feeling suspicious of it at first, yet knowing that some part of it was necessary.

The Bay Area in 1979 could not have provided a more fertile environment for our work. In Silicon Valley, the number of computer companies was growing so fast that no one's Rolodex (yes, we had Rolodexes back then) was ever up to date. Also growing exponentially were the number of tasks that computers were being assigned to tackle. Not long after I got to California, Microsoft's Bill Gates agreed to create an operating system for the new IBM personal computer—which would, of course, go on to transform the way Americans worked. One year later, Atari released the first in-home game console, meaning that its popular arcade games like Space Invaders and Pac-Man could be played in living rooms across America, opening up a market that now accounts for more than $65 billion in global sales.

To get a sense of how quickly things were changing, consider that when I was a graduate student, in 1970, we'd used huge computers made by IBM and seven other mainframe companies (a group that was nicknamed "IBM and the Seven Dwarves"). Picture a room filled with racks and racks of equipment measuring six feet tall, two feet wide, and 30 inches deep. Five years later, when I arrived at NYIT, the minicomputer—which was about the size of an armoire—was on the rise, with Digital Equipment in Massachusetts being the most significant player. By the time I got to Lucasfilm in 1979, the momentum was swinging to workstation computers such as those made by Silicon Valley upstarts Sun Microsystems and Silicon Graphics, as well as IBM, but by that time, everyone could see that workstations were only another stop on the way to PCs and, eventually, personal desktop computers. The swiftness of this evolution created seemingly endless opportunities for those who were willing and able to innovate. The allure of getting rich was a magnet for bright, ambitious people, and the resulting competition was intense—as were the risks. The old business models were undergoing continual disruptive change.

Lucasfilm was based in Marin County, one hour north of Silicon Valley by car and one hour from Hollywood by plane. This was no accident. George saw himself, first and foremost, as a filmmaker, so Silicon Valley wasn't for him. But he also had no desire to be too close to Los Angeles, because he thought there was something a bit unseemly and inbred about it. Thus, he created his own island, a community that embraced films and computers but pledged allegiance to neither of the prevailing cultures that defined those businesses. The resulting environment felt as protected as an academic institution—an idea that would stay with me and help shape what I would later try to build at Pixar. Experimentation was highly valued, but the urgency of a for-profit enterprise was definitely in the air. In other words, we felt like we were solving problems for a reason.

I put Alvy in charge of our graphics group, which was dedicated initially to creating a digital approach to blue-screen matting—the process by which one image (say, a man on a surfboard) can be dropped into a separate image (say, a 100-foot wave). Before digital, this effect was accomplished on film with the use of sophisticated optical devices, and the special effects wizards at the time had no interest in leaving that painstaking method behind. Our job was to convince them otherwise. Alvy's team set out to design a highly specialized standalone computer that had the resolution and processing power to scan film, combine special-effects images with live-action footage, and then record the final result back onto film. It took us roughly four years, but our engineers built just such a device, which we named the Pixar Image Computer.

Why "Pixar"? The name emerged from a back-and-forth between Alvy and another of our colleagues, Loren Carpenter. Alvy, who spent much of his childhood in Texas and New Mexico, had a fondness for the Spanish language, and he was intrigued by how certain nouns in English looked like Spanish verbs—words like "laser," for example. So Alvy lobbied for "Pixer," which he imagined to be a (fake) Spanish verb meaning "to make pictures." Loren countered with "Radar," which he thought sounded more high-tech. That's when it hit them: Pixer + radar = Pixar! It stuck.

Within Lucasfilm, the special effects experts were relatively indifferent to our computer graphics technology. Their film editor colleagues, however, were outright opposed. This was driven home when, at George's request, we developed a video-editing system that would enable editors to do their work on the computer. George envisioned a program that would allow shots to be banked and filed easily and cuts to be made far more quickly than they were on film. Ralph Guggenheim, a computer programmer (with a degree in filmmaking from Carnegie Mellon as well) I'd lured away from NYIT, took the lead on this project, which was so ahead of its time that the hardware needed to support it didn't even exist yet. (In order to approximate it, Ralph had to mock up an elaborate makeshift system using laser disks). But as challenging as that problem proved to be, it paled in comparison to the bigger, and eternal, impediment to our progress: the human resistance to change.

While George wanted this new video-editing system in place, the film editors at Lucasfilm did not. They were perfectly happy with the system they had already mastered, which involved actually cutting film into snippets with razor blades and then pasting them back together. They couldn't have been less interested in making changes that would slow them down in the short term. They took comfort in their familiar ways, and change meant being uncomfortable. So when it came time to test our work, the editors refused to participate. Our certainty that video editing would revolutionize the process didn't matter, and neither did George's backing. Because the people our new system was intended to serve were resistant to it, progress screeched to a halt.

What to do?

If left up to the editors, no new tool would ever be designed and no improvements would be possible. They saw no advantage to change and couldn't imagine how using a computer would make their work easier or better. But if we designed the new system in a vacuum, moving ahead without the editors' input, we would end up with a tool that didn't address their needs. Being confident about the value of our innovation was not enough. We needed buy-in from the community we were trying to serve. Without it, we were forced to abandon our plans.

Clearly, it wasn't enough for managers to have good ideas—they had to be able to engender support for those ideas among the people who'd be charged with employing them. I took that lesson to heart.

During the Lucasfilm years, I definitely had my periods of feeling overwhelmed as a manager, periods when I wondered about my own abilities and asked myself if I should try to adopt a more forceful, alpha male management style. I'd put my version of hierarchy in place by delegating to other managers, but I was also part of a chain of command in the greater Lucasfilm empire. I remember going home at night, exhausted, feeling like I was balancing on the backs of a herd of horses—only some of the horses were thoroughbreds, some were completely wild, and some were ponies who were struggling to keep up. I found it hard enough to hold on, let alone steer.

Simply put, managing was hard. No one took me aside to give me tips. The books I read that promised insight on the topic were mostly devoid of content. So I looked to George to see how he did it. I saw that his way seemed to reflect some of the philosophy he had put into Yoda. Just as Yoda said things like, "Do, or do not. There is no try," George had a fondness for folksy analogies that sought to describe, neatly, the mess of life. He would compare the often arduous process of developing his 4,700-acre Skywalker Ranch compound (a minicity of residences and production facilities) to a ship going down river . . . that had been cut in half . . . and whose captain had been thrown overboard. "We're still going to get there," he would say. "Grab the paddles and let's keep going!"

Another of his favorite analogies was that building a company was like being on a wagon train headed west. On the long journey to the land of plenty, the pioneers would be full of purpose and united by the goal of reaching their destination. Once they arrived, he'd say, people would come and go, and that was as it should be. But the process of moving *toward* something—of having not yet arrived—was what he idealized.

Whether evoking wagons or ships, George thought in terms of a long view; he believed in the future and his ability to shape it. The story has been told and retold about how, as a young filmmaker, in the wake of *American Graffiti*'s success, he was advised to demand a higher salary on his next movie, *Star Wars*. That would be the expected move in Hollywood: Bump up your quote. Not for George, though. He skipped the raise altogether and asked instead to retain ownership of licensing and merchandising rights to *Star Wars*. The studio that was distributing the film, 20th Century Fox, readily agreed to his request, thinking it was not giving up much. George would prove them wrong, setting the stage for major changes in the industry he loved. He bet on himself—and won.

Lucasfilm, in those post–*Star Wars* days, was a magnet for big names. Famous directors, from Steven Spielberg to Martin Scorsese, were always stopping by to see what we were working on and what new effects or innovations they might use in their films. But more than the drop-ins from A-listers, the visit that would stick with me most was the group of Disney animators who came for a tour just after Valentine's Day, 1983. As I showed them around, I noted that one of them—a kid in baggy jeans named John—seemed particularly excited about what we were up to. In fact, the first thing I noticed was his curiosity. When I showed everyone a computer-animated image that we were so proud of we'd given it a name—"The Road to Point Reyes"—he just stood there, transfixed. I told him we'd developed the image of a gently curving road overlooking the Pacific Ocean using a software program we'd developed called Reyes (for Renders Everything You Ever Saw), and the pun was intended: Point Reyes, California, is a seaside village on Route 1, not far from Lucasfilm. Reyes represented the cutting edge of computer graphics at the time. And it bowled this John guy over.

Soon, I learned why. He had an idea, he told me, for a film called *The Brave Little Toaster* about a toaster, a blanket, a lamp, a radio, and a vacuum cleaner who journey to the city to find their master after being abandoned in their cabin in the woods. He told me that his film, which he was about to pitch to his bosses at Disney Animation, would be the first to place hand-drawn characters inside computer-generated backgrounds, much like the one I'd just shown him. He wanted to know if we could work together to make this happen.

That animator was John Lasseter. Unbeknownst to me, soon after our meeting at Lucasfilm, he would lose his job at Disney. Apparently, his supervisors felt that *The Brave Little Toaster* was—like him—a little *too* avant-garde. They listened to his pitch and, immediately afterward, fired him. A few months later, I ran into John again on the Queen Mary, of all places. The historic Long Beach hotel, which also happens to be a docked ocean liner, was the site of the annual Pratt Institute Symposium on Computer Graphics. Not knowing of his newly unemployed status, I asked if there was any way he could come up to Lucasfilm and help us make our first short film. He said yes without hesitation. I remember thinking it was almost as if Professor Sutherland's exchange program idea was finally getting its moment. To have a Disney animator on our team, even temporarily, would be a huge leap forward. For the first time, a true storyteller would be joining our ranks.

John was a born dreamer. As a boy, he lived mostly in his head and in the tree houses and tunnels and spaceships he drew in his sketchbook. His dad was the parts manager at the local Chevrolet dealership in Whittier, California—instilling in John a lifelong obsession with cars—and his mom was a high school art teacher. Like me, John remembers discovering that there were people who made animation for a living and thinking he'd found his place in the world. For him, as for me, that realization was Disney-related; it came when he stumbled upon a well-worn copy of *The Art of Animation,* Bob Thomas's history of the Disney Studios, in his high school library. By the time I met John, he was as connected to Walt Disney as any twenty-six-year-old on earth. He had graduated from CalArts, the legendary art school founded by Walt, where he'd learned from some of the greatest artists of Disney's Golden Age; he'd worked as a river guide on the Jungle Cruise at Disneyland; and he'd won a Student Academy Award in 1979 for his short film *The Lady and the Lamp*—an homage to Disney's *Lady and the Tramp*—whose main character, a white desk lamp, would later evolve into our Pixar logo.

What John hadn't realized when he joined Disney Animation, however, was that the studio was going through a rough, fallow period. The animation there had plateaued much earlier—no significant technical advances had been made since 1961's *101 Dalmatians,* and many of its young, talented animators had left the studio, reacting in part to an increasingly hierarchical culture that didn't value their ideas. When John arrived in 1979, Frank Thomas, Ollie Johnston, and the rest of the Nine Old Men were getting up in years—the youngest was 65—and had stepped away from the day-to-day business of moviemaking, leaving the studio in the hands of a group of lesser artists who had been waiting in the wings for decades. These men felt that it was their turn to be in charge but were so insecure about their standing within the company that they clung to their newfound status by stifling—not encouraging—younger talents. Not only were they not interested in the ideas of their fledgling animators, they exercised a sort of punitive power. They were seemingly determined that those beneath them not rise in the ranks any faster than they already had. John was almost immediately unhappy in this noncollaborative environment, though it was still a shock when he got fired. No wonder he was so eager to join us at Lucasfilm.

The project we enlisted John's help on was originally going to be called *My Breakfast with André,* an homage of sorts to a 1981 movie we all loved called *My Dinner with André.* The idea was simple: an android named André was supposed to wake up, yawn, and stretch as the sun rose, revealing a lush, computer-rendered world. Alvy had drawn the first storyboards and was taking the lead on the project, which was a way for us to test some of the new animation technology we'd developed, and he was thrilled that John was coming aboard to help. John was an effusive presence with a knack for bringing out the best in others. His energy would enliven the film.

"Do you mind if I say a couple of things?" John asked Alvy after being shown the early storyboards.

"Of course not," Alvy responded. "That's why you're here."

As Alvy tells it, John then "proceeded to save the piece. I'd foolishly thought I'd be the animator, but frankly, I didn't have the magic. I could make things move very nicely, but not think, emote and have consciousness. That's John." John made some suggestions about the look of the main character, a simple, human-like figure with a sphere for a head and another sphere for a nose. But his most brilliant stroke was adding a second character, a bumblebee named Wally for André to interact with. (And who, by the way, was named for Wallace Shawn, who'd starred in the movie our short was inspired by.) The film was renamed *The Adventures of*

André and Wally B., and it opened with André on his back, asleep in the forest, waking to find Wally B. hovering just above his face. Frightened, he flees as Wally B. gives chase, buzzing right behind him. That is the entire plot, if you can call it that—frankly, we weren't as focused on story as we were on showing what was possible to render with a computer. John's genius was in creating an emotional tension, even in this briefest of formats.

The movie was designed to run two minutes, but we were still racing against time to complete it. It wasn't just that the animation process was labor-intensive, though it surely was; it was that we were inventing the animation process as we went along. Adding to the stress was the fact that we'd left ourselves so little time to get it all done. We had a self-imposed deadline of July 1984—just eight months after John came aboard—because that was when the annual SIGGRAPH Conference would be held in Minneapolis. This week-long computer graphics summit was a great place to find out what everyone in the field was up to, the one time every year that academics, educators, artists, hardware salesmen, graduate students, and programmers all came together under one roof. According to tradition, the Tuesday of conference week was reserved for "movie night," with a showing of the most exciting visual work produced in the field that year. Up until then, that had meant mostly 15-second snippets of flying network news logos (think spinning globes and rippling American flags) and scientific visualization (everything from the NASA's Voyager 2 fly-by of Saturn to illustrations of Contac time-release cold capsules). *Wally B.* would be the first computerized character animation ever shown at SIGGRAPH.

As the deadline approached, however, we realized that we weren't going to make it. We'd worked so hard to create images that were better and clearer and, to make things really hard, we'd set the movie in a forest (whose foliage tested the limits of our animation chops at the time). But we hadn't accounted for how much computer power those images would require to render and how long that process would take. We could complete a rough version of the film in time, but portions of it would be unfinished, appearing as wire frame images—mock-ups, made from grid polygons, of the finished characters—instead of fully colored images. The night of our premiere, we watched, mortified, as these segments appeared on the screen, but something surprising happened. Despite our worries, the majority of the people I talked to after the screening said that they hadn't even noticed that the movie had switched from full color to black and white wireframes! They were so caught up in the emotion of the story that they hadn't noticed its flaws.

This was my first encounter with a phenomenon I would notice again and again, throughout my career: For all the care you put into artistry, visual polish frequently doesn't matter if you are getting the story right.

In 1983, George and his wife Marcia split up, and the settlement would significantly affect the cash position of Lucasfilm. George hadn't lost an ounce of his ambition, but the new financial realities meant that he had to streamline his business. At the same time, I was coming to realize that while we in the computer division wanted more than anything to make an animated feature film, George didn't share our dream. He had always been most interested in what computers could do to enhance live-action films. For a while our goals, though disparate, had overlapped and pushed each other forward. But now, under pressure to consolidate his investments, George decided to sell us. The computer division's primary asset was the business we'd created around the Pixar Image Computer. Although we originally designed it to handle frames of film, it had proven to have multiple applications, including everything from medical imaging to design prototyping to image processing for the many three-letter agencies around Washington, D.C.

The next year would be one of the most stressful of my life.

A management team brought in by George to restructure Lucasfilm seemed concerned mostly with cash flow, and as time went on, they became openly skeptical that our division would ever attract a buyer. This team was headed by two men with the same first name, whom Alvy and I nicknamed "the Dweebs" because they didn't understand a thing about the business we were in. Those two guys threw around management consulting terms (they loved to tout their "corporate intuition" and constantly urged us to make "strategic alliances"), but they didn't seem at all insightful about how to make us attractive to buyers or about which buyers to pursue. At one point, they called us into an office, sat us down, and said that to cut costs, we should lay off all our employees until after our division was sold—at which point we could discuss rehiring them. In addition to the emotional toll we knew this would take, what bugged us about this suggestion was that our real selling point—the thing that had attracted potential suitors thus far—was the talent we'd gathered. Without that, we had nothing.

So, when our two like-minded overlords demanded a list of names of people to lay off, Alvy and I gave them two: his and mine. That temporarily halted that plan, but as we headed into 1985, I was keenly aware that if we weren't sold off, and fast, we could be shut down at any moment.

Lucasfilm wanted to walk away from the deal with $15 million in cash, but there was a hitch: Our computer division came with a business plan that required an additional infusion of $15 million to take us from prototype to product and ensure that we'd be able to stand on our own. This structure did not sit well with the venture capitalists they hoped would buy us, who didn't typically make such significant cash commitments when they acquired companies. We were shopped to twenty prospective buyers, none of whom bit. When that list was exhausted, a string of manufacturing companies stopped in to kick our tires. Again, no luck.

At long last, our group reached an agreement with General Motors and Philips, the Dutch electronics and engineering conglomerate. Philips was interested because, with our Pixar Image Computer, we had developed the foundational technology for rendering volumes of data, such as you get from CT scans or MRIs. General Motors was intrigued because we were leading the way in the modeling of objects, which they felt could be used in car design. We were within one week of signing the deal when it fell apart.

At this point, I remember feeling a mixture of despair and relief. We'd known from the outset that entering into a relationship with GM and Philips would likely put an end to our dream of making the first animated feature film, but that was a risk no matter who we joined up with: Each investor was going to have its own agenda, and that was the price of our survival. To this day, I am thankful that the deal went south. Because it paved the way for Steve Jobs.

I first met Steve in February of 1985, when he was the director of Apple Computer, Inc. Our meeting had been arranged by Apple's chief scientist, Alan Kay, who knew that Alvy and I were looking for investors to take our graphics division off George's hands. Alan had been at the U of U with me and at Xerox PARC with Alvy, and he told Steve that he should visit us if he wanted to see the cutting edge in computer graphics. We met in a conference room with a white board and a large table surrounded by chairs—not that Steve stayed seated for very long. Within minutes, he was standing at the white board, drawing us a chart of Apple's revenues.

I remember his assertiveness. There was no small talk. Instead, there were questions. Lots of questions. *What do you want?* Steve asked. *Where are you heading? What are your long-term goals?* He used the phrase "insanely great products" to explain what he believed in. Clearly, he was the sort of person who didn't let presentations happen to him, and it wasn't long before he was talking about making a deal.

To be honest, I was uneasy about Steve. He had a forceful personality, whereas I do not, and I felt threatened by him. For all of my talk about the importance of surrounding myself with people smarter than myself, his intensity was at such a different level, I didn't know how to interpret it. It put me in the mind of an ad campaign that the Maxell cassette tape company released around this time, featuring what would become an iconic image: a guy sitting low in a leather-and-chrome Le Corbusier chair, his long hair being literally blown back by the sound from the stereophonic speaker in front of him. That's what it was like to be with Steve. He was the speaker. Everyone else was the guy.

For nearly two months after that initial meeting, we heard nothing. Total silence.

We were perplexed, given how intent Steve had been in our meetings. We finally learned why when, in late May, we read in the papers of Steve's blowup with Apple CEO John Sculley. Sculley had persuaded Apple's board of directors to remove Steve from his duties as head of the company's Macintosh division after rumors surfaced that Steve was trying to stage a boardroom coup.

When the dust settled, Steve sought us out again. He wanted a new challenge and thought maybe we were it.

He came to Lucasfilm one afternoon for a tour of our hardware lab. Again, he pushed and prodded and poked. *What can the Pixar Image Computer do that other machines on the market can't? Who do you envision using it? What's your long-term plan?* His aim didn't seem to be to absorb the intricacies of our technology as much as to hone his own argument, to temper it by sparring with us. Steve's domineering nature could take one's breath away. At one point he turned to me and calmly explained that he wanted my job. Once he took my place at the helm, he said, I would learn so much from him that in just two years I would be able to run the enterprise all by myself. I was, of course, already running the enterprise by myself, but I marveled at his chutzpah. He not only planned to displace me in the day-to-day management of the company, he expected me to think it was a great idea!

Steve was hard-charging—relentless, even—but a conversation with him took you places you didn't expect. It forced you not just to defend but also to engage. And that in itself, I came to believe, had value.

The next day, several of us drove out to meet with Steve at his place in Woodside, a lovely neighborhood near Menlo Park. The house was almost empty but for a motorcycle, a grand piano, and two personal chefs who had once worked at Chez Panisse. Sitting on the grass looking out over his seven-acre lawn, he formally proposed that he buy the graphics group from Lucasfilm and showed us a proposed organizational chart for the new company. As he spoke, it became clear to us that his goal was not to build an animation studio; his goal was to build the next generation of home computers to compete with Apple.

This wasn't merely a deviation from our vision, it was the total abandonment of it, so we politely declined. We returned to the task of trying to find a buyer. Time was running out.

Months passed. As we approached the one-year anniversary of our unveiling of *The Adventures of André and Wally B.,* our anxiety—the kind that builds when survival is at stake and saviors are in short supply—was showing on our faces. Still, we had fortune on our side—or, at least, geography. The 1985 SIGGRAPH conference was being held in San Francisco, right up the 101 freeway from Silicon Valley. We had a booth on the trade show floor where we showcased our Pixar Image Computer. Steve Jobs dropped by on the first afternoon.

Immediately, I sensed a change. Since I'd last seen him, Steve had founded a personal computer company, NeXT. I think that gave him the ability to approach us with a different mindset. He had less to prove. Now, he looked around our booth and proclaimed our machine the most interesting thing in the room. "Let's go for a walk," he said, and we set off on a stroll around the hall. "How are things going?"

"Not great," I confessed. We were still hoping to find an outside investor, but we were nearly out of options. It was then that Steve raised the idea of resuming our talks. "Maybe we can work something out," he said.

As we talked, we came upon Bill Joy, one of the founders of Sun Computer. Bill, like Steve, was an extraordinarily bright, competitive, articulate, and opinionated person. I don't remember what they talked about as we stood there, but I'll never forget the *way* they talked: standing nose to nose, their arms behind their backs, swaying from side to side—in perfect sync—completely oblivious to anything going on around them. This went on for quite a while, until Steve had to break off to go meet someone.

After Steve left, Bill turned to me and said, "Boy, is he arrogant."

When Steve came by our booth again later, he walked up to me and said of Bill: "Boy, is he arrogant."

I remember being struck by this clash-of-the-titans moment. I was amused by the fact that each man could see ego in the other but not in himself.

It took another few months, but on the third day of January, 1986, Steve said he was ready to make a deal and addressed, right off, the issue that had concerned me most—his previous insistence on controlling and running the company. He was willing to back off on that, he said, and not only that, he was open to letting us explore making a business out of the nexus of computers and graphics. By the end of the meeting, Alvy and I felt comfortable with his proposal—and his intentions. The only wild card was what he was going to be like as a partner. We were well aware of his reputation for being difficult. Only time would tell whether he would live up to it.

At one point in this period, I met with Steve and gently asked him how things got resolved when people disagree with him. He seemed unaware that what I was really asking him was how things would get resolved if we worked together and *I* disagreed with him, for he gave a more general answer.

He said, "When I don't see eye to eye with somebody, I just take the time to explain it better, so they understand the way it should be."

Later, when I relayed this to my colleagues at Lucasfilm, they laughed. Nervously. I remember one of Steve's attorneys telling us that if we were acquired by his client, we had better be ready to "get on the Steve Jobs roller coaster." Given our dire straits, this was a ride Alvy and I were ready to board.

The acquisition process was complicated by the fact that the negotiators for Lucasfilm weren't very good. The chief financial officer, in particular, underestimated Steve, assuming he was just another rich kid in over his head. This CFO told me that the way to establish his authority in the room was to arrive last. His thinking, which he articulated out loud to me, was that this would establish him as the "most powerful player," since he and only he could afford to keep everyone else waiting.

All that it ended up establishing, however, was that he'd never met anyone like Steve Jobs.

The morning of the big negotiating session, all of us but the CFO were on time—Steve and his attorney; me, Alvy, and our attorney; Lucasfilm's attorneys; and an investment banker. At precisely 10 A.M., Steve looked around and, finding the CFO missing, started the meeting without him! In one swift move, Steve had not only foiled the CFO's attempt to place himself atop the pecking order, but he had grabbed control of the meeting. This would be the kind of strategic, aggressive play that would define Steve's stewardship of Pixar for years to come—once we joined forces, he became our protector, as fierce on our behalf as he was on his own. In the end, Steve paid $5 million to spin Pixar off of Lucasfilm—and then, after the sale, he agreed to pay another $5 million to fund the company, with 70 percent of the stock going to Steve and 30 percent to the employees.

The closing took place on a Monday morning in February 1986, and the mood in the room was decidedly muted because everyone was so worn out by the negotiations. After we signed our names, Steve pulled Alvy and me aside, put his arms around us and said, "Whatever happens, we have to be loyal to each other." I took that as an expression of his still-bruised feelings in the wake of his ouster from Apple, but I never forgot it. The gestation had been trying, but the feisty little company called Pixar had been born.

CHAPTER 3

A DEFINING GOAL

There is nothing quite like ignorance combined with a driving need to succeed to force rapid learning. I know this from firsthand experience. In 1986, I became the president of a new hardware company whose main business was selling the Pixar Image Computer.

The only problem was, I had no idea what I was doing.

From the outside, Pixar probably looked like your typical Silicon Valley startup. On the inside, however, we were anything but. Steve Jobs had never manufactured or marketed a high-end machine before, so he had neither the experience nor the intuition about how to do so. We had no sales people and no marketing people and no idea where to find them. Steve, Alvy Ray Smith, John Lasseter, me—none of us knew the first thing about how to run the kind of business we had just started. We were drowning.

While I was used to working within a budget, I had never been responsible for a profit-and-loss statement. I knew nothing about how to manage inventory, how to ensure quality, or any of the other things that a company purporting to sell products must master.

Not knowing where else to turn, I remember buying a copy of Dick Levin's *Buy Low, Sell High, Collect Early, and Pay Late: The Manager's Guide to Financial Survival,* a popular business title at the time, and devouring it in one sitting.

I read many such books as I set about trying to become a better, more effective manager. Most, I found, trafficked in a kind of simplicity that seemed harmful in that it offered false reassurance. These books were stocked with catchy phrases like "Dare to fail!" or "Follow people and people will follow you!" or "Focus, focus, focus!" (This last one was a particular favorite piece of nonadvice. When people hear it, they nod their heads in agreement as if a great truth has been presented, not realizing that they've been diverted from addressing the far harder problem: deciding what it is that they should be focusing on. There is nothing in this advice that gives you any idea how to figure out where the focus should be, or how to apply your energy to it. It ends up being advice that doesn't mean anything.) These slogans were offered as conclusions—as wisdom—and they may have been, I suppose. But none of them gave me any clue as to what to do or what I should focus on.

One thing we had to figure out in the early days of Pixar was the yin and yang of working with Steve. His determination to succeed and his willingness to think big were often inspiring. For example, he insisted that Alvy and I open sales offices for the Pixar Image Computer across the country—a bold move that we would never have dreamed of proposing right out of the gate. Alvy and I felt that, yes, we were selling a sexy product, but it was a highly specialized sexy product, which meant that there was a natural limit on the size of the market for it. Steve, however, coming from the world of consumer computers, pushed us to think past that. If we were going to sell this thing, he reasoned, we needed to establish a national presence. Alvy and I weren't sure how to go about it at first, but we appreciated Steve's vision.

With that vision came something else, however: an unusual style of interacting with people. Steve was often impatient and curt. When he attended meetings with potential customers, he wouldn't hesitate to call them out if he sniffed mediocrity or lack of preparation—hardly a helpful tactic when trying to make a deal or develop a loyal client base. He was young and driven and not yet attuned to his impact on others. In our first years together, he didn't "get" normal people—meaning people who did not run companies or who lacked personal confidence. His method for taking the measure of a room was saying something definitive and outrageous— "These charts are bullshit!" or "This deal is crap!"—and watching people react. If you were brave enough to come back at him, he often respected it—poking at you, then registering your response, was his way of deducing what you thought and whether you had the guts to champion it. Watching him reminded me of a principle of engineering: Sending out a sharp impulse—like a dolphin uses echolocation to determine the location of a school of fish—can teach you crucial things about your environment. Steve used aggressive interplay as a kind of biological sonar. It was how he sized up the world.

My first order of business as Pixar's president was to find and hire good people, a core staff that could help us begin to address our inadequacies. If we were going to make a business out of selling hardware, then we'd need to set up proper manufacturing, sales, service, and marketing departments. I sought out friends who'd started their own Silicon Valley companies and solicited their input on everything from profit margins and prices to commissions and customer relationships. While they were generous with their advice, the most valuable lessons I learned were gleaned from the flaws in that advice.

The first question was pretty basic: How do we figure out how much to charge for our machine? I was told by the presidents of Sun and Silicon Graphics to start with a high number. If you start high, they said, you can always reduce the price; if you lowball it and then need to raise the price later, you will only upset your customers. So based on the profit margins we wanted, we decided on a price of $122,000 per unit. Big mistake. The Pixar Image Computer quickly gained a reputation for being powerful but too expensive. When we lowered the price later, we discovered that our reputation for being overpriced was all anyone remembered. Regardless of our attempts to correct it, the first impression stuck.

The pricing advice I was given—by people who were smart and experienced and well-meaning—was not merely wrong, it kept us from asking the right questions. Instead of talking about whether it's easier to lower a price than raise it, we should have been addressing more substantive issues such as how to meet the expectations of customers and how to keep investing in software development so that the customers who *did* buy our product could put it to better use. In retrospect, when I sought the counsel of these more experienced men, I had been seeking simple answers to complex questions—do this, not that—because I was unsure of myself and stressed by the demands of my new job. But simple answers like the "start high" pricing advice—so seductive in its rationality—had distracted me and kept me from asking more fundamental questions.

At the time, we were a computer manufacturing company, so we had to learn very quickly what it meant to produce computers. It was at this time that I happened upon one of the most valuable lessons from the early days of Pixar. And the lesson came from an unexpected source—the history of Japanese manufacturing. No one thinks about the assembly line as a place that engenders creativity. Until that point, I'd associated manufacturing more with efficiency than with inspiration. But I soon discovered that the Japanese had found a way of making production a creative endeavor that engaged its workers—a completely radical and counterintuitive idea at the time. Indeed, the Japanese would have much to teach me about building a creative environment.

In the aftermath of World War II, as America embarked on a sustained period of prosperity, Japan struggled mightily to rebuild its infrastructure. Its economy had been driven to its knees, and its manufacturing base was chronically subpar, crippled by its reputation for extremely poor quality. I remember as a kid growing up in the 1950s, Japanese goods were seen as inferior—even trash. (There is no comparable stigma today. If you see "Made in Mexico" or "Made in China" on a label, it doesn't carry anything close to the negative connotation that "Made in Japan" had back then.) America, by contrast, was a manufacturing powerhouse in these years, and the auto industry led the way. The Ford Motor Company had pioneered the smoothly flowing assembly line, which was the key to producing large quantities of goods at low prices and which, in effect, had revolutionized the manufacturing process. Before long, every automobile maker in America had adopted the practice of moving the product from one worker to another via some sort of conveyor until its assembly was complete. The time saved translated into massive profits, and many other industries, from appliances to furniture to electronics, followed Ford's lead.

The mantra of mass production became: Keep the assembly line going, no matter what, because that was how you kept efficiency up and costs down. Lost time meant lost money. If a particular product in the chain was faulty, you pulled it off immediately, but you *always kept the line rolling*. To make sure the rest of the products were okay, you relied on quality-control inspectors. Hierarchy prevailed. Only upper managers were given the authority to halt the line.

But in 1947, an American working in Japan turned that thinking on its head. His name was W. Edwards Deming, and he was a statistician who was known for his expertise in quality control. At the request of the U.S. Army, he had traveled to Asia to assist with planning the 1951 Japanese census. Once he arrived, he became deeply involved with the country's reconstruction effort and ended up teaching hundreds of Japanese engineers, managers, and scholars his theories about improving productivity. Among those who came to hear his ideas was Akio Morita, the co-founder of Sony Corp.—one of many Japanese companies that would apply his ideas and reap their rewards. Around this time, Toyota also instituted radical new ways of thinking about production that jibed with Deming's philosophies.

Several phrases would later be coined to describe these revolutionary approaches—phrases like "just-in-time manufacturing" or "total quality control"—but the essence was this: The responsibility for finding and fixing problems should be assigned to *every* employee, from the most senior manager to the lowliest person on the production line. If anyone at any level spotted a problem in the manufacturing process, Deming believed, they should be encouraged (and expected) to stop the assembly line. Japanese companies that implemented Deming's ideas made it easy for workers to do so: They installed a cord that anyone could pull in order to bring production to a halt. Before long, Japanese companies were enjoying unheard-of levels of quality, productivity, and market share.

Deming's approach—and Toyota's, too—gave ownership of and responsibility for a product's quality to the people who were most involved in its creation. Instead of merely repeating an action, workers could suggest changes, call out problems, and—this next element seemed particularly important to me—feel the pride that came when they helped fix what was broken. This resulted in continuous improvement, driving out flaws and improving quality. In other words, the Japanese assembly line became a place where workers' engagement strengthened the resulting product. And that would eventually transform manufacturing around the world.

As we struggled to get Pixar off the ground, Deming's work was like a beacon that lit my way. I was fascinated by the fact that, for years, so many American business leaders had been unable to even conceive of the wisdom of his thinking. It wasn't that they were rejecting Deming's ideas as much as they were utterly blind to them. Their certainty about their existing systems had rendered them unable to see. They'd been on top for a while, after all. Why did they need to change their ways?

It would be decades before Deming's ideas took hold here. In fact, it wasn't until the 1980s when a few companies in Silicon Valley, such as Hewlett Packard and Apple, began to incorporate them. But Deming's work would make a huge impression on me and help frame my approach to managing Pixar going forward. While Toyota was a hierarchical organization, to be sure, it was guided by a democratic central tenet: You don't have to ask permission to take responsibility.

A few years ago, when Toyota stumbled—initially failing to acknowledge serious problems with their braking systems, which led to a rare public embarrassment—I remember being struck that a company as smart as Toyota could act in a way that ran so counter to one of its deepest cultural values. Whatever these forces are that make people do dumb things, they are powerful, they are often invisible, and they lurk even in the best of environments.

In the late 1980s, while we were building Pixar, Steve Jobs was spending most of his time trying to establish NeXT, the personal computer company he'd started after being forced out at Apple. He came to the Pixar offices only once a year—so rarely, in fact, that we had to give him directions each time so that he wouldn't get lost. But I was a regular visitor to NeXT. Every few weeks, I'd head down to Steve's office in Redwood City to brief him on our progress. I didn't relish the meetings, to be honest, because they were often frustrating. As we struggled to figure out how to make Pixar profitable, we needed frequent infusions of Steve's money to stay afloat. He often tried to put conditions on the money, which was understandable but also complicated because the conditions he imposed—whether they involved marketing or engineering new products—didn't always correspond to our realities. My memory of that period is that it was one of constant searching for a business model that would put us in the black. There was always reason to believe that the next thing we tried would be the thing that finally worked.

In the first years of Pixar's existence, we had a few triumphs—*Luxo Jr.,* a short film directed by John starring the lamp that is now the Pixar logo, was nominated for an Academy Award in 1987, and the next year, *Tin Toy,* a short film about a wind-up, one-man band toy and the drooling human baby who torments him, garnered Pixar's first Oscar. But we were mostly just hemorrhaging money. For obvious reasons, this increased tensions with Steve. We didn't feel that he understood what we needed, and he didn't feel that we understood how to run a business. We were both right. Steve had every reason to be anxious about us. At Pixar's lowest point, as we floundered and failed to make a profit, Steve had sunk $54 million of his own money into the company—a significant chunk of his net worth, and more money than any venture capital firm would have considered investing, given the sorry state of our balance sheet.

Why were we so deep in the red? Because our initial flurry of sales died away almost instantly—only three hundred Pixar Image Computers were ever sold—and we weren't big enough to design new products quickly. We had grown to more than seventy people, and our overhead was threatening to consume us. As the losses mounted, it became clear that there was only one path forward: We needed to abandon selling hardware. After trying everything we could to sell our Pixar Image Computer, we were finally facing the fact that hardware could not keep us going. Like an explorer perched on the edge of a melting ice floe, we needed to leap to more stable ground. Of course, we had no way of knowing whether where we landed next would support our weight. The only thing that made this leap easier was that we had decided to go all in on what we'd yearned to do from the outset: computer animation. This was where our true passion resided, and the only option left was to go after it with everything we had.

Starting in 1990, around the same time we moved into a concrete box of a building in the warehouse district of Point Richmond, north of Berkeley, we began to focus our energies on the creative side. We started making animated commercials for Trident gum and Tropicana orange juice and almost immediately won awards for the creative content while continuing to hone our technical and storytelling skills. The problem was, we still were taking in significantly less money than we spent. In 1991, we laid off more than a third of our employees.

Three times between 1987 and 1991, a fed-up Steve Jobs tried to sell Pixar. And yet, despite his frustrations, he could never quite bring himself to part with us. When Microsoft offered $90 million for us, he walked away. Steve wanted $120 million, and felt their offer was not just insulting but proof that they weren't worthy of us. The same thing happened with Alias, the industrial and automotive design software company, and with Silicon Graphics. With each suitor, Steve started with a high price and was unwilling to budge. I came to believe that what he was really looking for was not an exit strategy as much as external validation. His reasoning went like this: If Microsoft was willing to go to $90 million, then we must be worth hanging on to. It was difficult—and enervating—to watch this dance.

Pixar could not have survived without Steve, but more than once in those years, I wasn't sure if we'd survive *with* him. Steve could be brilliant and inspirational, capable of diving deeply and intelligently into any problem we faced. But he could also be impossible: dismissive, condescending, threatening, even bullying. Perhaps of most concern, from a management standpoint, was the fact that he exhibited so little empathy. At that point in his life, he was simply unable to put himself in other people's shoes, and his sense of humor was nonexistent. At Pixar, we have always had a pretty deep bench of jokesters and a core belief in having fun, but everything we tried with Steve fell painfully flat. Known for holding forth in meetings to the exclusion of all others, he once briefed a group of us who were about to go into a session with Disney execs by stressing how important it was that we "listen and not talk." The irony was so obvious, I couldn't resist saying: "Okay, Steve, I'll try to restrain myself." Everyone in the room laughed, but he didn't crack a smile. Then we went into the meeting and Steve held court for the full hour, barely letting the folks from Disney finish a sentence.

By this time, I'd spent enough time with Steve to know that he wasn't insensitive at his core—the problem was that he had not yet figured out how to behave in a way that let everyone see that. At one point, in a fit of pique, he called me to say that he refused to make payroll; he only relented after I called him, furious, and read him the riot act about all of the families that were depending on those paychecks. In my entire career, that may be the only time I've ever slammed my door in frustration. Even if Pixar doubled in value, Steve told me, we still wouldn't be worth anything. I felt increasingly burned out. I even thought about resigning.

A funny thing happened, though, as we went through these trials. Steve and I gradually found a way to work together. And as we did so, we began to understand each other. You'll recall the question I asked Steve just before he bought Pixar: How would we resolve conflicts? And his answer, which I found comically egotistical at the time, was that he simply would continue to explain why he was right until I understood. The irony was that this soon became the technique I used with Steve. When we disagreed, I would state my case, but since Steve could think much faster than I could, he would often shoot down my arguments. So I'd wait a week, marshal my thoughts, and then come back and explain it again. He might dismiss my points again, but I would keep coming back until one of three things happened: (1) He would say "Oh, okay, I get it" and give me what I needed; (2) I'd see that he was right and stop lobbying; or (3) our debate would be inconclusive, in which case I'd just go ahead and do what I had proposed in the first place. Each outcome was equally likely, but when this third option occurred,

Steve never questioned me. For all his insistence, he respected passion. If I believed in something that strongly, he seemed to feel, it couldn't be all wrong.

Jeffrey Katzenberg sat at the end of a long, dark wood conference table in the Team Disney building on the studio's lot in Burbank. The head of Disney's motion picture division was in wooing mode—at least up to a point. "It's clear that the talent here is John Lasseter," he said, as John, Steve, and I sat there, trying not to be offended. "And John, since you won't come work for me, I guess I'll have to make it work this way."

Katzenberg wanted Pixar to make a feature film, and he wanted Disney to own and distribute it.

This offer, though surprising to us, did not come entirely out of the blue. Early in Pixar's existence, we'd entered into a contract to write a graphics system for Disney—called the Computer Animation Production System, or CAPS—that would paint and manage animation cels. While CAPS was being created, Disney was producing *The Little Mermaid*, which would become a massive hit in 1989 and, all by itself, launch a second Golden Age of Animation that would also include *Beauty and the Beast, Aladdin,* and *The Lion King.* These films were so successful that they inspired Disney Animation to begin looking for partners to increase its feature film output, and since our track record with the studio was good, they looked to us.

Hammering out our deal with Disney meant coming to terms with Katzenberg—a notoriously wily and tough negotiator. Steve took the reins, rejecting Jeffrey's logic that since Disney was investing in Pixar's first movie, it deserved to own our technology as well. "You're giving us money to *make* the film," Steve said, "not to buy our trade secrets." What Disney brought to the table was its marketing and distribution muscle; what we brought were our technical innovations, and they were not for sale. Steve made this a deal breaker and stuck to his guns until, ultimately, Jeffrey agreed. When the stakes were highest, Steve could go to what seemed another level of play.

In 1991, we struck a three-picture deal under which Disney would provide majority financing for Pixar movies, which Disney would distribute and own. It felt like it had taken a lifetime to get to this point, and in a sense it had. While Pixar, the company, was just five years old, my dream of making a computer-animated feature film was pushing twenty. Once again, we were embarking on something we knew very little about. None of us had ever made a movie before—at least not one longer than five minutes—and since we were using computer animation, there was no one to ask for help. Given the millions of dollars at stake and the realization that we'd never get another chance if we blew it, we had to figure it out fast.

Luckily, John already had an idea. *Toy Story* would be about a group of toys and a boy—Andy—who loves them. The twist was that it would be told from the toys' point of view. The plot would transform again and again over many months, but it would eventually come to revolve around Andy's favorite toy, a cowboy named Woody, whose world is rocked when a shiny new rival, a space ranger named Buzz Lightyear, arrives on the scene and becomes the apple of Andy's eye. John pitched the basic idea to Disney, and after much revising, we got the green light on the script in January 1993.

By this point, John had begun assembling a team, surrounding himself with a number of talented and ambitious young people. He'd hired Andrew Stanton and Pete Docter, who would go on to become two of our most inspired directors, back when we were making commercials. Forceful to the point of red-faced when asserting something he held dear, Andrew was a writer-director with a deep insight into story structure; he loved nothing more than stripping a plot down to its emotional load-bearing sequences and then rebuilding it from the ground up. Pete was a supremely talented draftsman with a knack for capturing emotion on screen. In the fall of 1992, John's former Disney colleague Joe Ranft had come aboard, fresh from working on Tim Burton's *The Nightmare Before Christmas*. Joe, a bear of a man, had a warm and twisted sense of humor that made his criticisms, when he had them, easier to take. Our team was strong but fairly inexperienced. You've probably heard the maxim that it's best to assemble your parachute before you jump out of a plane. Well, in our case we were already in free fall—and not one of us had ever made a parachute before.

For the first year, John and his team would storyboard sequences and then fly down to Disney headquarters to get notes from Jeffrey Katzenberg and his two top executives, Peter Schneider and Tom Schumacher. Jeffrey pushed relentlessly for more "edge." Woody was too perky, too earnest, he thought. That didn't necessarily jibe with our sense of the story, but being novices, we took his advice to heart. Gradually, over a period of months, the character of Woody—originally imagined as affable and easygoing—became darker, meaner . . . and wholly unappealing. Woody was jealous. He threw Buzz out the window for spite. He bossed the other toys around and called them demeaning names. He had, in short, become a jerk. On November 19, 1993, we went to Disney to unveil the new, edgier Woody in a series of story reels—a mock-up of the film, like a comic book version with temporary voices, music, and drawings of the story. That day will forever be known at Pixar as "Black Friday" because Disney's completely reasonable reaction was to shut down the production until an acceptable script was written.

The shutdown was terrifying. With our first feature film suddenly on life support, John quickly summoned Andrew, Pete, and Joe. For the next several months, they spent almost every waking minute together, working to rediscover the heart of the movie, the thing that John had first envisioned: a toy cowboy who wanted to be loved. They also learned an important lesson—to trust their own storytelling instincts.

Meanwhile, as we struggled to finish *Toy Story,* the work that we'd started at Lucasfilm was beginning to have a noticeable impact in Hollywood. In 1991, two of the year's biggest blockbusters— *Beauty and the Beast* and *Terminator 2*—had relied heavily on technology that had been developed at Pixar, and people in Hollywood were starting to pay attention. By 1993, when *Jurassic Park* was released, computer-generated special effects would no longer be considered some nerdy sideline experiment; they were coming to be seen for what they were: tools that enable the making of mainstream entertainment. The digital revolution—with its special effects, crystalline sound quality, and video editing capabilities—had arrived.

John once described Steve's story as the classic Hero's Journey. Banished for his hubris from the company he founded, he wandered through the wilderness having a series of adventures that, in the end, changed him for the better. I have much to say about Steve's transformation and the role Pixar played in it, but for now, I will simply assert that failure made him better, wiser, and kinder. We'd all been affected and humbled by the failures and challenges of our first nine years, but we'd also gained something important along the way. Backing each other through difficulties increased our trust and deepened our bond.

Of course, one thing we could count on was that, at some point, Steve would throw us a curve ball. As we approached *Toy Story*'s release, it was becoming clear that Steve had something much bigger in mind. This wasn't just about a movie—this film, he believed, was going to change the field of animation. And, before that happened, he wanted to take us public.

"Bad idea," John and I told Steve. "Let's get a couple films under our belt first. We'll only increase our value that way."

Steve disagreed. "This is our moment," he said.

He went on to lay out his logic: Let's assume that *Toy Story* is a success, he said. Not only that, let's assume it is a *big* success. When that happens, Disney CEO Michael Eisner will realize that he has created his worst nightmare: a viable competitor to Disney. (We only owed his studio two more films under our contract, then we could go out on our own.) Steve predicted that as soon as *Toy Story* came out, Eisner would try to renegotiate our deal and keep us close, as a partner. In this scenario, Steve said, he wanted to be able to negotiate better terms. Specifically, he wanted a 50/50 split with Disney on returns—a demand, he pointed out, that also happened to be the moral high ground. In order to fulfill these terms, however, we would have to be able to put up the cash for our half of the production budgets—a significant amount of money. And to do that, we would have to go public.

His logic, as it often did, won the day.

Soon, I found myself criss-crossing the country with Steve, in what we called our "dog and pony show," trying to drum up interest in our initial public offering. As we traveled from one investment house to another, Steve (in a costume he rarely wore: suit and tie) pushed to secure early commitments, while I added a professorial presence by donning, at Steve's insistence, a tweed jacket with elbow patches. I was supposed to embody the image of what a "technical genius" looks like—though, frankly, I don't know anyone in computer science who dresses that way. Steve, as pitch man, was on fire. Pixar was a movie studio the likes of which no one had ever seen, he said, built on a foundation of cutting-edge technology and original storytelling. We would go public one week after *Toy Story* opened, when no one would question that Pixar was for real.

Steve turned out to be right. As our first movie broke records at the box office and as all our dreams seemed to be coming true, our initial public offering raised nearly $140 million for the company—the biggest IPO of 1995. And a few months later, as if on cue, Eisner called, saying that he wanted to renegotiate the deal and keep us as a partner. He accepted Steve's offer of a 50/50 split. I was amazed; Steve had called this exactly right. His clarity and execution were stunning.

For me, this moment was the culmination of such a lengthy series of pursuits, it was almost impossible to take in. I had spent twenty years inventing new technological tools, helping to found a company, and working hard to make all the facets of this company communicate and work well together. All of this had been in the service of a single goal: making a computer-animated feature film. And now, we'd not only done it; thanks to Steve, we were on steadier financial ground than we'd ever been before. For the first time since our founding, our jobs were safe.

I wish I could bottle how it felt to come into work during those first heady days after *Toy Story* came out. People seemed to walk a little taller, they were so proud of what we'd done. We'd been the first to make a movie with computers, and—even better—audiences were touched, and touched deeply, by the story we told. As my colleagues went about their work—and we had much to do, including getting more films going and finalizing our negotiations with Disney—every interaction was informed by a sense of pride and accomplishment. We had succeeded by holding true to our ideals; nothing could be better than that. The core team of John, Andrew, Pete, Joe, and Lee Unkrich, who had joined us in 1994 to edit *Toy Story,* immediately moved on to *A Bug's Life,* our movie about the insect world. There was excitement in the air.

But while I could *feel* that euphoria, I was oddly unable to participate in it.

For twenty years, my life had been defined by the goal of making the first computer graphics movie. Now that that goal had been reached, I had what I can only describe as a hollow, lost feeling. As a manager, I felt a troubling lack of purpose. *Now what?* The thing that had replaced it seemed to be the act of running a company, which was more than enough to keep me busy, but it wasn't *special.*

Pixar was now public and successful, yet there was something unsatisfying about the prospect of merely keeping it running.

It took a serious and unexpected problem to give me a new sense of mission.

For all of my talk about the leaders of thriving companies who did stupid things because they'd failed to pay attention, I discovered that, during the making of *Toy Story*, I had completely missed something that was threatening to undo us. And I'd missed it even though I *thought* I'd been paying attention.

Throughout the making of the movie, I had seen my job, in large part, as minding the internal and external dynamics that could divert us from our goal. I was determined that Pixar not make the same mistakes I'd watched other Silicon Valley companies make. To that end, I'd made a point of being accessible to our employees, wandering into people's offices to check in and see what was going on. John and I had very conscientiously tried to make sure that everyone at Pixar had a voice, that every job and every employee was treated with respect. I truly believed that self-assessment and constructive criticism had to occur at all levels of a company, and I had tried my best to walk that talk.

Now, though, as we assembled the crew to work on our second film, *A Bug's Life,* drawing on people who'd been key to *Toy Story*'s evolution, I discovered we'd completely missed a serious, ongoing rift between our creative and production departments. In short, production managers told me that working on *Toy Story* had been a nightmare. They felt disrespected and marginalized—like second-class citizens. And while they were gratified by *Toy Story*'s success, they were very reluctant to sign on to work on another film at Pixar.

I was floored. How had we missed this?

The answer, at least in part, was rooted in the role production managers play in making our films. Production managers are the people who keep track of the endless details that ensure that a movie is delivered on time and on budget. They monitor the overall progress of the crew; they keep track of the thousands of shots; they evaluate how resources are being used; they persuade and cajole and nudge and say no when necessary. In other words, they do something essential for a company whose success relies on hitting deadlines and staying on-budget: They manage people and safeguard the process.

If there was one thing we prided ourselves on at Pixar, it was making sure that Pixar's artists and technical people treated each other as equals, and I had assumed that that same mutual respect would be afforded to those who managed the productions. I had assumed wrong. Sure enough, when I checked with the artists and technical staff, they *did* believe that production managers were second-class and that they impeded—not facilitated—good filmmaking by overcontrolling the process, by micromanaging. Production managers, the folks I consulted told me, were just sand in the gears.

My total ignorance of this dynamic caught me by surprise. My door had always been open! I'd assumed that that would guarantee me a place in the loop, at least when it came to major sources of tension like this. Not a single production manager had dropped by to express frustration or make a suggestion in the five years we worked on *Toy Story*. Why was that? It took some digging to figure it out.

First, since we didn't know what we were doing as we'd geared up to do *Toy Story*, we'd brought in experienced production managers from Los Angeles to help us get organized. They felt that their jobs were temporary and thus that their complaints would not be welcome. In their world—conventional Hollywood productions—freelancers came together to make a film, worked side by side for several months, and then scattered to the winds. Complaining tended to cost you future work opportunities, so they kept their mouths shut. It was only when asked to stay on at Pixar that they voiced their objections.

Second, despite their frustrations, these production managers felt that they were making history and that John was an inspired leader. *Toy Story* was a meaningful project to work on. That they liked so much of what they were doing allowed them to put up with the parts of the job they came to resent. This was a revelation to me: The good stuff was hiding the bad stuff. I realized that this was something I needed to look out for: When downsides coexist with upsides, as they often do, people are reluctant to explore what's bugging them, for fear of being labeled complainers. I also realized that this kind of thing, if left unaddressed, could fester and destroy Pixar.

For me, this discovery was bracing. Being on the lookout for problems, I realized, was not the same as *seeing* problems. This would be the idea—the challenge—around which I would build my new sense of purpose.

While I felt I now understood *why* we had failed to detect this problem, we still needed to understand what it was they were upset about. To that end, I started sticking my head into people's offices, pulling up a chair and asking them for their view on how Pixar was and wasn't working. These conversations were intentionally open-ended. I didn't ask for a list of specific complaints. Bit by bit, conversation by conversation, I came to understand how we'd arrived in this thicket.

There had been a great deal riding on *Toy Story*, of course, and since making a film is an extremely complicated proposition, our production leaders had felt tremendous pressure to control the process—not just the budgets and schedules but the flow of information. If people went willy-nilly to anybody with their issues, they believed, the whole project could spiral out of control. So, to keep things on track, it was made clear to everyone from the get-go: If you have something to say, it needs to be communicated through your direct manager. If an animator wanted to talk to a modeler, for example, they were required to go through "proper channels."

The artists and technical people experienced this everything-goes-through-me mentality as irritating and obstructionist. I think of it as well-intentioned micromanaging.

Because making a movie involves hundreds of people, a chain of command is essential. But in this case, we had made the mistake of confusing the communication structure with the organizational structure. Of course an animator should be able to talk to a modeler directly, without first talking with his or her manager. So we gathered the company together and said: Going forward, anyone should be able to talk to anyone else, at any level, at any time, without fear of reprimand. Communication would no longer have to go through hierarchical channels. The exchange of information was key to our business, of course, but I believed that it could—and frequently should—happen out of order, without people getting bent out of shape. People talking directly to one another, then letting the manager find out later, was more efficient than trying to make sure that everything happened in the "right" order and through the "proper" channels.

Improvement didn't happen overnight. But by the time we finished *A Bug's Life,* the production managers were no longer seen as impediments to creative progress, but as peers—as first-class citizens. We had become better.

This was a success in itself, but it came with an added and unexpected benefit: The act of thinking about the problem and responding to it was invigorating and rewarding. We realized that our purpose was not merely to build a studio that made hit films but to foster a creative culture that would continually ask questions. Questions like: If we had done some things right to achieve success, how could we ensure that we understood what those things were? Could we replicate them on our next projects? Perhaps as important, was replication of success even the right thing to do? How many serious, potentially disastrous problems were lurking just out of sight and threatening to undo us? What, if anything, could we do to bring them to light? How much of our success was luck? What would happen to our egos if we continued to succeed? Would they grow so large they could hurt us, and if so, what could we do to address that overconfidence? What dynamics would arise now that we were bringing new people into a successful enterprise as opposed to a struggling startup?

What had drawn me to science, all those years ago, was the search for understanding. Human interaction is far more complex than relativity or string theory, of course, but that only made it more interesting and important; it constantly challenged my presumptions. As we made more movies, I would learn that some of my beliefs about why and how Pixar had been successful were wrong. But one thing could not have been more plain: Figuring out how to build a sustainable creative culture—one that didn't just pay lip service to the importance of things like honesty, excellence, communication, originality, and self-assessment but really *committed* to them, no matter how uncomfortable that became—wasn't a singular assignment. It was a day-in-day-out, full-time job. And one that I wanted to do.

As I saw it, our mandate was to foster a culture that would seek to keep our sightlines clear, even as we accepted that we were often trying to engage with and fix what we could not see. My hope was to make this culture so vigorous that it would survive when Pixar's founding members were long gone, enabling the company to continue producing original films that made money, yes, but also contributed positively to the world. That sounds like a lofty goal, but it was there for all of us from the beginning. We were blessed with a remarkable group of employees who valued change, risk, and the unknown and who wanted to rethink how we create. How could we enable the talents of these people, keep them happy, and not let the inevitable complexities that come with any collaborative endeavor undo us along the way? That was the job I assigned myself—and the one that still animates me to this day.

CHAPTER 4

ESTABLISHING PIXAR'S IDENTITY

Two defining creative principles emerged in the wake of *Toy Story*. They became mantras, of a sort, phrases we clung to and repeated endlessly in meetings. We believed that they had guided us through the crucible of *Toy Story* and the early stages of *A Bug's Life*, and as a result we took enormous comfort in them.

The first principle was "Story Is King," by which we meant that we would let nothing—not the technology, not the merchandising possibilities—get in the way of our story. We took pride in the fact that reviewers talked mainly about the way *Toy Story* made them *feel* and not about the computer wizardry that enabled us to get it up on the screen. We believed that this was the direct result of our always keeping story as our guiding light.

The other principle we depended on was "Trust the Process." We liked this one because it was so reassuring: While there are inevitably difficulties and missteps in any complex creative endeavor, you can trust that "the process" will carry you through. In some ways, this was no different than any optimistic aphorism ("Hang in there, baby!"), except that because our process was so different from other movie studios, we felt that it had real power. Pixar was a place that gave artists running room, that gave directors control, that trusted its people to solve problems. I have always been wary of maxims or rules because, all too often, they turn out to be empty platitudes that impede thoughtfulness, but these two principles actually seemed to help our people.

Which was good, because we would soon need all the help we could get.

In 1997, executives at Disney came to us with a request: Could we make *Toy Story 2* as a direct-to-video release—that is, not release it in theaters? At the time, Disney's suggestion made a lot of sense. In its history, the studio had only released one animated sequel in theaters, 1990's *The Rescuers Down Under,* and it had been a flop. In the years since, the direct-to-video market had become extremely lucrative, so when Disney proposed *Toy Story 2* for video release only—a niche product with a lower artistic bar—we said yes. While we questioned the quality of most sequels made for the video market, we thought that we could do better.

Right away, we realized that we'd made a terrible mistake. Everything about the project ran counter to what we believed in. We didn't know how to aim low. We had nothing against the direct-to-video model, in theory; Disney was doing it and making heaps of money. We just couldn't figure out how to go about it without sacrificing quality. What's more, it soon became clear that scaling back our expectations to make a direct-to-video product was having a negative impact on our internal culture, in that it created an A-team (*A Bug's Life*) and a B-team (*Toy Story 2*). The crew assigned to work on *Toy Story 2* was not interested in producing B-level work, and more than a few came into my office to say so. It would have been foolish to ignore their passion.

A few months into the project, we called a meeting with the Disney execs to sell them on the idea that the direct-to-video model wasn't going to work for us. It wasn't what Pixar was about. We proposed changing course and making *Toy Story 2* for theatrical release. To our surprise, they readily agreed. Suddenly, we were making two ambitious feature films at once—doubling our theatrical output overnight. This was a little scary, but it also felt like an affirmation of our core values. As we staffed up, I felt proud that we had insisted on quality. Decisions like that, I believed, would ensure future success.

The production of *Toy Story 2,* however, would be severely hindered by a series of faulty assumptions on our part. Since this was "only" a sequel, we told ourselves, it wouldn't be as arduous to make as the original. While the creative team that had led *Toy Story* focused on *A Bug's Life,* we picked two skilled animators (and first-time directors) to helm *Toy Story 2*. All of us assumed that an inexperienced team—when backed up by an experienced team—would be able to simply replicate the success of our first film. Bolstering our confidence was the fact that the outlines of the *Toy Story 2* plot had already been worked out by John Lasseter and the original *Toy Story* team: By mistake, Woody would be sold at a yard sale to a toy collector who—to preserve the toys' value—locked them away, never to be played with again, in order to sell them to a museum in Japan. The characters were known, the look was established, the technical crew was experienced and nimble, and we as a company had a fuller understanding of the filmmaking process. We thought we had it figured out.

We were wrong.

A year into production, I began to notice signs of trouble. Mainly, the directors were lobbing a continuous stream of requests for more "John time"—seeking to get on his calendar to pick his brain. This was worrisome. To me, it signaled that, as talented as the *Toy Story 2* directors were individually, they lacked confidence and weren't gelling as a team.

And then there were the reels. At Pixar, our directors gather every few months to screen "reels" of their film—spliced-together drawings, paired with what's called "temp" music and voices. First reels are a very rough approximation of what the final product will be; they're flawed and messy, no matter how good the team is that's making them. But looking at them is the only way to see what needs fixing. You cannot judge a team by the early reels. You do hope, however, that over time, the reels get better. In this case, they weren't getting better—months would pass, and the reels were still varying degrees of bad. Alarmed, some of us shared our worries with John and the original *Toy Story* creative team. They advised us to give it more time, to trust the process.

Only after *A Bug's Life* opened on Thanksgiving weekend 1998 did John finally have the time to sit down and take a hard look at what the *Toy Story 2* directors had produced up to that point. He went into one of our screening rooms to watch the reels. A couple of hours later, he emerged, walked right into my office, and shut the door. *Disaster* is the word he used. The story was hollow, predictable, without tension; the humor fell flat. We'd gone to Disney and insisted on swinging for the fences, rejecting the idea of settling for a B-level product. Now we wondered: Were we doing just that? There was no question that we couldn't go forward with the film as it was. This was a full-fledged crisis.

Before we could come up with a plan for fixing it, however, a meeting at Disney loomed—a previously scheduled screening to keep the Disney executives in the *Toy Story 2* loop. In December, Andrew (who often functioned as John's right hand) took the deeply flawed version of the film down to Burbank. A group of executives gathered in one of the screening rooms, the lights went down, and Andrew sat there, gritting his teeth, waiting for it to end. When the lights came up, he jumped right in.

"We know the film needs major changes," he said. "And we're in the process of mapping them out."

To his surprise, the Disney execs disagreed—the movie was good enough, and besides, there wasn't time to do an overhaul. *It's only a sequel.* Politely but firmly, Andrew demurred. "We're going to redo it," he said.

Back at Pixar, John told everyone to get some rest over the holidays, because starting January 2, we were re-boarding the entire movie. Together, we sought to send a swift, clear message: Righting this ship would require all hands on deck.

But first, we had to make a difficult decision. It was obvious that to save the film, a change was needed at the top. This would be the first time I would have to tell the directors of a film that we were replacing them, and it was anything but easy. Neither John nor I relished breaking the news that they were out and that John would now be taking over on *Toy Story 2*. But it had to be done. We couldn't lobby Disney for the chance to make a theatrical release, insist on our excellence, and then deliver something subpar.

The directors were shaken, and so were we. In a sense, we had failed them—causing them pain by putting them in a position they weren't ready for. Our role in that failure required some soul searching on my part. What was it that we missed? What led us to make such flawed assumptions, and to fail to intervene when the evidence was mounting that the film was in trouble? It was the first time we gave a position to someone believing they could do it, only to find that they couldn't. I wanted to understand why. While I pondered these things, the press of deadline forced us to move forward. We had nine months to deliver the film—not nearly enough time, even for the most experienced crew. But we were determined. It was unthinkable that we not do our best.

Our first job was fixing the story. Addressing its flaws would be the responsibility of a group that had emerged organically during the making of *Toy Story*. The members of this group, which at some point we'd started calling the Braintrust, were proven problem solvers who worked magnificently together to dissect scenes that were falling flat. I'll say more about the Braintrust and how it functions in the next chapter, but its most important characteristic was an ability to analyze the emotional beats of a movie without any of its members themselves getting emotional or defensive. To be clear, this wasn't a group that we had set out to create. But it was an enormous help to the company. The group would later expand, but at this point it consisted of just five members: John, Andrew Stanton, Pete Docter, Joe Ranft, and Lee Unkrich, a virtuosic editor from a small town in Ohio whose name sounds straight out of a Pixar movie: Chagrin Falls. Lee had joined us in 1994 and had quickly become known for his superb sense of timing. Now, John tapped him as co-director of *Toy Story 2*. The next nine months would be the most grueling production schedule we would ever undertake—the crucible in which Pixar's true identity was forged.

As John and his creative team went to work, I considered the stark reality we faced. We were asking our people to pull off the cinematic equivalent of a heart transplant. We had less than a year before *Toy Story 2* was due in theaters. Getting it there in time would drive our workforce to the breaking point, and there would surely be a price to pay for that. But I also believed that the alternative—acceptance of mediocrity—would have consequences that were far more destructive.

The most fundamental problem with the film, when John first called his team together, was that it was an escape saga with a predictable, and not very emotional, arc. The story, which took place about three years after the events in *Toy Story,* revolved around whether Woody would choose to flee the pampered and protected (but isolated) existence—the life of a "collectible"—that Al, the collector, had forced upon him. Would he or would he not fight for the chance to go home to his original owner, Andy? For the film to work, viewers would have to believe that the choice Woody was weighing—whether to return to a world where Andy will someday outgrow and discard him or to remain in a place of security, with no one to love him—was real. But since viewers knew that this film was from Pixar and Disney, they would just assume that there would be a happy ending—meaning that Woody would choose to go back to reunite with Andy. What the film needed were reasons to believe that Woody was facing a real dilemma, and one that viewers could relate to. What it needed, in other words, was drama.

The movie always began with Woody preparing to go to cowboy camp with Andy, only to suffer a rip in his arm that caused Andy to leave him behind (and Andy's mother to put him away on a shelf). At this point, the Braintrust made the first of two key changes: They added a character named Wheezy the penguin, who tells Woody that he has been on that same shelf for months because of a broken squeaker. Wheezy introduces the idea early on that no matter how cherished, when a toy gets damaged, it is likely to be shelved, tossed aside—maybe for good. Wheezy, then, establishes the emotional stakes of the story.

The second fundamental tweak the Braintrust made was to beef up the story of Jessie, a cowgirl doll who had loved her little girl owner, just as Woody loved Andy, only to be abandoned when the girl outgrew her toys. Jessie's message to Woody—which would now be wrenchingly told in a montage sequence, accompanied by the Sarah McLachlan song "When She Loved Me"—was that no matter what you want or how much you care, Andy is someday going to put away childish things. Jessie picks up the theme that Wheezy set in motion, and her sassy interactions with Woody allow that theme—once implicit—to be discussed openly.

With the addition of Wheezy and Jessie, Woody's choice became more fraught: He could stay with someone he loves, knowing that he will eventually be discarded, or he could flee to a world where he could be pampered forever, but without the love that he was built for. That is a real choice, a real question. The way the creative team phrased it to each other was: Would *you* choose to live forever without love? When you can feel the agony of that choice, you have a movie.

While Woody would choose Andy in the end, he would make that choice with the awareness that doing so guaranteed future sadness. "I can't stop Andy from growing up," he tells Stinky Pete the Prospector. "But I wouldn't miss it for the world."

With the story reconceived, the entire company gathered one morning in the lunchroom of a building we had taken over across the street from our original warehouse in Point Richmond. The name of this annex, which we'd commandeered as the company grew, was Frogtown (the site had once been a marsh). At the appointed time, John walked to the front of the room and pitched the new, more emotionally wrenching throughline of *Toy Story 2* to our colleagues, who applauded when he was done. In another, smaller meeting with just the *Toy Story 2* crew, Steve Jobs added his endorsement. "Disney doesn't think we can do this," he said. "So let's prove them wrong."

Then the heavy lifting began.

For the next six months, our employees rarely saw their families. We worked deep into the night, seven days a week. Despite two hit movies, we were conscious of the need to prove ourselves, and everyone gave everything they had. With several months still to go, the staff was exhausted and starting to fray.

One morning in June, an overtired artist drove to work with his infant child strapped into the backseat, intending to deliver the baby to day care on the way. Some time later, after he'd been at work for a few hours, his wife (also a Pixar employee) happened to ask him how drop-off had gone—which is when he realized that he'd left their child in the car in the broiling Pixar parking lot. They rushed out to find the baby unconscious and poured cold water over him immediately. Thankfully, the child was okay, but the trauma of this moment—the what-could-have-been—was imprinted deeply on my brain. Asking this much of our people, even when they wanted to give it, was not acceptable. I had expected the road to be rough, but I had to admit that we were coming apart. By the time the film was complete, a full third of the staff would have some kind of repetitive stress injury.

In the end, we would meet our deadline—and release our third hit film. Critics raved that *Toy Story 2* was one of the only sequels ever to outshine the original, and the total box office would eventually top $500 million. Everyone was fried to the core, yet there was also a feeling that despite all the pain, we had pulled off something important, something that would define Pixar for years to come.

As Lee Unkrich says, "We had done the impossible. We had done the thing that everyone told us we couldn't do. And we had done it spectacularly well. It was the fuel that has continued to burn in all of us."

The gestation of *Toy Story 2* offers a number of lessons that were vital to Pixar's evolution. Remember that the spine of the story—Woody's dilemma, to stay or to go—was the same before and after the Braintrust worked it over. One version didn't work at all, and the other was deeply affecting. Why? Talented storytellers had found a way to make viewers care, and the evolution of this story-line made it abundantly clear to me: If you give a good idea to a mediocre team, they will screw it up. If you give a mediocre idea to a brilliant team, they will either fix it or throw it away and come up with something better.

The takeaway here is worth repeating: Getting the team right is the necessary precursor to getting the ideas right. It is easy to say you want talented people, and you do, but the way those people interact with one another is the real key. Even the smartest people can form an ineffective team if they are mismatched. That means it is better to focus on how a team is performing, not on the talents of the individuals within it. A good team is made up of people who complement each other. There is an important principle here that may seem obvious, yet—in my experience—is not obvious at all. Getting the right people and the right chemistry is more important than getting the right idea.

This is an issue I have thought a lot about over the years. Once, I was having lunch with the president of another movie studio, who told me that his biggest problem was not finding good people; it was finding good ideas. I remember being stunned when he said that—it seemed patently false to me, in part because I'd found the exact opposite to be true on *Toy Story 2*. I resolved to test whether what seemed a given to me was, in fact, a common belief. So for the next couple of years I made a habit, when giving talks, of posing the question to my audience: Which is more valuable, good ideas or good people? No matter whether I was talking to retired business executives or students, to high school principals or artists, when I asked for a show of hands, the audiences would be split 50-50. (Statisticians will tell you that when you get a perfect split like this, it doesn't mean that half know the right answer—it means that they are all guessing, picking at random, as if flipping a coin.)

People think so little about this that, in all these years, only one person in an audience has ever pointed out the false dichotomy. To me, the answer should be obvious: Ideas come from people. Therefore, people are more important than ideas.

Why are we confused about this? Because too many of us think of ideas as being singular, as if they float in the ether, fully formed and independent of the people who wrestle with them. Ideas, though, are not singular. They are forged through tens of thousands of decisions, often made by dozens of people. In any given Pixar film, every line of dialogue, every beam of light or patch of shade, every sound effect is there because it contributes to the greater whole. In the end, if you do it right, people come out of the theater and say, "A movie about talking toys—what a clever idea!" But a movie is not one idea, it's a multitude of them. And behind these ideas are people. This is true of products in general; the iPhone, for example, is not a singular idea—there is a mind-boggling depth to the hardware and software that supports it. Yet too often, we see a single object and think of it as an island that exists apart and unto itself.

To reiterate, it is the focus on people—their work habits, their talents, their values—that is absolutely central to any creative venture. And in the wake of *Toy Story 2*, I saw that more clearly than I ever had. That clarity, in turn, led me to make some changes. Looking around, I realized we had a few traditions that didn't put people first. For example, we had a development department, as do all movie studios, that was charged with seeking out and developing ideas to make into films. Now I saw that this made no sense. Going forward, the development department's charter would be not to develop scripts but to hire good people, figure out what they needed, assign them to projects that matched their skills, and make sure they functioned well together. To this day, we keep adjusting and fiddling with this model, but the underlying goals remain the same: Find, develop, and support good people, and they in turn will find, develop, and own good ideas.

In a sense, this was related to my thinking about W. Edward Deming's work in Japan. Though Pixar didn't rely on a traditional assembly line—that is, with conveyor belts connecting each work station—the making of a film happened in order, with each team passing the product, or idea, off to the next, who pushed it further down the line. To ensure quality, I believed, any person on any team needed to be able to identify a problem and, in effect, pull the cord to stop the line. To create a culture in which this was possible, you needed more than a cord within easy reach. You needed to show your people that you meant it when you said that while efficiency was *a* goal, quality was *the* goal. More and more, I saw that by putting people first—not just *saying* that we did, but *proving* that we did by the actions we took—we were protecting that culture.

On the most basic level, *Toy Story 2* was a wakeup call. Going forward, the needs of a movie could never again outweigh the needs of our people. We needed to do more to keep them healthy. As soon as we wrapped the film, we set about addressing the needs of our injured, stressed-out employees and coming up with strategies to prevent future deadline pressures from hurting our workers again. These strategies went beyond ergonomically designed workstations, yoga classes, and physical therapy. *Toy Story 2* was a case study in how something that is usually considered a plus—a motivated, workaholic workforce pulling together to make a deadline—

could destroy itself if left unchecked. Though I was immensely proud of what we had accomplished, I vowed that we would never make a film that way again. It was management's job to take the long view, to intervene and protect our people from their willingness to pursue excellence at all costs. Not to do so would be irresponsible.

This is trickier than you might think. As a group, Pixar's people take pride in their work. They're ambitious high achievers who want to do their best and then some. On the management side, we want the next product to be better than the last, while at the same time we need to meet budget and schedule requirements. Inspiring managers push their people to excel. That's what we expect them to do. But when the powerful forces that create this positive dynamic turn negative, they are hard to counteract. It's a fine line. On any film, there are inevitable periods of extreme crunch and stress, some of which can be healthy if they don't go on too long. But the ambitions of both managers and their teams can exacerbate each other and become unhealthy. It is a leader's responsibility to see this, and guide it, not exploit it.

If we are in this for the long haul, we have to take care of ourselves, support healthy habits, and encourage our employees to have fulfilling lives outside of work. Moreover, everyone's home lives change as they—and their children, if they have them—age. This means creating a culture in which taking maternity or paternity leave is not seen as an impediment to career advancement. That may not sound revolutionary, but at many companies, parents know that taking that leave comes at a cost; a truly committed employee, they are wordlessly told, *wants* to be at work. That's not true at Pixar.

Supporting your employees means encouraging them to strike a balance not merely by saying, "Be balanced!" but also by making it easier for them to achieve balance. (Having a swimming pool, a volleyball court, and a soccer field on-site tells our workers that we value exercise and a life beyond the desk.) But leadership also means paying close attention to ever-changing dynamics in the workplace. For example, when our younger employees—those without families—work longer hours than those who are parents, we must be mindful not to compare the output of these two groups without being mindful of the context. I'm not talking just about the health of our employees here; I'm talking about their long-term productivity and happiness. Investing in this stuff pays dividends down the line.

I know of one gaming company in Los Angeles that had a stated goal of turning over 15 percent of its workforce every year. The reasoning behind such a policy was that productivity shoots up when you hire smart, hungry kids fresh out of school and work them to death. Attrition was inevitable under such conditions, but that was okay, because the company's needs outweighed those of the worker. Did it work? Sure, maybe. To a point. But if you ask me, that kind of thinking is not just misguided, it is immoral. At Pixar, I have made it known that we must always have the flexibility to recognize and support the need for balance in all of our employees' lives. While all of us believed in that principle—and had from the beginning—*Toy Story 2* helped me see how those beliefs could get pushed aside in the face of immediate pressures.

I began this chapter by talking about two phrases that, to my mind, both helped us and deluded us in the early days of Pixar. Coming out of *Toy Story,* we thought that "Story Is King" and "Trust the Process" were core principles that would carry us forward and keep us focused—that the phrases themselves had the power to help us do better work. It's not just Pixar people who believe this, by the way. Try it yourself. Say to somebody in the creative world that "story is king," and they will nod their heads vigorously. Of course! It just rings true. Everyone knows how important a well-wrought, emotionally affecting storyline is to any movie.

"Story Is King" differentiated us, we thought, not just because we said it but also because we believed it and acted accordingly. As I talked to more people in the industry and learned more about other studios, however, I found that *everyone* repeated some version of this mantra—it didn't matter whether they were making a genuine work of art or complete dreck, they *all* said that story is the most important thing. This was a reminder of something that sounds obvious but isn't: Merely repeating ideas means nothing. You must act—and think—accordingly. Parroting the phrase "Story Is King" at Pixar didn't help the inexperienced directors on *Toy Story 2* one bit. What I'm saying is that this guiding principle, while simply stated and easily repeated, didn't protect us from things going wrong. In fact, it gave us false assurance that things would be okay.

Likewise, we "trusted the process," but the process didn't save *Toy Story 2* either. "Trust the Process" had morphed into "Assume that the Process Will Fix Things for Us." It gave us solace, which we felt we needed. But it also coaxed us into letting down our guard and, in the end, made us passive. Even worse, it made us sloppy.

Once this became clear to me, I began telling people that the phrase was meaningless. I told our staff that it had become a crutch that was distracting us from engaging, in a meaningful way, with our problems. We should trust in *people,* I told them, not processes. The error we'd made was forgetting that "the process" has no agenda and doesn't have taste. It is just a tool—a framework. We needed to take more responsibility and ownership of our own work, our need for self-discipline, and our goals.

Imagine an old, heavy suitcase whose well-worn handles are hanging by a few threads. The handle is "Trust the Process" or "Story Is King"—a pithy statement that seems, on the face of it, to stand for so much more. The suitcase represents all that has gone into the formation of the phrase: the experience, the deep wisdom, the truths that emerge from struggle. Too often, we grab the handle and—without realizing it—walk off without the suitcase. What's more, we don't even think about what we've left behind. After all, the handle is so much easier to carry around than the suitcase.

Once you're aware of the suitcase/handle problem, you'll see it everywhere. People glom onto words and stories that are often just stand-ins for real action and meaning. Advertisers look for words that imply a product's value and use that as a substitute for value itself. Companies constantly tell us about their commitment to excellence, implying that this means they will make only top-shelf products. Words like *quality* and *excellence* are misapplied so relentlessly that they border on meaningless. Managers scour books and magazines looking for greater understanding but settle instead for adopting a new terminology, thinking that using fresh words will bring them closer to their goals. When someone comes up with a phrase that sticks, it becomes a meme, which migrates around even as it disconnects from its original meaning.

To ensure quality, then, *excellence* must be an *earned* word, attributed by others to us, not proclaimed by us about ourselves. It is the responsibility of good leaders to make sure that words remain attached to the meanings and ideals they represent.

I should say here that even as I rail against "Trust the Process" as a flawed motivational tool, I still understand the need for faith in a creative context. Because we are often working to invent something that doesn't yet exist, it can be scary to come to work. Early on in the production of a film, chaos reigns. The bulk of what the directors and their teams are doing is not cohering, and the responsibilities, pressures, and expectations are intense. How, then, do you move forward when so little is visible and so much is unknown?

I have seen directors and writers who were stuck and could not get unstuck, because they couldn't see where to go next. It is here that some of my colleagues have insisted that I am wrong, that "Trust the Process" has meaning—they see it as code for "Keep on going, even when things look bleak." When we trust the process, they argue, we can relax, let go, take a flyer on something radical.

We can accept that any given idea may not work and yet minimize our fear of failure because we believe we will get there in the end. When we trust the process, we remember that we are resilient, that we've experienced discouragement before, only to come out the other side. When we trust the process—or perhaps more accurately, when we trust the people who *use* the process—we are optimistic but also realistic. The trust comes from knowing that we are safe, that our colleagues will not judge us for failures but will encourage us to keep pushing the boundaries. But to me, the key is not to let this trust, our faith, lull us into the abdication of personal responsibility. When that happens, we fall into dull repetition, producing empty versions of what was made before.

As Brad Bird, who joined Pixar as a director in 2000, likes to say, "The process either makes you or unmakes you." I like Brad's way of looking at it because while it gives the process power, it implies that we have an active role to play in it as well. Katherine Sarafian, a producer who's been at Pixar since *Toy Story,* tells me she prefers to envision *triggering* the process over *trusting* it— observing it to see where it's faltering, then slapping it around a bit to make sure it's awake. Again, the individual plays the active role, not the process itself. Or, to put it another way, it is up to the individual to remember that it's okay to use the handle, just as long as you don't forget the suitcase.

At Pixar, *Toy Story 2* taught us this lesson—that we must always be alert to shifting dynamics, because our future depends on it—once and for all. Begun as a direct-to-video sequel, the project proved not only that it was important to everyone that we weren't tolerating second-class films but also that *everything* we did— everything associated with our name—needed to be good. Thinking this way was not just about morale; it was a signal to everyone at Pixar that they were part owners of the company's greatest asset—its quality.

Around this time, John coined a new phrase: "Quality is the best business plan." What he meant was that quality is not a consequence of following some set of behaviors. Rather, it is a prerequisite and a mindset you must have *before* you decide what you are setting out to do. Everyone says quality is important, but they must do more than say it. They must live, think, and breathe it. When our people asserted that they only wanted to make films of the highest quality and when we pushed ourselves to the limit in order to prove our commitment to that ideal, Pixar's identity was cemented. We would be a company that would never settle. That didn't mean that we wouldn't make mistakes. Mistakes are part of creativity. But when we did, we would strive to face them without defensiveness and with a willingness to change. Struggling through the production of *Toy Story 2* twisted our heads around, causing us to look inward, to be self-critical and to change the way we thought about ourselves. When I say this was the defining moment for Pixar, I mean it in the most dynamic sense. Our need for and embrace of introspection was just beginning.

In the next section of the book, I want to explore how that introspection developed. The chapters revolve around the questions we would soon be tackling as a company: What is the nature of honesty? If everyone agrees about its importance, why do we find it hard to be frank? How do we think about our own failures and fears? Is there a way to make our managers more comfortable with unexpected results—the inevitable surprises that arise, no matter how well you've planned? How can we address the imperative many managers feel to overcontrol the process? With what we have learned so far, can we finally get the process right? Where are we still deluded?

These questions would continue to challenge us for years to come—indeed, even to this day.

PART II

PROTECTING THE NEW

CHAPTER 5

HONESTY AND CANDOR

Ask anyone, "Should people be honest?" and of course their answer will be yes. It has to be! Saying no is to endorse dishonesty, which is like coming out against literacy or childhood nutrition—it sounds like a moral transgression. But the fact is, there are often good reasons *not* to be honest. When it comes to interacting with other people in a work environment, there are times when we choose not to say what we really think.

This creates a dilemma. On one level, the only way to get a grip on the facts, issues, and nuances we need to solve problems and collaborate effectively is by communicating fully and openly, by *not* withholding or misleading. There is no doubt that our decision-making is better if we are able to draw on the collective knowledge and unvarnished opinions of the group. But as valuable as the information is that comes from honesty and as loudly as we proclaim its importance, our own fears and instincts for self-preservation often cause us to hold back. To address this reality, we need to free ourselves of *honesty*'s baggage.

One way to do that is to replace the word *honesty* with another word that has a similar meaning but fewer moral connotations: *candor*. Candor is forthrightness or frankness—not so different from honesty, really. And yet, in common usage, the word communicates not just truth-telling but a lack of reserve. Everyone knows that sometimes, being reserved is healthy, even necessary for survival. Nobody thinks that being less than candid makes you a bad person (while no one wants to be called dishonest). People have an easier time talking about their level of candor because they don't think they will be punished for admitting that they sometimes hold their tongues. This is essential. You cannot address the obstacles to candor until people feel free to say that they exist (and using the word *honesty* only makes it harder to talk about those barriers).

Of course, there are sometimes legitimate reasons not to be candid. Politicians, for example, can pay a steep price for speaking too bluntly about contentious issues. CEOs can get dinged for being too open with the press or with shareholders, and they certainly don't want competitors to know their plans. I will be less than candid at work if it means not embarrassing or offending someone or in any number of situations where choosing my words carefully feels like the smart strategy. But that's not to say lack of candor should be celebrated. A hallmark of a healthy creative culture is that its people feel free to share ideas, opinions, and criticisms. Lack of candor, if unchecked, ultimately leads to dysfunctional environments.

So how can a manager ensure that his or her working group, department, or company is embracing candor? I look for ways to institutionalize it by putting mechanisms in place that explicitly say it is valuable. In this chapter, we will look into the workings of one of Pixar's key mechanisms: the Braintrust, which we rely upon to push us toward excellence and to root out mediocrity. The Braintrust, which meets every few months or so to assess each movie we're making, is our primary delivery system for straight talk. Its premise is simple: Put smart, passionate people in a room together, charge them with identifying and solving problems, and encourage them to be candid with one another. People who would feel obligated to be honest somehow feel freer when asked for their candor; they have a choice about whether to give it, and thus, when they do give it, it tends to be genuine. The Braintrust is one of the most important traditions at Pixar. It's not foolproof—sometimes its interactions only serve to highlight the difficulties of achieving candor—but when we get it right, the results are phenomenal. The Braintrust sets the tone for everything we do.

In many ways, it is no different than any other group of creative people—within it, you will find humility and ego, openness and generosity. It varies in size and purpose, depending on what it has been called upon to examine. But always, its most essential element is candor. This isn't just some pie-in-the-sky idea—without the critical ingredient that is candor, there can be no trust. And without trust, creative collaboration is not possible.

Over the years, as the Braintrust has evolved, the dynamics within the group have evolved along with it, and this has required continual attention on our part. While I attend and participate in almost all Braintrust meetings and enjoy discussing the storytelling, I see my primary role (and that of my colleague Jim Morris, who is Pixar's general manager) as making sure that the compact upon which the meetings are based is protected and upheld. This part of our job is never done because, as it turns out, you can't address or eliminate the blocks to candor once and for all. The fear of saying something stupid and looking bad, of offending someone or being intimidated, of retaliating or being retaliated against—they all have a way of reasserting themselves, even once you think they've been vanquished. And when they do, you must address them squarely.

There is some dispute about when, exactly, the Braintrust came into being. That's because it developed organically, growing out of the rare working relationship among the five men who led and edited the production of *Toy Story*—John Lasseter, Andrew Stanton, Pete Docter, Lee Unkrich, and Joe Ranft. From Pixar's earliest days, this quintet gave us a solid example of what a highly functional working group should be. They were funny, focused, smart, and relentlessly candid with each other. Most crucially, they never allowed themselves to be thwarted by the kinds of structural or personal issues that can render meaningful communication in a group setting impossible. It was only when we rallied to fix *Toy Story 2*, coming together to solve a crisis, that the "Braintrust" entered the Pixar lexicon as an official term.

Over those nine months in 1999, when we were rushing to reboot this broken film, the Braintrust would evolve into an enormously beneficial and efficient entity. Even in its earliest meetings, I was struck by how constructive the feedback was. Each of the participants focused on the film at hand and not on some hidden personal agenda. They argued—sometimes heatedly—but always about the project. They were not motivated by the kinds of things—getting credit for an idea, pleasing their supervisors, winning a point just to say you did—that too often lurk beneath the surface of work-related interactions. The members saw each other as peers. The passion expressed in a Braintrust meeting was never taken personally because everyone knew it was directed at solving problems. And largely because of that trust and mutual respect, its problem-solving powers were immense.

After the release of *Toy Story 2*, our production slate expanded rapidly. Suddenly, we had several projects going at once, which meant that we couldn't have the same five people working exclusively on every film. We were not a little startup anymore. Pete was off working on *Monsters, Inc.*, Andrew had started *Finding Nemo*, and Brad Bird had joined us to begin work on *The Incredibles*. The Braintrust had to evolve, then, from a tight, well-defined group that worked on one film together until it was done to a larger, more fluid group that assembled, as needed, to solve problems on all our films.

While we still called it the Braintrust, there was no hard-and-fast membership list. Over the years, its ranks have grown to include a variety of people—directors, writers, and heads of story—whose only requirement is that they display a knack for storytelling. (Among those talented additions: Mary Coleman, the head of Pixar's story department; development executives Kiel Murray and Karen Paik; and writers Michael Arndt, Meg LeFauve, and Victoria Strouse.) The one thing that has never changed is the demand for candor—which, while its value seems obvious, is harder to achieve than one might think.

Let's imagine that you just joined a Braintrust meeting for the first time and sat down in a room full of smart and experienced people to discuss a film that has just been screened. There are many good reasons to be careful about what you say, right? You want to be polite, you want to respect or defer to others, and you don't want to embarrass yourself or come off as having all the answers. Before you speak up, no matter how self-assured you are, you will check yourself: Is this a good idea or a stupid one? How many times am I allowed to say something stupid before others begin to doubt me? Can I tell the director that his protagonist is unlikable or that his second act is incomprehensible? It's not that you want to be dishonest or to withhold from others. At this stage, you aren't even thinking about candor. You're thinking about not looking like an idiot.

Compounding matters is the fact that you aren't the only one who's struggling with these doubts. Everyone is; societal conditioning discourages telling the truth to those perceived to be in higher positions. Then there's human nature. The more people there are in the room, the more pressure there is to perform well. Strong and confident people can intimidate their colleagues, subconsciously signaling that they aren't interested in negative feedback or criticism that challenges their thinking. When the stakes are high and there is a sense that people in the room don't understand a director's project, it can feel to that director like everything they've worked so hard on is in jeopardy, under attack. Their brains go into overdrive, reading all of the subtexts and fighting off the perceived threats to what they've built. When so much is on the line, the barriers to truly candid discussions are formidable.

And yet, candor could not be more crucial to our creative process. Why? Because early on, *all* of our movies suck. That's a blunt assessment, I know, but I make a point of repeating it often, and I choose that phrasing because saying it in a softer way fails to convey how bad the first versions of our films really are. I'm not trying to be modest or self-effacing by saying this. Pixar films are not good at first, and our job is to make them so—to go, as I say, "from suck to not-suck." This idea—that all the movies we now think of as brilliant were, at one time, terrible—is a hard concept for many to grasp. But think about how easy it would be for a movie about talking toys to feel derivative, sappy, or overtly merchandise-driven. Think about how off-putting a movie about rats preparing food could be, or how risky it must've seemed to start WALL-E with 39 dialogue-free minutes. We dare to attempt these stories, but we don't get them right on the first pass. And this is as it should be. Creativity has to start somewhere, and we are true believers in the power of bracing, candid feedback and the iterative process— reworking, reworking, and reworking again, until a flawed story finds its throughline or a hollow character finds its soul.

As I've discussed, first we draw storyboards of the script and then edit them together with temporary voices and music to make a crude mock-up of the film, known as reels. Then the Braintrust watches this version of the movie and discusses what's not ringing true, what could be better, what's not working at all. Notably, they do not *prescribe* how to fix the problems they diagnose. They test weak points, they make suggestions, but it is up to the director to settle on a path forward. A new version of the movie is generated every three to six months, and the process repeats itself. (It takes about twelve thousand storyboard drawings to make one 90-minute reel, and because of the iterative nature of the process I'm describing, story teams commonly create ten times that number by the time their work is done.) In general, the movie steadily improves with each iteration, although sometimes a director becomes stuck, unable to address the feedback he or she is being given. Luckily, another Braintrust meeting is usually around the corner.

To understand what the Braintrust does and why it is so central to Pixar, you have to start with a basic truth: People who take on complicated creative projects become lost at some point in the process. It is the nature of things—in order to create, you must internalize and almost *become* the project for a while, and that near-fusing with the project is an essential part of its emergence. But it is also confusing. Where once a movie's writer/director had perspective, he or she loses it. Where once he or she could see a forest, now there are only trees. The details converge to obscure the whole, and that makes it difficult to move forward substantially in any one direction. The experience can be overwhelming.

All directors, no matter how talented, organized, or clear of vision, become lost somewhere along the way. That creates a problem for those who seek to give helpful feedback. How do you get a director to address a problem he or she cannot see? The answer depends, of course, on the situation. The director may be right about the potential impact of his central idea, but maybe he simply hasn't set it up well enough for the Braintrust to understand that. Maybe he doesn't realize that much of what he *thinks* is visible on screen is, in fact, only visible in his own head. Or maybe the ideas presented in the reels don't work and won't ever work, and the only path forward is to blow something up or start over. No matter what, the process of coming to clarity takes patience and candor.

In Hollywood, studio executives typically communicate their criticisms of an early cut of a film by giving extensive "notes" to the director. The movie will be screened and suggestions will be typed up and delivered a few days later. The problem is, directors don't want the notes, because they are usually coming from people who aren't filmmakers and are seen as ignorant and interfering. There is a built-in tension, then, between directors and the studios that employ them; to put it in stark terms, the studios are paying the bills and want the films to be commercially successful, while the directors want to preserve their artistic vision. I should add that some notes offered by studio executives are quite astute—people outside of the production can often see more clearly. But when you add oft-held resentments about input from "non-creative" people to how difficult it is to be a director in the first place—presiding over a project that, as I've said, sucks for months before it gets good—this tension makes it difficult to bridge the divide between art and commerce.

Which is why we don't give notes this way at Pixar. We have developed our own model, based on our determination to be a filmmaker-led studio. That does not mean there is no hierarchy here. It means that we try to create an environment where people want to hear each other's notes, even when those notes are challenging, and where everyone has a vested interest in one another's success. We give our filmmakers both freedom and responsibility. For example, we believe that the most promising stories are not assigned to filmmakers but emerge from within them. With few exceptions, our directors make movies that they have conceived of and are burning to make. Then, because we know that this passion will at some point blind them to their movie's inevitable problems, we offer them the counsel of the Braintrust.

You may be thinking, *How is the Braintrust different from any other feedback mechanism?*

There are two key differences, as I see it. The first is that the Braintrust is made up of people with a deep understanding of storytelling and, usually, people who have been through the process themselves. While the directors welcome critiques from many sources along the way (and in fact, when our films are screened in-house, *all* Pixar employees are asked to send notes), they particularly prize feedback from fellow directors and storytellers.

The second difference is that the Braintrust has no authority. This is crucial: The director does not have to follow any of the specific suggestions given. After a Braintrust meeting, it is up to him or her to figure out how to address the feedback. Braintrust meetings are not top-down, do-this-or-else affairs. By removing from the Braintrust the power to mandate solutions, we affect the dynamics of the group in ways I believe are essential.

While problems in a film are fairly easy to identify, the sources of those problems are often extraordinarily difficult to assess. A mystifying plot twist or a less-than-credible change of heart in our main character is often caused by subtle, underlying issues elsewhere in the story. Think of it like a patient complaining of knee pain that stems from his fallen arches. If you operated on the knee, it wouldn't just fail to alleviate the pain, it could easily compound it. To alleviate the pain, you have to identify and deal with the root of the problem. The Braintrust's notes, then, are intended to bring the true causes of problems to the surface—not to demand a specific remedy.

Moreover, we don't *want* the Braintrust to solve a director's problem because we believe that, in all likelihood, our solution won't be as good as the one the director and his or her creative team comes up with. We believe that ideas—and thus, films—only become great when they are challenged and tested. In academia, peer review is the process by which professors are evaluated by others in their field. I like to think of the Braintrust as Pixar's version of peer review, a forum that ensures we raise our game—not by being prescriptive but by offering candor and deep analysis.

That doesn't mean it doesn't get tough sometimes. Naturally, every director would prefer to be told that his film is a masterpiece. But because of the way the Braintrust is structured, the pain of being told that flaws are apparent or revisions are needed is mini-

mized. Rarely does a director get defensive, because no one is pulling rank or telling the filmmaker what to do. The film itself—not
the filmmaker—is under the microscope. This principle eludes
most people, but it is critical: You are not your idea, and if you
identify too closely with your ideas, you will take offense when they
are challenged. To set up a healthy feedback system, you must remove power dynamics from the equation—you must enable yourself, in other words, to focus on the problem, not the person.

Here's how it works: On an appointed morning, the Braintrust
gathers for a screening of the film-in-progress. After the screening,
we head for a conference room, have some lunch, gather our
thoughts, and sit down to talk. The director and producer of the
film give a summary of where they think they are. "We've locked
down the first act, but we know the second act is still gelling,"
they'll say. Or "The ending still isn't connecting like we want it to."
Then, the feedback usually begins with John. While everyone has
an equal voice in a Braintrust meeting, John sets the tone, calling
out the sequences he liked best, identifying some themes and ideas
he thinks need to be improved. That's all it takes to launch the
back-and-forth. Everybody jumps in with observations about the
film's strengths and weaknesses.

Before we get to the forces that shape that discussion, let's take
a moment to look at things from the filmmakers' point of view. To
a one, they regard these sessions as essential. Michael Arndt, who
wrote *Toy Story 3*, says he thinks to make a great film, its makers
must pivot, at some point, from creating the story for themselves to
creating it for others. To him, the Braintrust provides that pivot,
and it is necessarily painful. "Part of the suffering involves giving
up control," he says. "I can think it's the funniest joke in the world,
but if nobody in that room laughs, I have to take it out. It hurts that
they can see something you can't."

Rich Moore, whose first animated feature for Disney was
Wreck-It Ralph, likens the Braintrust to a bunch of people who are
each working on their own puzzles. (Since John and I took over at

Disney Animation, that studio has adopted this tradition of candor as well.) Somehow, and perhaps especially because they have less invested, a director who's struggling with his own dilemmas can see another director's struggles more clearly than his own. "It's like I can put my crossword puzzle away and help you with your Rubik's Cube a little bit," is how he puts it.

Bob Peterson, a member of the Braintrust who has helped write (and provide voices for) eleven Pixar films, uses another analogy to describe the Braintrust. He calls it "the grand eye of Sauron"— a reference to the lidless, all-seeing character in the *Lord of the Rings* trilogy—because when it focuses on you, there's no avoiding its gaze.

But the Braintrust is benevolent. It wants to help. And it has no selfish agenda.

Andrew Stanton, who has been on the giving or the receiving end of almost every Braintrust meeting we've ever had, likes to say that if Pixar is a hospital and the movies are the patients, then the Braintrust is made up of trusted doctors. In this analogy, it's important to remember that the movie's director and producer are doctors, too. It's as if they've gathered a panel of consulting experts to help find an accurate diagnosis for an extremely confounding case. But ultimately, it's the filmmakers, and no one else, who will make the final decisions about the wisest course of treatment.

Jonas Rivera, who started as an office assistant on *Toy Story* and has gone on to produce two films for us, alters Andrew's hospital analogy slightly, adding this: If the movies are patients, then they are in utero when the Braintrust first evaluates them. "The Braintrust meetings," he says, "are where the movie is born."

To get a clearer sense of how candor is delivered at Pixar, I want to take you inside a Braintrust meeting. This one followed an early screening of a Pete Docter film, then known as *The Untitled Pixar Movie That Takes You Inside the Mind*. The premise for the film had emerged straight out of Pete's cranium, and it was predictably ambitious, layered, and complex. Already, Pete and his team had spent months hashing out whose mind, exactly, he was going to take viewers inside of and what those viewers would ultimately find when they got there. As Braintrusts go, this was a crowded one, with about twenty people at the table and fifteen more in chairs against the walls. Everyone grabbed plates of food on the way in and, after a little small talk, got down to business.

Earlier, before the screening, Pete had described what they'd come up with so far in terms of the overall conceit of the film and the specific story points that he hoped would connect with the audience. "What's inside the mind?" he asked his colleagues. "Your emotions—and we've worked really hard to make these characters look the way those emotions feel. We have our main character, an emotion called Joy, who is effervescent. She literally glows when she's excited. Then we have Fear. He thinks of himself as confident and suave, but he's a little raw nerve and tends to freak out. The other characters are Anger, Sadness—her shape is inspired by teardrops—and Disgust, who basically turns up her nose at everything. And all these guys work at what we call Head-quarters."

That got a laugh—as did many scenes in the roughed-out ten-minute preview that followed, which everyone agreed had the potential to be, like Pete's previous film *Up,* among our most original and affecting. As I've said, Pete is superb at teasing out subtle moments that are both funny and emotionally authentic, and this idea of bringing a person's competing emotions to life was inspired, rich with possibility. But as the Braintrust came to life, there seemed to be a consensus that one of the movie's major scenes—an argument between two characters about why certain memories fade while others burn bright forever—was too minor to sufficiently connect audiences to the profound ideas the film was attempting to tackle.

Pete is a big guy—6 foot 4½—but despite his size, he projects an undaunted gentleness. This was in evidence in the conference room now, as he listened to us parse what was amiss in this pivotal scene. His face was open, not pained. He'd been through this many times before, and he believed in its power to help him get where he was trying to go.

Midway down the table, Brad Bird shifted in his chair. Brad joined Pixar in 2000, after having written and directed *The Iron Giant* at Warner Bros., and his first movie for us was *The Incredibles,* which opened in 2004. Brad is a born rebel who fights against creative conformity in any guise. The smell of artistic victory is his drug, and with his rapid, high-energy delivery, he will turn almost everything into a battle to win for the cause of creativity (even if there isn't anybody around to fight). So it was no surprise that he was among the first to articulate his worries about the core of the story feeling too slight. "I understand that you want to keep this simple and relatable," he told Pete, "but I think we need something that your audience can get a little more *invested* in."

Andrew Stanton spoke next. Andrew is fond of saying that people need to be wrong as fast as they can. In a battle, if you're faced with two hills and you're unsure which one to attack, he says, the right course of action is to hurry up and choose. If you find out it's the wrong hill, turn around and attack the other one. In that scenario, the only unacceptable course of action is running *between* the hills. Now, he seemed to be suggesting that Pete and his team had stormed the wrong hill. "I think you need to spend more time settling on the rules of your imagined world," he said.

Every Pixar movie has its own rules that viewers have to accept, understand, and enjoy understanding. The voices of the toys in the *Toy Story* films, for example, are never audible to humans. The rats in *Ratatouille* walk on four paws, like normal vermin, except for Remy, our star, whose upright posture sets him apart. In Pete's film, one of the rules—at least at this point—was that memories (depicted as glowing glass globes) were stored in the brain by traveling through a maze of chutes into a kind of archive. When retrieved or remembered, they'd roll back down another tangle of chutes, like bowling balls being returned to bowlers at the alley.

That particular construct was elegant and effective, but Andrew suggested that another rule needed to be firmed up and clarified: how memories and emotions change over time, as the brain gets older. This was the moment in the film, Andrew said, to establish some key themes. Listening to this, I remembered how in *Toy Story 2,* the addition of Wheezy immediately helped establish the idea that damaged toys could be discarded, left to sit, unloved, on the shelf. Andrew felt there was a similarly impactful opportunity here that was being missed—and, thus, was keeping the film from working—and he said so candidly. "Pete, this movie is about the inevitability of change," he said. "And of growing up."

This set Brad off. "A lot of us in this room have *not* grown up— and I mean that in the best way," he said. "The conundrum is how to become mature, how to take on responsibility and become reliable while at the same time preserving your childlike wonder. People have come up to me many times, as I'm sure has happened to many people in this room, and said, 'Gee, I wish I could be creative like you. That would be something, to be able to draw.' But I believe that *everyone* begins with the ability to draw. Kids are instinctively there. But a lot of them unlearn it. Or people tell them they can't or it's impractical. So yes, kids have to grow up, but maybe there's a way to suggest that they could be better off if they held onto some of their childish ideas.

"Pete, the thing I want to give you a huge round of applause for is: This is a frickin' *big* idea to try to make a movie about," Brad continued, his voice full of affection. "I've said to you on previous films, 'You're trying to do a triple back flip into a gale force wind, and you're mad at yourself for not sticking the landing. Like, it's amazing you're *alive.*' What you're doing with this film is the same—and it's the kind of thing that nobody else in the movie industry is doing with a sizable budget. So, huge round of applause." Brad paused as everyone clapped. Then he grinned at Pete, who grinned back. "And you're in for a world of hurt," Brad said.

An important corollary to the assertion that the Braintrust

must be candid is that filmmakers must be ready to hear the truth; candor is only valuable if the person on the receiving end is open to it and willing, if necessary, to let go of things that don't work. Jonas Rivera, the producer of Pete's film, tries to make that painful process easier by doing something he calls "headlining" the main points of a Braintrust session for whichever director he's assisting—distilling the many observations down to a digestible takeaway. Once this Braintrust meeting wrapped up, this is exactly what he did for Pete, ticking off the areas that seemed the most problematic, reminding him of the scenes that resonated most. "So what do we blow up?" Jonas asked. "What do we go backwards on? And what do you love? Is what you loved about the film different now than it was when we started?"

"The way the movie opens," Pete responded, "I love."

Jonas raised his hand in a salute. "Okay, that's the movie, then," he said. "How we set up the story has to handshake with that."

"I agree," Pete said.

They were on their way.

Frank talk, spirited debate, laughter, and love. If I could distill a Braintrust meeting down to its most essential ingredients, those four things would surely be among them. But newcomers often notice something else first: the volume. Routinely, Braintrust attendees become so energized and excited that they talk over each other, and voices tend to rise. I'll admit that there have been times when outsiders think they've witnessed a heated argument or even some kind of intervention. They haven't—though I understand their confusion, which stems from their inability (after such a brief visit) to grasp the Braintrust's *intent*. A lively debate in a Braintrust meeting is not being waged in the hopes of any one person winning the day. To the extent there is "argument," it seeks only to excavate the truth.

That is part of the reason why Steve Jobs didn't come to Braintrust meetings at Pixar—a mutually agreed prohibition, based on my belief that his bigger-than-life presence would make it harder to be candid. We had reached this agreement way back in 1993, on a day that I happened to be visiting Microsoft, and Steve reached me by phone, worried that I was being wooed to take a job there. I had no intention of working at Microsoft, and it wasn't why I was there, but I knew he was nervous, and I took the opportunity to exert some leverage. "This group works well together," I told him of the Braintrust. "But if you go to its meetings it will change what they are." He agreed, and believing that John and the story people knew more about narrative than he did, he left it to them. At Apple, he had the reputation for being deeply involved in the most minute detail of every product, but at Pixar, he didn't believe that his instincts were better than the people here, so he stayed out. That's how much candor matters at Pixar: It overrides hierarchy.

Braintrust meetings require giving candid notes, but they do a great deal more than that. The most productive creative sessions allow for the exploration of myriad trains of thought. Take *WALL-E,* for example, which was known, early on, as *Trash Planet.* For a long time, that movie ended with our googly-eyed trash compactor robot saving his beloved droid, EVE, from destruction in a dumpster. But there was something about that ending that nagged, that never quite felt right. We had countless discussions about it, but Andrew Stanton, the director, was having difficulty putting his finger on what was wrong, let alone finding a solution. The confusing thing was that the romantic plotline *seemed* right. Of course WALL-E would save EVE—he'd fallen in love with her the moment he saw her. In a sense, that was precisely the flaw. And it was Brad Bird who pointed that out to Andrew in a Braintrust meeting. "You've denied your audience the moment they've been waiting for," he said, "the moment where EVE throws away all her programming and goes all out to save WALL-E. Give it to them. The audience wants it." As soon as Brad said that, it was like: *Bing!* After the meeting, Andrew went off and wrote an entirely new ending in which EVE saves WALL-E, and at the next screening, there wasn't a dry eye in the house.

Michael Arndt remembers it was Andrew, meanwhile, who gave a Braintrust note on *Toy Story 3* that fundamentally altered the end of that movie's second act. At that point in the film, Lotso— the pink teddy bear and mean-spirited leader of the day-care center toys—is overthrown after the toys mutiny. But the problem was, the mutiny wasn't believable, because the impetus behind it didn't ring true. "In that draft," Michael told me, "I had Woody giving this big, heroic speech about what a mean guy Lotso was, and it changed everyone's mind about Lotso. But in the Braintrust, Andrew said, 'Nope, I don't buy it. These toys aren't stupid. They *know* Lotso isn't a good guy. They've only aligned themselves with him because he's the most powerful.'" This sparked a pitched discussion in the room, until, finally, Michael hit on an analogy: If you think of Lotso as Stalin and the other toys as his cowering subjects, then Big Baby—the bald-headed doll with one droopy eye who acts as Lotso's enforcer—was Stalin's army. At that point, a fix began to emerge at last. "If you flip the army, then you can get rid of Stalin," Michael said. "So the question was, What can Woody do that will turn Big Baby's sympathies against Lotso? That was the problem I faced."

The solution—a reveal of a previously unknown injustice: that Lotso's duplicity had led Big Baby to be abandoned by his little girl owner—was all Michael's, but he never would have found it if not for the Braintrust.

It is natural for people to fear that such an inherently critical environment will feel threatening and unpleasant, like a trip to the dentist. The key is to look at the viewpoints being offered, in any successful feedback group, as additive, not competitive. A competitive approach measures other ideas against your own, turning the discussion into a debate to be won or lost. An additive approach, on the other hand, starts with the understanding that each participant contributes something (even if it's only an idea that fuels the discussion—and ultimately doesn't work). The Braintrust is valuable because it broadens your perspective, allowing you to peer—at least briefly—through others' eyes.

Brad Bird has a terrific example of exactly this—an instance when the Braintrust helped him fix something he didn't realize was a problem. It was during production on *The Incredibles*, when people raised concerns about a scene in which Helen and Bob Parr (a.k.a. Elastigirl and Mr. Incredible) are having an argument. Many people in the Braintrust thought the scene, in which Bob is caught sneaking into his house late one night after doing a little superhero moonlighting, felt all wrong. What Brad likes best about this example is that the Braintrust helped him find a solution even though it failed to diagnose what was truly amiss! The fix that was suggested in the Braintrust session wasn't the right one—and yet, Brad says that it helped him immensely.

"Sometimes the Braintrust will know something's wrong, but they will identify the wrong symptom," he told me. "I knew what the film's tone was—I had pitched the tone, and everybody bought the tone that was pitched. But this was one of the first scenes that the Braintrust was seeing illustrated, with voices. And I think they were privately thinking, are we doing a Bergman film? Bob was yelling at Helen, and the note I got was, 'God, it seems like he's bullying her. I really don't like him. You've got to rewrite it.' So I go in to rewrite it, and I look at it, and think, 'No, that *is* what he would say. And that *is* how she would respond.' I don't want to change a damn thing—but I know I can't say that, because something's not working. And then I realize the problem: Physically, Bob is the size of a house, and Helen is this little tiny thing. Even though Helen is his equal, what you're seeing on the screen is this big threatening guy yelling and it felt like he was abusing her. Once I figured that out, all I did was have Helen stretch when she holds her ground and says, 'This is not about you.' I didn't change any of the dialogue. I just changed the drawings to make her body bigger, as if to say, 'I'm a match for you.' And when I played the revised scene, the Braintrust said, 'That's *much* better. What lines did you change?' I said, 'I didn't change a comma.' That's an example of the group knowing something was wrong, but not having the solution. I had to go deep and ask, 'If the dialogue is not wrong, what is?' And then I saw it: Oh, *that*."

In the very early days of Pixar, John, Andrew, Pete, Lee, and Joe made a promise to one another. No matter what happened, they would always tell each other the truth. They did this because they recognized how important and rare candid feedback is and how, without it, our films would suffer. Then and now, the term we use to describe this kind of constructive criticism is "good notes."

A good note says what is wrong, what is missing, what isn't clear, what makes no sense. A good note is offered at a timely moment, not too late to fix the problem. A good note doesn't make demands; it doesn't even have to include a proposed fix. But if it does, that fix is offered only to illustrate a potential solution, not to prescribe an answer. Most of all, though, a good note is specific. "I'm writhing with boredom," is not a good note.

As Andrew Stanton says, "There's a difference between criticism and constructive criticism. With the latter, you're constructing at the same time that you're criticizing. You're building as you're breaking down, making new pieces to work with out of the stuff you've just ripped apart. That's an art form in itself. I always feel like whatever notes you're giving should inspire the recipient—like, 'How do I get that kid to want to redo his homework?' So, you've got to act like a teacher. Sometimes you talk about the problems in fifty different ways until you find that one sentence that you can see makes their eyes pop, as if they're thinking, 'Oh, I want to do it.' Instead of saying, 'The writing in this scene isn't good enough,' you say, 'Don't you want people to walk out of the theater and be quoting those lines?' It's more of a challenge. 'Isn't this what you want? I want that too!' "

Telling the truth is difficult, but inside a creative company, it is the only way to ensure excellence. It is the job of the manager to watch the dynamics in the room, although sometimes a director will come in after a meeting to say that some people were holding back. In these cases, the solution is often to convene a smaller group—a sort of mini-Braintrust—to encourage more direct communication by limiting the number of participants. Other times there are problems that require special attention, people dodging and weaving without even knowing it. In my experience, people usually don't intend to be evasive, and a gentle nudge is all it takes to put them back on the right path.

Candor isn't cruel. It does not destroy. On the contrary, any successful feedback system is built on empathy, on the idea that we are all in this together, that we understand your pain because we've experienced it ourselves. The need to stroke one's own ego, to get the credit we feel we deserve—we strive to check those impulses at the door. The Braintrust is fueled by the idea that every note we give is in the service of a common goal: supporting and helping each other as we try to make better movies.

It would be a mistake to think that merely gathering a bunch of people in a room for a candid discussion every couple of months will automatically cure your company's ills. First, it takes a while for any group to develop the level of trust necessary to be truly candid, to express reservations and criticisms without fear of reprisal, and to learn the language of good notes. Second, even the most experienced Braintrust can't help people who don't understand its philosophies, who refuse to hear criticism without getting defensive, or who don't have the talent to digest feedback, reset, and start again. Third, as I'll discuss in later chapters, the Braintrust is something that evolves over time. Creating a Braintrust is not something you do once and then check off your to-do list. Even when populated with talented and generous people, there is plenty that can go wrong. Dynamics change—between people, between departments—and so the only way to ensure that your Braintrust is doing its job is to watch and protect it continually, making adaptations as needed.

I want to stress that you don't have to work at Pixar to create a Braintrust. Every creative person, no matter their field, can draft into service those around them who exhibit the right mixture of intelligence, insight, and grace. "You can and should make your own solution group," Andrew Stanton says, adding that on each of his own films, he has made a point of doing this on a smaller scale, separate from the official Braintrust. "Here are the qualifications required: The people you choose must (a) make you think smarter and (b) put lots of solutions on the table in a short amount of time. I don't care who it is, the janitor or the intern or one of your most trusted lieutenants: If they can help you do that, they should be at the table."

Believe me, you don't want to be at a company where there is more candor in the hallways than in the rooms where fundamental ideas or matters of policy are being hashed out. The best inoculation against this fate? Seek out people who are willing to level with you, and when you find them, hold them close.

CHAPTER 6

FEAR AND FAILURE

The production of *Toy Story 3* could be a master class in how to make a film. At the beginning of the process, in 2007, the team that had made the original *Toy Story* gathered for a two-day off-site in a rustic cabin, 50 miles north of San Francisco, that often functions as our unofficial retreat center. The place, called the Poet's Loft, is all redwood and glass—perched on stilts over Tomales Bay, a perfect place to think. The team's goal, this day, was to rough out a movie they could imagine paying to see.

Sitting on couches with a whiteboard in the center of the room, the participants started by asking some basic questions: Why even do a third movie? What was left to say? What are we still curious about? The *Toy Story* team knew and trusted each other—over the years, they'd made stupid mistakes together and solved seemingly insurmountable problems together. The key was to focus less on the end goal and more on what still intrigued them about the characters who, by this point, felt like people we actually knew. Every so often, someone would stand up and road test what they had so far—trying to summarize a three-part story as if it were the blurb on the back of a DVD cover. Feedback would be given, and they'd go back—literally—to the drawing board.

Then somebody said the one thing that snapped everything into focus. *We've talked so much over the years, in so many different ways, about Andy growing up and growing out of his toys. So what if we just leaped right into that idea directly? How would the toys feel if Andy left for college?* While no one knew exactly how they'd answer that question, everyone present knew that we'd landed on the idea—the line of tension—that would animate *Toy Story 3*.

From that moment forward, the film seemed to fall right into place. Andrew Stanton wrote a treatment, Michael Arndt wrote a script, Lee Unkrich and Darla Anderson, the director and producer, rocked the production, and we hit our deadlines. Even the Braintrust found relatively little to argue with. I don't want to overstate this—the project had its problems—but since our founding, we'd been striving for a production as smooth as this. At one point, Steve Jobs called me to check in on our progress.

"It's really strange," I told him. "We haven't had a single big problem on this film."

Many people would have been happy with this news. Not Steve. "Watch out," he said. "That's a dangerous place to be."

"I wouldn't be too alarmed," I said. "This is our first time, in eleven movies, without a major meltdown. And besides, we have a few more meltdowns coming up."

I wasn't being glib. Over the next two years, we were about to rack up a string of costly misfires. Two of those—*Cars 2* and *Monsters University*—were solved by replacing the films' original directors. Another, a film we spent three years developing, proved so confounding that we shut it down altogether.

I'm going to talk more about our misfires, but I'm gratified to say that because we caught them midstream, before they were finished and released to the public, we were able to treat them as learning experiences. Yes, they cost us money, but the losses were not as sizable as they would have been had we not intervened. And yes, they were painful, but we emerged better and stronger because of them. I came to think of our meltdowns as a necessary part of doing our business, like investments in R&D, and I urged everyone at Pixar to see them the same way.

For most of us, failure comes with baggage—a lot of baggage—that I believe is traced directly back to our days in school. From a very early age, the message is drilled into our heads: Failure is bad; failure means you didn't study or prepare; failure means you slacked off or—worse!—aren't smart enough to begin with. Thus, failure is something to be ashamed of. This perception lives on long into adulthood, even in people who have learned to parrot the oft-repeated arguments about the upside of failure. How many articles have you read on that topic alone? And yet, even as they nod their heads in agreement, many readers of those articles still have the emotional reaction that they had as children. They just can't help it: That early experience of shame is too deep-seated to erase. All the time in my work, I see people resist and reject failure and try mightily to avoid it, because regardless of what we say, mistakes feel embarrassing. There is a visceral reaction to failure: It hurts.

We need to think about failure differently. I'm not the first to say that failure, when approached properly, can be an opportunity for growth. But the way most people interpret this assertion is that mistakes are a necessary evil. Mistakes aren't a necessary evil. They aren't evil at all. They are an inevitable consequence of doing something new (and, as such, should be seen as valuable; without them, we'd have no originality). And yet, even as I say that embracing failure is an important part of learning, I also acknowledge that acknowledging this truth is not enough. That's because failure is painful, and our feelings about this pain tend to screw up our understanding of its worth. To disentangle the good and the bad parts of failure, we have to recognize both the reality of the pain and the benefit of the resulting growth.

Left to their own devices, most people don't want to fail. But Andrew Stanton isn't most people. As I've mentioned, he's known around Pixar for repeating the phrases "fail early and fail fast" and "be wrong as fast as you can." He thinks of failure like learning to ride a bike; it isn't conceivable that you would learn to do this without making mistakes—without toppling over a few times. "Get a bike that's as low to the ground as you can find, put on elbow and knee pads so you're not afraid of falling, and go," he says. If you apply this mindset to everything new you attempt, you can begin to subvert the negative connotation associated with making mistakes. Says Andrew: "You wouldn't say to somebody who is first learning to play the guitar, 'You better think *really* hard about where you put your fingers on the guitar neck before you strum, because you only get to strum once, and that's it. And if you get that wrong, we're going to move on.' That's no way to learn, is it?"

This doesn't mean that Andrew enjoys it when he puts his work up for others to judge, and it is found wanting. But he deals with the possibility of failure by addressing it head on, searching for mechanisms that turn pain into progress. To be wrong as fast as you can is to sign up for aggressive, rapid learning. Andrew does this without hesitation.

Even though people in our offices have heard Andrew say this repeatedly, many still miss the point. They think it means accept failure with dignity and move on. The better, more subtle interpretation is that failure is a manifestation of learning and exploration. If you aren't experiencing failure, then you are making a far worse mistake: You are being driven by the desire to avoid it. And, for leaders especially, this strategy—trying to avoid failure by out-thinking it—dooms you to fail. As Andrew puts it, "Moving things forward allows the team you are leading to feel like, 'Oh, I'm on a boat that is actually going towards land.' As opposed to having a leader who says, 'I'm still not sure. I'm going to look at the map a little bit more, and we're just going to float here, and all of you stop rowing until I figure this out.' And then weeks go by, and morale plummets, and failure becomes self-fulfilling. People begin to treat the captain with doubt and trepidation. Even if their doubts aren't fully justified, you've become what they see you as because of your inability to move."

Rejecting failure and avoiding mistakes seem like high-minded goals, but they are fundamentally misguided. Take something like the Golden Fleece Awards, which were established in 1975 to call attention to government-funded projects that were particularly egregious wastes of money. (Among the winners were things like an $84,000 study on love commissioned by the National Science Foundation, and a $3,000 Department of Defense study that examined whether people in the military should carry umbrellas.) While such scrutiny may have seemed like a good idea at the time, it had a chilling effect on research. No one wanted to "win" a Golden Fleece Award because, under the guise of avoiding waste, its organizers had inadvertently made it dangerous and embarrassing for everyone to make mistakes.

The truth is, if you fund thousands of research projects every year, some will have obvious, measurable, positive impacts, and others will go nowhere. We aren't very good at predicting the future—that's a given—and yet the Golden Fleece Awards tacitly implied that researchers should know *before* they do their research whether or not the results of that research would have value. Failure was being used as a weapon, rather than as an agent of learning. And that had fallout: The fact that failing could earn you a very public flogging distorted the way researchers chose projects. The politics of failure, then, impeded our progress.

There's a quick way to determine if your company has embraced the negative definition of failure. Ask yourself what happens when an error is discovered. Do people shut down and turn inward, instead of coming together to untangle the causes of problems that might be avoided going forward? Is the question being asked: Whose fault was this? If so, your culture is one that vilifies failure. Failure is difficult enough without it being compounded by the search for a scapegoat.

In a fear-based, failure-averse culture, people will consciously or unconsciously avoid risk. They will seek instead to repeat something safe that's been good enough in the past. Their work will be derivative, not innovative. But if you can foster a positive understanding of failure, the opposite will happen.

How, then, do you make failure into something people can face without fear?

Part of the answer is simple: If we as leaders can talk about our mistakes and our part in them, then we make it safe for others. You don't run from it or pretend it doesn't exist. That is why I make a point of being open about our meltdowns inside Pixar, because I believe they teach us something important: Being open about problems is the first step toward learning from them. My goal is not to drive fear out completely, because fear is inevitable in high-stakes situations. What I want to do is loosen its grip on us. While we don't want too many failures, we must think of the cost of failure as an investment in the future.

If you create a fearless culture (or as fearless as human nature will allow), people will be much less hesitant to explore new areas, identifying uncharted pathways and then charging down them. They will also begin to see the upside of decisiveness: The time they've saved by not gnashing their teeth about whether they're on the right course comes in handy when they hit a dead end and need to reboot.

It isn't enough to pick a path—you must go down it. By doing so, you see things you couldn't possibly see when you started out; you may not like what you see, some of it may be confusing, but at least you will have, as we like to say, "explored the neighborhood." The key point here is that even if you decide you're in the wrong place, there is still time to head toward the *right* place. And all the thinking you've done that led you down that alley was not wasted. Even if most of what you've seen doesn't fit your needs, you inevitably take away ideas that will prove useful. Relatedly, if there are parts of the neighborhood you like but that don't seem helpful in the quest you're on, you will remember those parts and possibly use them later.

Let me explain what I mean by exploring the neighborhood. Years before it evolved into the funny, affecting tale of a fierce, shaggy behemoth (Sulley) and his unlikely friendship with the little girl it's his job to scare (Boo), *Monsters, Inc.* was an altogether different story. As first imagined by Pete Docter, it revolved around a thirty-year-old man who was coping with a cast of frightening characters that only he could see. As Pete describes it, the man "is an accountant or something, and he hates his job, and one day his mom gives him a book with some drawings in it that he did when he was a kid. He doesn't think anything of it, and he puts it on the shelf, and that night, monsters show up. And nobody else can see them. He thinks he's starting to go crazy. They follow him to his job, and on his dates, and it turns out these monsters are all the fears that he never dealt with as a kid. He becomes friends with them eventually, and as he conquers the fears, they slowly begin to disappear."

Anyone who's seen the movie knows that the final product bears no resemblance to that description. But what nobody knows is how many wrong turns the story took, over a period of years, before it found its true north. The pressure on Pete, all along, was enormous—*Monsters, Inc.* was the first Pixar film not directed by John Lasseter, so in some very real ways Pete and his crew were under the microscope. Every unsuccessful attempt to crack the story only heightened the pressure.

Fortunately, Pete had a basic concept that he held to throughout: "Monsters are real, and they scare kids for a living." But what was the strongest manifestation of that idea? He couldn't know until he'd tried a few options. At first, the human protagonist was a six-year-old named Mary. Then she was changed to a little boy. Then back to a six-year-old girl. Then she was seven, named Boo, and bossy—even domineering. Finally, Boo was turned into a fearless, preverbal toddler. The idea of Sulley's buddy character—the round, one-eyed Mike, voiced by Billy Crystal—wasn't added until more than a year after the first treatment was written. The process of determining the rules of the incredibly intricate world Pete created also took him down countless blind alleys—until, eventually, those blind alleys converged on a path that led the story where it needed to go.

"The process of developing a story is one of discovery," Pete says. "However, there's always a guiding principle that leads you as you go down the various roads. In *Monsters, Inc.,* all of our very different plots shared a common feeling—the bittersweet goodbye you feel once a problem"—in this case, Sulley's quest to return Boo to her own world—"has been solved. You suffer through it as you struggle to solve it, but by the end you've developed a sort of fondness for it, and you miss it when it is gone. I knew I wanted to express that, and I was eventually able to get it in the film."

While the process was difficult and time consuming, Pete and his crew never believed that a failed approach meant that *they* had failed. Instead, they saw that each idea led them a bit closer to finding the better option. And that allowed them to come to work each day engaged and excited, even while in the midst of confusion. This is key: When experimentation is seen as necessary and productive, not as a frustrating waste of time, people will enjoy their work—even when it is confounding them.

The principle I'm describing here—iterative trial and error—has long-recognized value in science. When scientists have a question, they construct hypotheses, test them, analyze them, and draw conclusions—and then they do it all over again. The reasoning behind this is simple: Experiments are fact-finding missions that, over time, inch scientists toward greater understanding. That means *any* outcome is a good outcome, because it yields new information. If your experiment proved your initial theory wrong, better to know it sooner rather than later. Armed with new facts, you can then reframe whatever question you're asking.

This is often easier to accept in the laboratory than in a business. Creating art or developing new products in a for-profit context is complicated and expensive. In our case, when we try to tell the most compelling story, how do we assess our attempts and draw conclusions? How do we determine what works best? And how do we put the need to succeed out of our minds long enough to identify a true emotional storyline that will carry a film?

There is an alternative approach to being wrong as fast as you can. It is the notion that if you carefully think everything through, if you are meticulous and plan well and consider all possible outcomes, you are more likely to create a lasting product. But I should caution that if you seek to plot out all your moves before you make them—if you put your faith in slow, deliberative planning in the hopes it will spare you failure down the line—well, you're deluding yourself. For one thing, it's easier to plan derivative work—things that copy or repeat something already out there. So if your primary goal is to have a fully worked out, set-in-stone plan, you are only upping your chances of being unoriginal. Moreover, you cannot plan your way out of problems. While planning is very important, and we do a lot of it, there is only so much you can control in a creative environment. In general, I have found that people who pour their energy into thinking about an approach and insisting that it is too early to act are wrong just as often as people who dive in and work quickly. The overplanners just take longer to be wrong (and, when things inevitably go awry, are more crushed by the feeling that they have failed). There's a corollary to this, as well: The more time you spend mapping out an approach, the more likely you are to get attached to it. The nonworking idea gets worn into your brain, like a rut in the mud. It can be difficult to get free of it and head in a different direction. Which, more often than not, is exactly what you must do.

There are arenas, of course, in which a zero failure rate is essential. Commercial flying has a phenomenal safety record because there is so much attention paid at every level to removing error, from manufacturing the engines to assembling and maintaining the planes to observing safety checks and the rules that govern air spaces. Likewise, hospitals have elaborate safeguards to make sure that they operate on the right patient, on the correct side of the body, on the right organ, and so on. Banks have protocols to prevent errors; manufacturing companies have a goal of eliminating production line errors; many industries set goals of having zero injuries.

But just because "failure free" is crucial in some industries does not mean that it should be a goal in all of them. When it comes to creative endeavors, the concept of zero failures is worse than useless. It is counterproductive.

To be sure, failure can be expensive. Making a bad product or suffering a major public setback damages your company's reputation and, often, your employees' morale. So we try to make it less expensive to fail, thereby taking some of the onus off it. For example, we've set up a system in which directors are allowed to spend years in the development phase of a movie, where the costs of iteration and exploration are relatively low. (At this point, we're paying the director's and story artists' salaries but not putting anything into production, which is where costs explode.)

It's one thing to talk about the value of people encountering a number of small failures as they grope their way to understanding, but what about a big, catastrophic failure? What about a project you sink millions of dollars into, commit to publicly, and then have to walk away from? This happened on a film we were developing a few years back, which was based on a terrific idea that originated in the mind of one of our most creative and trusted colleagues (but, notably, one who had never directed a feature film before). He wanted to tell the story of what happens when the last remaining male and female blue-footed newts on the planet are forced together by science to save the species—but they can't stand each other. When he got up and pitched the idea, we were blown away. The story was, like *Ratatouille,* a somewhat challenging concept, but if handled the right way, we could see that it would be a phenomenal movie.

Significantly, the pitch also came at a time when Jim Morris and I were thinking a lot about whether the success of Pixar was making us complacent. Among the questions we'd been asking ourselves and each other: Had we, in the interest of governing production and making it efficient, created habits and rules that were unnecessary? Were we in danger of growing lethargic and set in our ways? Were our budgets on each movie inching higher and higher for no reason? We were looking for an opportunity to change it up, to create our own little startup, within Pixar and yet separate from it, to try to tap back into the energy that permeated the place when we were young and small and striving. This project seemed to fit the bill. As we put it into production, we decided to treat it as an experiment: What if we brought in new people from the outside with fresh ideas, gave them the charter of rethinking the entire production process (and gave them experienced teammates to help carry this out), and then put them two blocks away from our main campus to minimize their contact with those who might encourage them to adopt the status quo? In addition to making a memorable movie, we were looking to challenge and improve our processes. We called the experiment the Incubator Project.

Within Pixar, some expressed doubts about this approach, but the spirit behind it—the desire not to rest on our laurels—was appealing to all. Andrew Stanton told me later that he worried from the outset about how isolated the project's crew was, even though it was by design. We were so enamored, he felt, of the possibilities of reinventing the wheel that we underestimated the impact of making so many changes at once. It was as if we'd picked four talented musicians, left them to their own devices, and hoped like hell they'd figure out how to be the Beatles.

But we didn't see that clearly then. The idea for the movie was strong, which was confirmed when we unveiled it at a presentation for the media on upcoming Pixar and Disney movies. As the website *Ain't It Cool News* reported with enthusiasm, the main character, who'd been in captivity since he was a tadpole, lived in a cage in a lab where he could see a flowchart on the wall that spelled out the mating rituals of his species. Because he was lonely, he would practice the steps day in and day out, getting ready for scientists to capture him a girlfriend. Unfortunately, he couldn't read the ninth and final mating ritual because it was obscured by the lab's coffee machine. Therein lay the mystery.

The presentation drew raves. It was classic Pixar, people gushed—offbeat, witty, while at the same time tackling meaningful, relatable ideas. But within the production, unbeknownst to us, the story was stalled. It had the beginnings of a plot—our hero gets his wish when scientists catch him a mate in the wild and bring her back to the lab—but when the unhappy couple ends up back in the natural world, the film began to fall apart. The movie was stuck, and even after a lot of thoughtful feedback, it wasn't getting better.

That fact evaded us at first because of the separateness of the enterprise. When we tried to assess how things were going, early reports seemed good. The director had a strong vision, and his crew was excited and working hard, but they didn't know what they didn't know: that the first two years of a movie's development should be a time of solidifying the story beats by relentlessly testing them—much like you temper steel. And that required decision-making, not just abstract discussion. While everyone working on it had the best intentions, it got bogged down in hypotheticals and possibilities. The bottom line was that while everyone was rowing the boat, to use Andrew's analogy, there was no forward movement.

When we finally figured this out—after a few experienced Pixar people were sent in to help and reported back about what they saw—it was too late. The Pixar way is to invest in a singular vision, and we'd done so, in a major way, on this project. We didn't consider replacing the director—the story was his, and without him as the engine, we didn't think we could push it to completion. So in May 2010, with heavy hearts, we shut it down.

There are some who will read this and conclude that putting this film into production in the first place was a mistake. An untested director, an unfinished script—it's easy to look back, after the shutdown, and say that those factors alone should have dissuaded us at the outset. But I disagree. While it cost us time and money to pursue, to my mind it was worth the investment. We learned better how to balance new ideas with old ideas, and we learned that we had made a mistake in not getting very explicit buy-in from all of Pixar's leaders about the nature of what we were trying to do. These are lessons that would serve us very well later as we adopted new software and changed some of our technical processes. While experimentation is scary to many, I would argue that we should be far more terrified of the opposite approach. Being too risk-averse causes many companies to stop innovating and to reject new ideas, which is the first step on the path to irrelevance. Probably more companies hit the skids for this reason than because they dared to push boundaries and take risks—and, yes, to fail.

To be a truly creative company, you must start things that might fail.

For all of this talk about accepting failure, if a movie—or any creative endeavor—isn't improving at a reasonable rate, there is a problem. If a director devises a series of solutions that are not making a movie better, one could come to the conclusion that he or she isn't right for the job. Which is sometimes precisely the right conclusion to reach.

But where to draw that line? How many errors are too many? When does failure go from a stop on the road to excellence to a red flag that signals change is needed? We put a lot of faith in our Braintrust meetings to make sure that our directors get all the feedback and support they need, but there are problems that process can't fix. What do you do when candor is not enough?

These were the questions we faced on our various meltdowns.

We are a filmmaker-driven studio, which means that our goal is to let the creative people guide our projects. But when a movie gets stuck and it becomes clear that not only is it broken but its directors are at a loss as to how to fix it, we must replace them or shut the project down. You may ask: *If it is true that all the movies suck at first, and if Pixar's way is to give filmmakers—not the Braintrust— the ultimate authority to fix what's broken, then how do you know when to step in?*

The criteria we use is that we step in if a director loses the confidence of his or her crew. About three hundred people work on each Pixar movie, and they are used to endless adjustments and changes being made while the story is finding its feet. In general, movie crews are an understanding bunch. They recognize that there are always problems, so while they can be judgmental, they don't tend to *rush* to judgment. Their first impulse is to work harder. When a director stands up in a meeting and says, "I realize this scene isn't working, I don't yet know how to fix it, but I'm figuring it out. Keep going!"—a crew will follow him or her to the ends of the earth. But when a problem is festering and everyone seems to be looking the other way or when people are sitting around waiting to be told what to do, the crew gets antsy. It's not that they don't like the director—they usually do. It's that they lose confidence in the director's ability to bring the movie home. Which is part of why, to me, they are the most reliable barometer. If the crew is confused, then their leader is, too.

When this happens, we must act. To know when to act, we much watch carefully for signs that a movie is stuck. Here is one: A Braintrust meeting will occur, notes will be given, and three months later, the movie will come back essentially unchanged. That is not okay. You may say, "Wait a minute—I thought you just said the directors didn't *have* to obey the notes!" They don't. But directors must find ways to address problems that are raised by the group because the Braintrust represents the audience; when they are confused or otherwise dissatisfied, there's a good chance moviegoers will be too. The implication of being director-led is that the director must lead.

But any failure at a creative company is a failure of many, not one. If you're a leader of a company that has faltered, any misstep that occurs is yours as well. Moreover, if you don't use what's gone wrong to educate yourself and your colleagues, then you'll have missed an opportunity. There are two parts to any failure: There is the event itself, with all its attendant disappointment, confusion, and shame, and then there is our reaction to it. It is this second part that we control. Do we become introspective, or do we bury our heads in the sand? Do we make it safe for others to acknowledge and learn from problems, or do we shut down discussion by looking for people to blame? We must remember that failure gives us chances to grow, and we ignore those chances at our own peril.

Which raises the question: When failure occurs, how should you get the most out of it? When it came to our meltdowns, we were determined to look inward. We had picked talented, creative people to preside over these projects, so we clearly were doing something that was making it hard for them to succeed. Some worried the meltdowns were an indication that we were losing our touch. I disagreed. We never said it was going to be easy—we'd only insisted that our movies be great. Had we not stepped in and taken action, I said, *then* we'd be abandoning our values. After several misfires, though, it was important that we take a moment to reassess and to try to absorb the lessons they had to teach us.

So in March 2011, Jim Morris, Pixar's general manager, arranged an off-site with the studio's producers and directors—twenty or so people in all. On the agenda was one question: Why did we have so many meltdowns in a row? We weren't looking to point fingers. We wanted to rally the company's creative leadership to figure out the underlying problems that were leading us astray.

Jim kicked the meeting off by thanking everyone for coming and reminding us why we were there. Nothing is more critical to our continued success as a studio, he said, than the ability to develop new projects and directors, and yet we were clearly doing something wrong. We had been trying to increase the number of movies we released, but we'd hit a roadblock. Over the next two days, he said, our goal was to figure out what was missing and to chart out ways to create it and put it in place.

What became immediately apparent was that no one in the room was running from his or her role in these failures. They neither blamed the existing problems on others nor asked for someone else to solve them. The language they used to talk about the issues showed that they thought of them as their own. "Is there a way, other than Braintrust notes, that we could do a better job of teaching our directors the importance of an emotional arc?" asked one person. "I feel like I should be formally sharing my experience with other people," said another. I could not have been prouder. It was obvious that they felt they owned the problem and the responsibility for its solution. Even though we had serious problems, the culture of the place—the willingness to roll up our pant legs and wade into the muck for the good of the company—felt more alive than ever.

As a team, we analyzed our assumptions, why we'd made such flawed choices. Were there essential qualities we needed to look for in our director candidates, going forward, that we'd overlooked in the past? More significantly, how had we failed to prepare new directors adequately for the daunting job they faced? How many times had we said, "We won't let him or her fail"—only to let them fail? We discussed how we had been blinded by the fact that the directors of our first films—John, Andrew, and Pete—had each figured out how to be a director without formal training, something that we now saw was much rarer than we'd previously believed. We talked about the fact that Andrew, Pete, and Lee had spent years working side by side with John, absorbing his lessons—the need for decisiveness, for example—and his collaborative way of teasing out ideas. Andrew and Pete, the first directors at Pixar to follow in John's footsteps, had been challenged by the process but in the end had succeeded spectacularly. We assumed that others would do the same. But we had to face the fact that as we'd gotten bigger, our newer directors did not have the benefit of that experience.

Then we turned to the future. We identified individuals who we thought had the potential to become directors, listing their strengths and weaknesses and being specific about what we would do to teach them, give them experience, and support them. In the wake of our failures, we still didn't want to make only "safe" choices going forward; we understood that taking creative and leadership risks is essential to who we are and that sometimes this means handing the keys to someone who may not fit the traditional conception of a movie director. And yet, as we made those unconventional choices, everyone agreed, we needed to outline better, more explicit steps to train and prepare those we felt had the necessary skills to make movies. Instead of hoping that our director candidates would absorb our shared wisdom through osmosis, we resolved to create a formal mentoring program that would, in a sense, give to others what Pete and Andrew and Lee had experienced working so closely with John in the early days. Going forward, every established director would check in weekly with his mentees—giving them both practical and motivational advice as they developed ideas they hoped would become feature films.

Later, when I was reflecting on the off-site with Andrew, he made what I think is a profound point. He told me that he thinks he and the other proven directors have a responsibility to be teachers—that this should be a central part of their jobs, even as they continue to make their own films. "The Holy Grail is to find a way that we can teach others how to make the best movie possible with whoever they've got on their crew, because it's just logic that someday we won't be here," he said. "Walt Disney didn't do that. And without him, Disney Animation wasn't able to survive without enduring a decade and a half, if not two, of a slump. That's the real goal: Can we teach in a way that our directors will think smart when we're not around?"

Who better to teach than the most capable among us? And I'm not just talking about seminars or formal settings. Our actions and behaviors, for better or worse, teach those who admire and look up to us how to govern their own lives. Are we thoughtful about how people learn and grow? As leaders, we should think of ourselves as teachers and try to create companies in which teaching is seen as a valued way to contribute to the success of the whole. Do we think of most activities as teaching opportunities and experiences as ways of learning? One of the most crucial responsibilities of leadership is creating a culture that rewards those who lift not just our stock prices but our aspirations as well.

Discussing failure and all its ripple effects is not merely an academic exercise. We face it because by seeking better understanding, we remove barriers to full creative engagement. One of the biggest barriers is fear, and while failure comes with the territory, fear shouldn't have to. The goal, then, is to uncouple fear and failure— to create an environment in which making mistakes doesn't strike terror into your employees' hearts.

How, exactly, do you do that? By necessity, the message companies send to their managers is conflicting: Develop your people, help them grow into strong contributors and team members, and oh, by the way, make sure everything goes smoothly because there aren't enough resources, and the success of our enterprise depends on your group doing its job on time and on budget. It is easy to be critical of the micromanaging many managers resort to, yet we must acknowledge the rock and the hard place we often place them between. If they have to choose between meeting a deadline and some less well defined mandate to "nurture" their people, they will pick the deadline every time. We tell ourselves that we will devote more time to our people if we, in turn, are given more slack in the schedule or budget, but somehow the requirements of the job always eat up the slack, resulting in increased pressure with even less room for error. Given these realities, managers typically want two things: (1) for everything to be tightly controlled, and (2) to appear to be in control.

But when control is the goal, it can negatively affect other parts of your culture. I've known many managers who hate to be surprised in meetings, for example, by which I mean they make it clear that they want to be briefed about any unexpected news in advance and in private. In many workplaces, it is a sign of disrespect if someone surprises a manager with new information in front of other people. But what does this mean in practice? It means that there are pre-meetings before meetings, and the meetings begin to take on a pro forma tone. It means wasted time. It means that the employees who work with these people walk on eggshells. It means that fear runs rampant.

Getting middle managers to tolerate (and not feel threatened by) problems and surprises is one of our most important jobs; they already feel the weight of believing that if they screw up, there will be hell to pay. How do we get people to reframe the way they think about the process and the risks?

The antidote to fear is trust, and we all have a desire to find something to trust in an uncertain world. Fear and trust are powerful forces, and while they are not opposites, exactly, trust is the best tool for driving out fear. There will always be plenty to be afraid of, especially when you are doing something new. Trusting others doesn't mean that they won't make mistakes. It means that if they do (or if you do), you trust they will act to help solve it. Fear can be created quickly; trust can't. Leaders must demonstrate their trustworthiness, over time, through their actions—and the best way to do that is by responding well to failure. The Braintrust and various groups within Pixar have gone through difficult times together, solved problems together, and that is how they've built up trust in each other. Be patient. Be authentic. And be consistent. The trust will come.

When I mention authenticity, I am referring to the way that managers level with their people. In many organizations, managers tend to err on the side of secrecy, of keeping things hidden from employees. I believe this is the wrong instinct. A manager's default mode should not be secrecy. What is needed is a thoughtful consideration of the cost of secrecy weighed against the risks. When you instantly resort to secrecy, you are telling people they can't be trusted. When you are candid, you are telling people that you trust them and that there is nothing to fear. To confide in employees is to give them a sense of ownership over the information. The result— and I've seen this again and again—is that they are less likely to leak whatever it is that you've confided.

The people at Pixar have been extremely good at keeping secrets, which is crucial in a business whose profits depend on the strategic release of ideas or products when they are ready and not before. Since making movies is such a messy process, we need to be able to talk candidly, among ourselves, about the mess without having it shared outside the company. By sharing problems and sensitive issues with employees, we make them partners and part-owners in our culture, and they do not want to let each other down.

Your employees are smart; that's why you hired them. So treat them that way. They know when you deliver a message that has been heavily massaged. When managers explain what their plan is without giving the reasons for it, people wonder what the "real" agenda is. There may be no hidden agenda, but you've succeeded in implying that there is one. Discussing the thought processes behind solutions aims the focus on the solutions, not on second-guessing. When we are honest, people know it.

Pixar's head of management development, Jamie Woolf, put together a mentoring program that pairs new managers with experienced ones. A key facet of this program is that mentors and mentees work together for an extended period of time—eight months. They meet about all aspects of leadership, from career development and confidence building to managing personnel challenges and building healthy team environments. The purposes are to cultivate deep connections and to have a place to share fears and challenges, exploring the skills of managing others by wrestling together with real problems, whether they be external (a volatile supervisor) or internal (an overly active inner critic). In other words, to develop a sense of trust.

While I work with a couple of mentees, I also speak every year to the entire group. In this talk, I tell the story of how, when I was first a manager at New York Tech, I didn't feel like a manager at all. And while I liked the idea of being in charge, I went to work every day feeling like something of a fraud. Even in the early years of Pixar, when I was the president, that feeling didn't go away. I knew many presidents of other companies and had a good idea of their personality characteristics. They were aggressive and extremely confident. Knowing that I didn't share many of those traits, again I felt like a fraud. In truth, I was afraid of failure.

Not until about eight or nine years ago, I tell them, did the imposter feeling finally go away. I have several things to thank for that evolution: my experience of both weathering our failures and watching our films succeed; my decisions, post–*Toy Story,* to recommit myself to Pixar and its culture; and my enjoyment of my maturing relationship with Steve and John. Then, after fessing up, I ask the group, "How many of *you* feel like a fraud?" And without fail, every hand in the room shoots up.

As managers, we all start off with a certain amount of trepidation. When we are new to the position, we imagine what the job is in order to get our arms around it, then we compare ourselves against our made-up model. But the job is never what we think it is. The trick is to forget our models about what we "should" be. A better measure of our success is to look at the people on our team and see how they are working together. Can they rally to solve key problems? If the answer is yes, you are managing well.

This phenomenon of not perceiving correctly what our job is occurs frequently with new directors. Even if a person works side by side with an experienced director in a supporting role, a role in which they repeatedly demonstrate the abilities to take the reins on their own film, when they actually get the job it isn't quite what they thought it was. There is something scary about discovering that they have responsibilities that were not part of their mental model. In the case of first-time directors, the weight of those responsibilities is not only new, it is further amplified by the track record of our previous films. Every director at Pixar worries that his or her movie will be the one that fails, that breaks our streak of number-one hits. "That pressure is there: You can't be the first bomb," says Bob Peterson, a longtime Pixar writer and voice artist. "What you want is for that pressure to light a fire under you to make you say, 'I'm going to do better.' But there's a fear of not knowing if you can find the right answer. The directors here who are successful are able to just relax and let ideas be born out of that pressure."

Bob jokes that to relieve that pressure, Pixar should intentionally do a bad film "just to correct the market." Of course we'd never set out to make something terrible, but Bob's idea is thought-provoking: Are there ways to prove to your employees that your company doesn't stigmatize failure?

All of this attention on not only allowing but even *expecting* errors has helped make Pixar a unique culture. For proof of just how unique, consider the example of *Toy Story 3* once again. As I said at the start of this chapter, this was the only Pixar production during which we didn't have a major crisis, and after the film came out, I repeatedly said so in public, lauding its crew for racking up not a single disaster during the film's gestation.

You might imagine that the *Toy Story 3* crew would have been happy when I said this, but you'd imagine wrong. So ingrained are the beliefs I've been describing about failure at Pixar that the people who worked on *Toy Story 3* were actually offended by my remarks. They interpreted them to mean that they hadn't tried as hard as their colleagues on other films—that they hadn't pushed themselves enough. That isn't at all what I meant, but I have to admit: I was thrilled by their reaction. I saw it as proof that our culture is healthy.

As Andrew Stanton puts it, "It's gotten to the point that we get worried if a film is not a problem child right away. It makes us nervous. We've come to recognize the signs of invention—of dealing with originality. We have begun to welcome the feeling of, 'Oh, we've never had this exact problem before—and it's incredibly recalcitrant and won't do what we want it to do.' That's familiar territory for us—in a good way."

Rather than trying to prevent all errors, we should assume, as is almost always the case, that our people's intentions are good and that they want to solve problems. Give them responsibility, let the mistakes happen, and let people fix them. If there is fear, there is a reason—our job is to find the reason and to remedy it. Management's job is not to prevent risk but to build the ability to recover.

CHAPTER 7

THE HUNGRY BEAST AND
THE UGLY BABY

During the late 1980s and early 1990s, as an ascendant Disney Animation was enjoying a remarkable string of hit films—*The Little Mermaid, Beauty and the Beast, Aladdin, The Lion King*—I began to hear a phrase being used again and again in the executive suites of its Burbank headquarters: "You've got to feed the Beast."

As you may recall, Pixar had entered into a contract to write a graphics system for Disney—the Computer Animation Production System, or CAPS—that would paint and manage animation cels. We began working on CAPS while Disney was producing *The Little Mermaid,* so I had a front-row seat from which to view the way that film's success led to the studio's expansion and to its need for more film projects to justify (and occupy) the growing staff. In other words, I was there to witness the creation of Disney's Beast— and by "Beast" I mean any large group that needs to be fed an uninterrupted diet of new material and resources in order to function.

I should say that none of this was happening by accident or for the wrong reasons. The Walt Disney Company's CEO, Michael

Eisner, and the studio's chairman, Jeffrey Katzenberg, had committed to reviving animation after the long fallow period that followed Walt's death. To their credit, the result was an artistic flourishing that drew on the talents of legendary artists who'd been at the studio for decades as well as the fresh thinking of more recent hires. The films they produced not only were huge economic drivers for the company, but they immediately became iconic in the popular culture and, in turn, prompted the animation explosion that would ultimately enable Pixar to make *Toy Story*.

But the success of each new Disney film also did something else: It created a hunger for more. As the infrastructure of the studio grew to service, market, and promote each successful film, the need for more product in the pipeline only expanded. The stakes were simply too high to let all those employees at all those desks in all those buildings sit idle. If you'd asked around Disney at the time, you would have had trouble finding someone who believed that animated storytelling was a product that could or should be made on an assembly line, even though the term "Feed the Beast" has that very idea embedded in it. In fact, the intentions and values of the high-caliber people working in production were surely admirable. But the Beast is powerful and can overwhelm even the most dedicated individuals. As Disney expanded its release schedule, its need for output increased to the point that it opened animation studios in Burbank, Florida, France, and Australia just to keep up with its appetites. The pressure to create—and quickly!—became the order of the day. To be clear, this happens at many companies, not just in Hollywood, and its unintended effect is always the same: It lessens quality across the board.

After *The Lion King* was released in 1994, eventually grossing $952 million worldwide, the studio began its slow decline. It was hard, at first, to deduce why—there had been some leadership changes, yet the bulk of the people were still there, and they still had the talent and the desire to do great work. Nevertheless, the drought that was beginning then would last for the next sixteen years: From 1994 to 2010, not a single Disney animated film would open at number one at the box office. I believe this was the direct result of its employees thinking that their job was to feed the Beast.

Seeing even the earliest manifestation of this trend at Disney, I felt an urgency to understand the hidden factors that were behind it. Why? Because I sensed that if we continued to be successful, whatever was happening at Disney Animation would almost certainly happen to us, too.

Originality is fragile. And, in its first moments, it's often far from pretty. This is why I call early mock-ups of our films "ugly babies." They are not beautiful, miniature versions of the adults they will grow up to be. They are truly ugly: awkward and unformed, vulnerable and incomplete. They need nurturing—in the form of time and patience—in order to grow. What this means is that they have a hard time coexisting with the Beast.

The Ugly Baby idea is not easy to accept. Having seen and enjoyed Pixar movies, many people assume that they popped into the world already striking, resonant, and meaningful—fully grown, if you will. In fact, getting them to that point involved months, if not years, of work. If you sat down and watched the early reels of any of our films, the ugliness would be painfully clear. But the natural impulse is to compare the early reels of our films to finished films—by which I mean to hold the new to standards only the mature can meet. Our job is to protect our babies from being judged too quickly. Our job is to protect the new.

Before I go on, I want to say something about the word *protection*. I worry that because it has such a positive connotation, by implication anything being protected seems, ipso facto, worth protecting. But that's not always the case. Sometimes within Pixar, for example, production tries to protect processes that are comfortable and familiar but that don't make sense; legal departments are famous for being overly cautious in the name of protecting their companies from possible external threats; people in bureaucracies often seek to protect the status quo. *Protection* is used, in these contexts, to further a (small-c) conservative agenda: Don't disrupt what already is. As a business becomes successful, meanwhile, that conservatism gains strength, and inordinate energy is directed toward protecting what has worked so far.

When I advocate for protecting the new, then, I am using the word somewhat differently. I am saying that when someone hatches an original idea, it may be ungainly and poorly defined, but it is also the opposite of established and entrenched—*and that is precisely what is most exciting about it*. If, while in this vulnerable state, it is exposed to naysayers who fail to see its potential or lack the patience to let it evolve, it could be destroyed. Part of our job is to protect the new from people who don't understand that in order for greatness to emerge, there must be phases of not-so-greatness. Think of a caterpillar morphing into a butterfly—it only survives because it is encased in a cocoon. It survives, in other words, because it is protected from that which would damage it. It is protected from the Beast.

Pixar's first battle with the Beast came in 1999, after we'd released two successful films and were putting what we hoped would be our fifth movie, *Finding Nemo*, into production.

I remember Andrew Stanton's initial pitch about Marlin, an overprotective clownfish, and his search for Nemo, his abducted son. It was a brisk day in October, and we had gathered in a crowded conference room to hear Andrew talk through his story beats. His presentation was nothing short of magnificent. The narrative, as he described it, would be intercut with a series of flashbacks that explained what had happened to make Nemo's father such an overprotective worrywart when it came to his son (Nemo's mother and siblings, Andrew said, had been slain by a barracuda). Standing there in the front of the room, Andrew seamlessly wove together two stories: what was happening in Marlin's world, during the epic search he undertakes after Nemo is scooped up by a scuba diver, and what was happening in the aquarium in Sydney, where Nemo had ended up with a group of tropical fish called "the Tank Gang." The tale Andrew wanted to tell got to the heart of the struggle for independence that often shapes the father-son relationship. And what's more, it was funny.

When Andrew finished his pitch, those of us in attendance were silent for a moment. Then, John Lasseter spoke for all of us when he said, "You had me at the word *fish.*"

At this point, the specter of *Toy Story 2,* which had taken such a devastating toll on our employees, still loomed large in our memories. Stretched to the breaking point, we'd emerged from that film with a clear understanding that what we had gone through was not healthy for our employees or our business. We had vowed not to repeat those mistakes on *Monsters, Inc.,* and for the most part, we hadn't. But our determination on that front also meant that *Monsters, Inc.* ended up taking nearly five years to make. In the wake of that, we were actively looking for ways to improve and speed up our process. In this, we were driven by a particular observation: It was obvious to us that a large portion of our costs stemmed from the fact that we never seemed to stop tinkering with the scripts of our movies, even long after we started making them. It didn't take a genius to see that if we could only settle on the story early on, our movies would be much easier—and thus cheaper—to make. This then became our goal—finalize the script *before* we start making the film. After Andrew's tour de force pitch, *Finding Nemo* seemed like the perfect project with which to test our new theory. As we gave Andrew the go-ahead, we were confident that locking in the story early would yield not just a phenomenal movie but a cost-efficient production.

Looking back, I realize we weren't just trying to be more efficient. We were hoping to avoid the messy (and at times uncomfortable) part of the creative process. We were trying to eliminate errors (and, in so doing, to efficiently feed our beast). Of course, it was not to be. All those flashbacks that we'd loved in Andrew's pitch?

They proved confusing when we saw them on early reels—in a Braintrust meeting, Lee Unkrich was the first to call them cryptic and impressionistic, and he lobbied for a more linear storytelling structure. When Andrew tried it, an unexpected benefit emerged. Before, Marlin had come off as unsympathetic and unlikable because it took too long to find out the reason he was being such a smothering father. Now, with a more chronological approach, Marlin was more appealing and sympathetic. Moreover, Andrew found that his intention to weave together two concurrent storylines—the action in the ocean vs. the action in the aquarium—was far more complicated than he had imagined. The tale of the Tank Gang, originally intended as a major throughline, became a subplot. And those were just two of many difficult changes that were made during the production as unforeseen problems presented themselves—and our goal of a predetermined story and a streamlined production fell apart.

Despite our hopes that *Finding Nemo* would be the film that changed the way we did business, we ended up making as many adjustments during production as we had on any other film we had made. The result, of course, was a movie we're incredibly proud of, one that went on to become the second-highest-grossing film of 2003 and the highest-grossing animated film ever.

The only thing it *didn't* do was transform our production process.

My conclusion at the time was that finalizing the story before production began was still a worthy goal—we just hadn't achieved it yet. As we continued to make films, however, I came to believe that my goal was not just impractical but naïve. By insisting on the importance of getting our ducks in a row early, we had come perilously close to embracing a fallacy. Making the process better, easier, and cheaper is an important aspiration, something we continually work on—but *it is not the goal*. Making something great is the goal.

I see this over and over again in other companies: A subversion takes place in which streamlining the process or increasing production supplants the ultimate goal, with each person or group thinking they're doing the right thing—when, in fact, they have strayed off course. When efficiency or consistency of workflow are not balanced by other equally strong countervailing forces, the result is that new ideas—our ugly babies—aren't afforded the attention and protection they need to shine and mature. They are abandoned or never conceived of in the first place. Emphasis is placed on doing safer projects that mimic proven money-makers just to keep something—anything!—moving through the pipeline (see *The Lion King 1½*, a direct-to-video effort that came out in 2004, six years after *The Lion King 2: Simba's Pride*). This kind of thinking yields predictable, unoriginal fare because it prevents the kind of organic ferment that fuels true inspiration. But it does feed the Beast.

When I talk about the Beast and the Baby, it can seem very black and white—that the Beast is all bad and the Baby is all good. The truth is, reality lies somewhere in between. The Beast is a glutton but also a valuable motivator. The Baby is so pure and unsullied, so full of potential, but it's also needy and unpredictable and can keep you up at night. The key is for your Beast and your Babies to coexist peacefully, and that requires that you keep various forces in balance.

How do we balance these forces that seem so at odds, especially when it always appears to be such an unfair fight? The needs of the Beast seem to trump the needs of the Baby every time, given that the Baby's true worth is often unknown or in doubt and can remain so for months on end. How do we hold off the Beast, curbing its appetites, without putting our companies in jeopardy? Because every company needs its Beast. The Beast's hunger translates into deadlines and urgency. That's a good thing, as long as the Beast is kept in its place. And that's the tough part.

Many talk of the Beast as if it is a greedy, unthinking creature, insistent and beyond our control. But in fact, any group that produces a product or drives revenue could be considered to be part of the Beast, including marketing and distribution. Each group operates according to its own logic, and many have neither the responsibility for the quality of what is produced nor a good understanding of their own impact on that quality. It simply isn't their problem; keeping the process going and the money flowing is. Each group has its own goals and expectations and acts according to its own appetites.

In many businesses, the Beast requires so much attention that it acquires inordinate power. The reason: It is expensive, accounting for the vast majority of most companies' costs. Any company's profit margin depends in large part on how effectively it uses its people: The auto workers on the assembly line who are being paid whether the line is in motion or not; the stock boys in Amazon's warehouses who come to work regardless of how many shoppers are online that day; the lighting and shading experts (to pick one of dozens of examples in the world of animation) who must wait for many others to complete their duties on a particular shot before they can begin to do their work. If inefficiencies result in anyone waiting for too long, if the majority of your people aren't engaged in the work that drives your revenue most of the time, you risk being devoured from the inside out.

The solution, of course, is to feed the Beast, to occupy its time and attention, putting its talents to use. Even when you do that, though, the Beast cannot be sated. It is one of life's cruel ironies that when it comes to feeding the Beast, success only creates more pressure to hurry up and succeed again. Which is why at too many companies, the schedule (that is, the need for product) drives the output, not the strength of the ideas at the front end. I want to be careful not to imply that it is the individual people who comprise the Beast who are the problem—they are doing the best they can to accomplish what they've been charged with doing. Despite good intentions, the result is troubling: Feeding the Beast becomes the central focus.

The Beast thrives not only within animation or movie companies, of course. No creative business is immune, from technology to publishing to manufacturing. But all Beasts have one thing in common. Frequently, the people in charge of the Beast are the most organized people in the company—people wired to make things happen on track and on budget, as their bosses expect them to do. When those people and their interests become too powerful—when there is not sufficient push-back to protect new ideas—things go wrong. The Beast takes over.

The key to preventing this is balance. I see the give and take between different constituencies in a business as central to its success. So when I talk about taming the Beast, what I really mean is that keeping its needs balanced with the needs of other, more creative facets of your company will make you stronger.

Let me give you an example of what I mean, drawn from the business I know best. In animation, we have many constituencies: story, art, budget, technology, finance, production, marketing, and consumer products. The people within each constituency have priorities that are important—and often opposing. The writer and director want to tell the most affecting story possible; the production designer wants the film to look beautiful; the technical directors want flawless effects; finance wants to keep the budgets within limits; marketing wants a hook that is easily sold to potential viewers; the consumer products people want appealing characters to turn into plush toys and to plaster on lunchboxes and T-shirts; the production managers try to keep everyone happy—and to keep the whole enterprise from spiraling out of control. And so on. Each group is focused on its own needs, which means that no one has a clear view of how their decisions impact other groups; each group is under pressure to perform well, which means achieving stated goals.

Particularly in the early months of a project, these goals—which are subgoals, really, in the making of a film—are often easier to articulate and explain than the film itself. But if the director is able to get everything he or she wants, we will likely end up with a film that's too long. If the marketing people get their way, we will only make a film that mimics those that have already been "proven" to succeed—in other words, familiar to viewers but in all likelihood a creative failure. Each group, then, is trying to do the right thing, but they're pulling in different directions.

If any one of those groups "wins," we lose.

In an unhealthy culture, each group believes that if their objectives trump the goals of the other groups, the company will be better off. In a healthy culture, all constituencies recognize the importance of balancing competing desires—they want to be heard, but they don't have to win. Their interaction with one another—the push and pull that occurs naturally when talented people are given clear goals—yields the balance we seek. But that only happens if they understand that achieving balance is a central goal of the company.

While the idea of balance always sounds good, it doesn't capture the dynamic nature of what it means to actually achieve balance. Our mental image of balance is somewhat distorted because we tend to equate it with stillness—the calm repose of a yogi balancing on one leg, a state without apparent motion. To my mind, the more accurate examples of balance come from sports, such as when a basketball player spins around a defender, a running back bursts through the line of scrimmage, or a surfer catches a wave. All of these are extremely dynamic responses to rapidly changing environments. In the context of animation, directors have told me that they see their engagement when making a film as extremely active. "It seems like it's good psychologically to expect these movies to be troublesome," Byron Howard, one of our directors at Disney, told me. "It's like someone saying, 'Here, take care of this tiger, but watch your butt, they're tricky.' I feel like my butt is safer when I *expect* the tiger to be tricky."

As director Brad Bird sees it, every creative organization—be it an animation studio or a record label—is an ecosystem. "You need all the seasons," he says. "You need storms. It's like an ecology. To view lack of conflict as optimum is like saying a sunny day is optimum. A sunny day is when the sun wins out over the rain. There's no conflict. You have a clear winner. But if every day is sunny and it doesn't rain, things don't grow. And if it's sunny all the time—if, in fact, we don't ever even *have* night—all kinds of things don't happen and the planet dries up. The key is to view conflict as *essential,* because that's how we know the best ideas will be tested and survive. You know, it can't only be sunlight."

It is management's job to figure out how to help others see conflict as healthy—as a route to balance, which benefits us all in the long run. I'm here to say that it can be done—but it is an unending job. A good manager must always be on the lookout for areas in which balance has been lost. For example, as we expand our animation staff at Pixar, which has the positive impact of allowing us to do more quality work, there is also a negative impact that we must deal with: Meetings have become larger and less intimate, with each participant having a proportionally smaller ownership in the final film (which can mean feeling less valued). In response, we created smaller subgroups in which departments and individuals are encouraged to feel they have a voice. In order to make corrections like this—to reestablish balance—managers must be diligent about paying attention.

In chapter 4, I talked about a key moment in Pixar's development, as we embarked on making *Toy Story 2,* when we realized that we never wanted to foster a culture in which some workers were viewed as first-class, and others as second-class, where some employees were held to a higher standard and others were effectively relegated to the B-team. This may have sounded vaguely idealistic to some, but it was just another way of saying that we believe in preserving balance in our culture. If some employees or constituencies or goals are perceived to matter more, or to "win," there can be no balance.

Imagine a balance board—one of those planks of wood that rests, at its midsection, on a cylinder. The trick is to place one foot on each end of the board, then shift your weight in order to achieve equilibrium as the cylinder rolls beneath you. If there's a better example of balance—and of the ability to manage two competing forces (the left and the right)—I can't think of one. But while I can try to explain to you how to do it, show you videos, and suggest different methods for getting started, I could never fully explain *how* to achieve balance. That you learn only by doing—by allowing your conscious and subconscious mind to figure it out while in motion. With certain jobs, there isn't any other way to learn than by doing—by putting yourself in the unstable place and then feeling your way.

I often say that managers of creative enterprises must hold lightly to goals and firmly to intentions. What does that mean? It means that we must be open to having our goals change as we learn new information or are surprised by things we thought we knew but didn't. As long as our intentions—our values—remain constant, our goals can shift as needed. At Pixar, we try never to waver in our ethics, our values, and our intention to create original, quality products. We are willing to adjust our goals as we learn, striving to get it right—*not* necessarily to get it right the first time. Because that, to my mind, is the only way to establish something else that is essential to creativity: a culture that protects the new.

For many years, I was on a committee that read and selected papers to be published at SIGGRAPH, the annual computer graphics conference I mentioned in chapter 2. These papers were supposed to present ideas that advanced the field. The committee was composed of many of the field's most prominent players, all of whom I knew; it was a group that took the task of selecting papers very seriously. At each of the meetings, I was struck that there seemed to be two kinds of reviewers: some who would look for flaws in the papers, and then pounce to kill them; and others who started from a place of seeking and promoting good ideas. When the "idea protectors" saw flaws, they pointed them out gently, in the spirit of improving the paper—not eviscerating it. Interestingly, the "paper killers" were not aware that they were serving some other agenda (which was often, in my estimation, to show their colleagues how high their standards were). Both groups thought they were protecting the proceedings, but only one group understood that by looking for something new and surprising, they were offering the most valuable kind of protection. Negative feedback may be fun, but it is far less brave than endorsing something unproven and providing room for it to grow.

You'll notice, I hope, that I'm in no way asserting that protecting the new should mean isolating the new. As much as I admire the efficiency of the caterpillar in its cocoon, I do not believe that creative products should be developed in a vacuum (arguably, that was one of the mistakes we made on the film about blue-footed newts). I know some people who like to keep their gem completely to themselves while they polish it. But allowing this kind of behavior isn't protection. In fact, it can be the opposite: a failure to protect your employees from themselves. Because if history is any guide, some are diligently trying to polish a brick.

At Pixar, protection means populating story meetings with idea protectors, people who understand the difficult, ephemeral process of developing the new. It means supporting our people, because we know that the best ideas emerge when we've made it safe to work through problems. (Remember: People are more important than ideas.) Finally, it does not mean protecting the new forever. At some point, the new has to engage with the needs of the company—with its many constituencies and, yes, with the Beast. As long as the Beast is not allowed to run roughshod over everyone else, as long as we don't let it invert our values, its presence can be an impetus for progress.

At some point, the new idea has to move from the cocoon of

protection into the hands of other people. This engagement process is typically very messy and can be painful. Once, after one of our special effects software guys resigned, he wrote me an email containing two complaints. First, he said, he didn't like that his job involved cleaning up so many little problems caused by the new software. Second, he wrote, he was disappointed that we weren't taking more technical risks in our movies. The irony was that his job was to help solve problems that arose precisely because we *were* taking a major technical risk by implementing new software systems. The mess that he encountered—the reason he quit—was, in fact, caused by the complexity of trying to do something new. I was struck by how he didn't understand that taking a risk necessitated a willingness to deal with the mess created by the risk.

So: When is that magic moment when we shift from protection to engagement? This is sort of like asking the mama bird how she knows it's time to nudge her baby out of the nest. Will the baby have the strength to fly on its own? Will it figure out how to use its wings on the way down, or will it crash to earth?

The fact is, we struggle with this question on every film. Hollywood famously uses the term *green light* to reference the moment in a project's development when a studio officially decides it is viable (and many, many projects remain stuck in "development hell," never to emerge to face the world). In Pixar's history, though, we have only developed one feature film that didn't make it through to completion.

One of my favorite examples of how protection can give way to engagement comes not from a Pixar film but from our intern program. In 1998, I decided that the company would benefit from a summer program—like those at many creative companies—that would bring bright young people into Pixar for a couple of months to learn from working with experienced production people. But when I ran the idea past our production managers, they said no thanks: They had no interest in taking interns on. At first, I thought this was because they were too busy to spend time attending to inexperienced college kids and teaching them the ropes. But when I probed more deeply, it became clear that the resistance wasn't a question of time but of money. They didn't want the added expense of paying the interns. They only had so much cash in their budget and would rather spend it on experienced people. They had only so much time and resources, and the Beast was bearing down upon them. Their reaction was a form of protection, I suppose, motivated by a desire to protect the film and to aim every dollar at making it a success. But this stance didn't benefit the company as a whole. Internship programs are mechanisms for spotting talent and seeing if outsiders fit in. Moreover, new people bring an infusion of energy. To me, it seemed like a win-win.

I suppose I could simply have mandated that our production managers add the cost of adding interns to their budgets. But that would have made this new idea the enemy—something to resent. Instead, I decided to make the interns a corporate expense—they would essentially be available, at no extra cost, to any department who wanted to take them on. The first year, Pixar hired eight interns who were placed in the animation and technical departments. They were so eager and hard-working and they learned so fast that every one of them, by the end, was doing real production work. Seven of them ultimately returned, after graduation, to work for us in a full-time capacity. Every year since then, the program has grown a little more, and every year more managers have found themselves won over by their young charges. It wasn't just that the interns lightened the workload by taking on projects. Teaching them Pixar's ways made our people examine how they did things, which led to improvements for all. A few years in, it became clear that we didn't need to fund interns out of the corporate coffers anymore; as the program proved its worth, people became willing to absorb the costs into their budgets. In other words, the intern program needed protection to establish itself at first, but then grew out of that need. Last year, we had ten thousand applications for a hundred spots.

Whether it's the kernel of a movie idea or a fledgling internship program, the new needs protection. Business-as-usual does not. Managers do *not* need to work hard to protect established ideas or ways of doing business. The system is tilted to favor the incumbent. The challenger needs support to find its footing. And protection of the new—of the future, not the past—must be a conscious effort.

I can't help but think of one of my favorite moments in any Pixar movie, when Anton Ego, the jaded and much-feared food critic in *Ratatouille,* delivers his review of Gusteau's, the restaurant run by our hero Remy, a rat. Voiced by the great Peter O'Toole, Ego says that Remy's talents have "challenged my preconceptions about fine cooking . . . [and] have rocked me to my core." His speech, written by Brad Bird, similarly rocked me—and, to this day, sticks with me as I think about my work.

"In many ways, the work of a critic is easy," Ego says. "We risk very little yet enjoy a position over those who offer up their work and their selves to our judgment. We thrive on negative criticism, which is fun to write and to read. But the bitter truth we critics must face is that in the grand scheme of things, the average piece of junk is probably more meaningful than our criticism designating it so. But there are times when a critic truly risks something, and that is in the discovery and defense of the new. The world is often unkind to new talent, new creations. The new needs friends."

CHAPTER 8

CHANGE AND RANDOMNESS

There's nothing quite like the feeling you get, deep in your gut, when you're about to stand up in front of your entire company and say something you know has the potential to be upsetting. The day Steve, John, and I called an all-employee meeting to announce our decision to sell Pixar to Disney in 2006 was definitely one of those moments. We knew that the prospect of our little studio being absorbed into a much larger entity would worry many people. While we'd worked hard to put safeguards in place that would ensure our independence, we still expected our employees to be fearful that the merger would negatively impact our culture. I'll say more about the specific steps we took to protect Pixar in a later chapter, but here I want to discuss what happened when, in my eagerness to ease my colleagues' fears, I stood up and assured them that Pixar would not change.

It was one of the dumbest things I've ever said.

For the next year or so, whenever we wanted to try something new or rethink an established way of working, a steady stream of alarmed and upset people would show up at my office. "You promised the merger wouldn't affect the way we work," they'd say. "You said that Pixar would never change."

This happened enough that I called another company-wide meeting to explain myself. "What I *meant*," I said, "was that we aren't going to change *because* we were acquired by a larger company. We will still go through the kinds of changes that we would have gone through anyway. Furthermore, we are *always* changing, because change is a good thing."

I was glad I'd cleared that up. Except that I hadn't. In the end, I had to give the "Of course we will continue to change" speech three times before it finally sunk in.

What was interesting to me was that the changes that sparked so much concern had nothing to do with the merger. These were the normal adjustments that have to be made when a business expands and evolves. It's folly to think you can avoid change, no matter how much you might want to. But also, to my mind, you *shouldn't* want to. There is no growth or success without change.

For example, around the time of the merger, we were evaluating how to strike a balance between original films and sequels. We knew that audiences who loved our films were eager to see more stories set in those worlds (and, of course, the marketing and consumer products people want films that are easier to sell, which sequels always are). However, if we only made sequels, Pixar would wither and die. I thought of sequels as a sort of creative bankruptcy. We needed a constant churn of new ideas, even though we knew that original films are riskier. We recognized that making sequels, which were likely to do well at the box office, gave us more leeway to take those risks. Therefore, we came to the conclusion that a blend—one original film each year and a sequel every other year, or three films every two years—seemed a reasonable way to keep us both financially and creatively healthy.

At that point, Pixar had undertaken only one sequel, *Toy Story 2*. So our decision, because it occurred in such proximity to the merger, made many people assume that Disney was pressuring us to make more sequels. This isn't what happened. In fact, Disney gave us a great deal of latitude. Though we said this at the time, our words were greeted with skepticism.

We experienced similar confusion around the issue of office space. As we staffed up to meet the more intense production demands, we quickly outgrew our main Pixar building. Needing more room, we leased an annex a few blocks away that would house the next production we were developing, *Brave,* as well as the engineers in the software tools group, who were working on the next generation of our animation software. Soon after, people began showing up in my office again. Why, they wanted to know, were we separating our tools engineers from all of our production artists except those working on *Brave*? Why were we splitting up our story and art departments, who were accustomed to sitting together?

In short, it seemed like every issue, big or small, that arose around this time was chalked up to the merger: "You said things wouldn't change! You're breaking your word! We don't want to lose the old Pixar!" I should say that this outcry came despite the fact that the measures we had put in place to protect Pixar's culture were *working*—and, in my view, were a model for how to maintain cultural integrity after a merger. Still, people felt vulnerable—and that bred suspicion. More and more, I began to think that many of our employees viewed *any* change as a threat to the Pixar way (and, as such, to our ability to be successful going forward).

People want to hang on to things that work—stories that work, methods that work, strategies that work. You figure something out, it works, so you keep doing it—this is what an organization that is committed to learning does. And as we become successful, our approaches are reinforced, and we become even more resistant to change.

Moreover, it is precisely because of the inevitability of change that people fight to hold on to what they know. Unfortunately, we often have little ability to distinguish between what works and is worth hanging on to and what is holding us back and worth discarding. If you polled the employees of any creative company, my guess is that the vast majority would say they *believe* in change. But my experience, postmerger, taught me something else: Fear of change—innate, stubborn, and resistant to reason—is a powerful force. In many ways, it reminded me of Musical Chairs: We cling as long as possible to the perceived "safe" place that we already know, refusing to loosen our grip until we feel sure another safe place awaits.

In a company like Pixar, each individual's processes are deeply interconnected with those of other people, and it is nearly impossible to get everyone to change in the same way, at the same pace, all at once. Frequently, trying to force simultaneous change just doesn't seem worth it. How, as managers, do we differentiate between sticking with the tried-and-true and reaching for some unknown that might—or might not—be better?

Here's what we all know, deep down, even though we might wish it weren't true: Change is going to happen, whether we like it or not. Some people see random, unforeseen events as something to fear. I am not one of those people. To my mind, randomness is not just inevitable; it is part of the beauty of life. Acknowledging it and appreciating it helps us respond constructively when we are surprised. Fear makes people reach for certainty and stability, neither of which guarantee the safety they imply. I take a different approach. Rather than fear randomness, I believe we can make choices to see it for what it is and to let it work for us. The unpredictable is the ground on which creativity occurs.

Our tenth movie, *Up*, would be one of our most emotionally rich and original films, but it was also a case study in change and randomness. Conceived and directed by Pete Docter, it would be heralded by critics as a heartfelt adventure impeccably crafted with wit and depth. But boy, did it ever change during its development.

In the first version, there was a castle floating in the sky, completely unconnected to the world below. In this castle lived a king and his two sons, who were each vying to inherit the kingdom. The sons were opposites—they couldn't stand each other. One day, they both fell to earth. As they wandered around, trying to get back to their castle in the sky, they came across a tall bird who helped them understand each other.

This version was intriguing, but ultimately it could not be made to work. Those who saw it had trouble empathizing with spoiled princes or understanding the rules of this strange, floating world. Pete recalls that he had to think hard, then, about what he was trying to express. "I was after a feeling—an experience of life," he says. "For me, there are days when the world is overwhelming—especially when I'm directing a crew of three hundred people. As a result, I often daydream of running away. I have lots of daydreams about getting marooned on a tropical island or walking alone across America. I think we can all relate to the idea of wanting to get away from everything. Once I was able to understand what I was after, we were able to retool the story to better communicate that feeling."

Only two things survived from that original version, the tall bird and the title: *Up*.

For the next pass, Pete and his team introduced an old man, Carl Fredrickson, whose lifelong love affair with his childhood sweetheart Ellie was summarized in a brilliant prologue that set the emotional tone for the rest of the film. After Ellie dies, a grief-stricken Carl attaches his house to a huge bouquet of balloons that makes the structure slowly lift into the sky. He soon discovers that he has an eight-year-old stowaway (and eager cub scout) with him named Russell. Eventually, the house lands on an abandoned Soviet-era spy dirigible that's camouflaged to look like a giant cloud. Much of this version of the story unfolded on this airship until someone noted that—while it worked okay story-wise—it bore a slight resemblance to an idea Pixar had optioned that had to do with clouds. Though Pete had not been inspired at all by that idea, the echo felt too strong. So it was back to the drawing board.

In the third version, Pete and his team dumped the cloud, but kept the seventy-eight-year-old Carl, his sidekick Russell, the tall bird, and the idea of the house being lifted into the sky by balloons. Together, Carl and Russell floated in the house to a flat-topped Venezuelan mountain, called a tepui, where they encountered a famous explorer named Charles Muntz, whom Frederickson had read about and been inspired by when he was a boy. The reason Muntz hadn't died of old age by this point was that the aforementioned bird laid eggs that had a magical, fountain-of-youth effect if you ate them. However, the egg mythology was complicated and got in the way of the core story—it felt like too much of an aside. So Pete revised again.

In the fourth iteration, there were no youth-prolonging eggs—Pete had taken them out. Which left us with a chronological problem: While the emotional throughline of the film was working, the age difference between Muntz and Carl (who'd admired him since childhood) should have meant that Muntz was pushing a hundred. But we were late in the game—too late to fix it—and in the end, we simply decided not to address it. We've found over the years that if people are enjoying the world you've created, they will forgive little inconsistencies, if they notice them at all. In this case, nobody noticed—or if they did, they didn't care.

Up had to go through these changes—changes that unfolded over not months but years—to find its heart. Which meant that the people working on *Up* had to be able to roll with that evolution without panicking, shutting down, or growing discouraged. It helped that Pete understood what they were feeling.

"It wasn't until I finished directing *Monsters, Inc.* that I realized failure is a healthy part of the process," he told me. "Throughout the making of that film, I took it personally—I believed my mistakes were personal shortcomings, and if I were only a better director I wouldn't make them." To this day, he says, "I tend to flood and freeze up if I'm feeling overwhelmed. When this happens, it's usually because I *feel* like the world is crashing down and all is lost. One trick I've learned is to force myself to make a list of what's actually wrong. Usually, soon into making the list, I find I can group most of the issues into two or three larger all-encompassing problems. So it's really not all that bad. Having a finite list of problems is much better than having an illogical feeling that *everything* is wrong."

It also helped that Pete never lost sight of his mission on *Up*, which was to drill down to the emotional core of his characters and then build the story around that. I've heard people who've been on Pete's crews say that they would volunteer to take out the trash if it meant getting to work with him again. He is beloved. But the path he followed on *Up* was difficult and unpredictable; there was nothing about where the movie started that indicated where it would end up. It wasn't a matter of unearthing a buried story; in the beginning, there *was* no story.

"If I start on a film and right away know the structure—where it's going, the plot—I don't trust it," Pete says. "I feel like the only reason we're able to find some of these unique ideas, characters, and story twists is through discovery. And, by definition, 'discovery' means you don't know the answer when you start. This could just be my Lutheran, Scandinavian upbringing, but I believe life should not be easy. We're meant to push ourselves and try new things—which will definitely make us feel uncomfortable. Living through a few big catastrophes helps. After people survived *A Bug's Life* and *Toy Story 2*, they realized the pressure led to some pretty cool ideas."

Pete has a few methods he uses to help manage people through the fears brought on by pre-production chaos. "Sometimes in meetings, I sense people seizing up, not wanting to even talk about changes," he says. "So I try to trick them. I'll say, 'This would be a big change if we were really going to do it, but just as a thought exercise, what if . . .' Or, 'I'm not actually suggesting this, but go with me for a minute . . .' If people anticipate the production pressures, they'll close the door to new ideas—so you have to pretend you're not actually going to do anything, we're just talking, just playing around. Then if you hit upon some new idea that clearly works, people are excited about it and are happier to act on the change."

Another trick is to encourage people to play. "Some of the best ideas come out of joking around, which only comes when you (or the boss) give yourself permission to do it," Pete says. "It can feel like a waste of time to watch YouTube videos or to tell stories of what happened last weekend, but it can actually be very productive in the long run. I've heard some people describe creativity as 'unexpected connections between unrelated concepts or ideas.' If that's at all true, you have to be in a certain mindset to make those connections. So when I sense we're getting nowhere, I just shut things down. We all go off to something else. Later, once the mood has shifted, I'll attack the problem again."

This idea—that change is our friend because only from struggle does clarity emerge—makes many people uncomfortable, and I understand why. Whether you're coming up with a fashion line or an ad campaign or a car design, the creative process is an expensive undertaking, and blind alleys and unforeseen snafus inevitably drive up your costs. The stakes are so high, and the crises that pop up can be so unpredictable, that we try to exert control. The potential cost of failure appears far more damaging than that of micromanaging. But if we shun such necessary investment—tightening up controls because we fear the risk of being exposed for having made a bad bet—we become the kind of rigid thinkers and managers who impede creativity.

What is it, exactly, that people are *really* afraid of when they say they don't like change? There is the discomfort of being confused or the extra work or stress the change may require. For many people, changing course is also a sign of weakness, tantamount to admitting that you don't know what you are doing. This strikes me as particularly bizarre—personally, I think the person who can't change his or her mind is dangerous. Steve Jobs was known for changing his mind instantly in the light of new facts, and I don't know anyone who thought he was weak.

Managers often see change as a threat to their existing business model—and, of course, it is. In the course of my life, the computer industry has moved from mainframes to minicomputers to workstations to desktop computers and now to iPads. Each machine had a sales, marketing, and engineering organization built around it, and thus the shift from one to the next required radical changes to the organization. In Silicon Valley, I have seen the sales forces of many computer manufacturers fight to maintain the status quo, even as their resistance to change caused their market share to be gobbled up by rivals—a short-term view that sank many companies. One good example is Silicon Graphics, whose sales force was so accustomed to selling large, expensive machines that they fiercely resisted the transition to more economical models. Silicon Graphics still exists, but I rarely hear about them anymore.

"Better the devil you know than the devil you don't." For many, these are words to live by. Politicians master whatever system it took to get elected, and afterward there is little incentive to change it. Companies of all sorts hire lobbyists to keep the government from changing anything that would disrupt their way of doing business. In Hollywood, there are throngs of agents, lawyers, and so-called talent (actors and other performers) who recognize that the system is seriously flawed, but they don't attempt to change it because stepping outside the norm could eat into their revenues, at least for the short-term. Why would anybody want to change a system in ways that would endanger—or even eliminate—one's own job?

Self-interest guides opposition to change, but lack of self-awareness fuels it even more. Once you master any system, you typically become blind to its flaws; even if you can see them, they appear far too complex and intertwined to consider changing. But to remain blind is to risk becoming the music industry, in which self-interest (trying to protect short-term gains) trumped self-awareness (few people realized that the old system was about to be overtaken altogether). Industry executives clung to their outdated business model—selling albums—until it was too late and file sharing and iTunes had turned everything upside down.

To be clear, I am not endorsing change for change's sake. There are often good reasons to hang on to things that work. The wrong kind of change can endanger our projects, which is why those who oppose it are in earnest when they say that they just want to protect the companies in which they work. When people who run bureaucracies balk at change, they are usually acting in the service of what they think is right. Many of the rules that people find onerous and bureaucratic were put in place to deal with real abuses, problems, or inconsistencies or as a way of managing complex environments. But while each rule may have been instituted for good reason, after a while a thicket of rules develops that may not make sense in the aggregate. The danger is that your company becomes overwhelmed by well-intended rules that only accomplish one thing: draining the creative impulse.

So we've covered change. Where does randomness fit in? Once, when I was on a retreat in Marin, I heard a delightful—and possibly apocryphal—story about what happened when the British introduced golf to India in the 1820s. Upon building the first golf course there, the Royal Calcutta, the British discovered a problem: Indigenous monkeys were intrigued by the little white balls and would swoop down out of the trees and onto the fairways, picking them up and carrying them off. This was a disruption, to say the least. In response, officials tried erecting fences to keep the monkeys out, but the monkeys climbed right over. They tried capturing and relocating the monkeys, but the monkeys kept coming back. They tried loud noises to scare them away. Nothing worked. In the end, they arrived at a solution: They added a new rule to the game—"Play the ball where the monkey drops it."

Randomness is part of the folklore of history and literature; it has been studied extensively by mathematicians, scientists, and statisticians; it is deeply embedded in everything we do. We are aware of it in the abstract sense, by which I mean we have developed methods to acknowledge its existence. We talk about lucky breaks, good days and bad days, crazy coincidences, fortune smiling upon us, or being in the wrong place at the wrong time; we know that a drunk driver can come out of nowhere or, as the saying goes, that we could be hit by a bus tomorrow. Yet randomness remains stubbornly difficult to understand.

The problem is that our brains aren't wired to think about it. Instead, we are built to look for patterns in sights, sounds, interactions, and events in the world. This mechanism is so ingrained that we see patterns even when they aren't there. There is a subtle reason for this: We can store patterns and conclusions in our heads, but we cannot store randomness itself. Randomness is a concept that defies categorization; by definition, it comes out of nowhere and can't be anticipated. While we intellectually accept that it exists, our brains can't completely grasp it, so it has less impact on our consciousness than things we can see, measure, and categorize.

Here's a simple example: You leave late for work but still arrive in time for your 9 A.M. meeting. Congratulating yourself, you are oblivious to the fact that two minutes behind you on the freeway, someone blew a tire and blocked traffic for a half-hour. Without knowing it, you narrowly missed being late. Perhaps you draw the conclusion that tomorrow, you can afford to sleep a little later. But if you'd been in that traffic jam, you'd draw the opposite conclusion: Never leave late again. Because it is our nature to attach great significance to the patterns we witness, we ignore the things we cannot see and make deductions and predictions accordingly.

This is the puzzle of trying to understand randomness: Real patterns are mixed in with random events, so it is extraordinarily difficult for us to differentiate between chance and skill. Did you arrive early to work because you left on time, planned ahead, and drove carefully? Or were you just in the right place at the right time? Most people would choose the former answer without a second thought—without even acknowledging the latter was an option. As we try to learn from the past, we form patterns of thinking based on our experiences, not realizing that the things that happened have an unfair advantage over the things that didn't. In other words, we can't see the alternatives that might well have happened if not for some small chance event. When a bad thing happens, people will draw conclusions that might include conspiracy or forces acting against them or, conversely, if a good thing happens, that they are brilliant and deserving. But these kinds of misperceptions ultimately deceive us. And this has consequences in business— and for the way we manage.

When companies are successful, it is natural to assume that this is a result of leaders making shrewd decisions. Those leaders go forward believing that they have figured out the key to building a thriving company. In fact, randomness and luck played a key role in that success.

If you run a business that is covered with any frequency by the media, you may face another challenge. Journalists tend to look for patterns that can be explained in a relatively small number of words. If you haven't done the work of teasing apart what is random and what you have intentionally set in motion, you will be overly influenced by the analysis of outside observers, which is often oversimplified. When managing a company that is often in the news, as Pixar is, we must be careful not to believe our own hype. I say this knowing that it is difficult to resist, especially when we are flying high and tempted to think we have done everything right. But the truth is, I have no way of accounting for all of the factors involved in any given success, and whenever I learn more, I have to revise what I think. That's not a weakness or a flaw. That's reality.

Physics is a discipline that is dedicated to trying to find the underlying mechanisms that govern how our world works. One truly influential idea in physics is the famous principle known as Occam's Razor, attributed to William of Ockham, a fourteenth-century English logician. On the most basic level, it says that if there are competing explanations for why something occurs the way it does, you should pick the one that relies on the fewest assumptions and is thus the simplest. When Renaissance astronomers were trying to explain the movement of the planets, for example, there were many complex theories. The prevailing belief was that orbits were perfect circles, or epicycles, but as planetary observation improved, the models based on circles had to be made extremely complex in order to work. Then, Johannes Kepler hit upon the comparatively simple idea that the orbit of every planet is an ellipse, with the sun at one of two foci within it. The explanation's simplicity seemed proof that it was the right one—and with that simplicity came great power.

Unlike some theoretical ideas, Occam's Razor accords easily with human nature. In general, we seek what we think are simple explanations for events in our lives because we believe the simpler something is, the more fundamental—the more true—it is. But when it comes to randomness, our desire for simplicity can mislead us. Not everything is simple, and to try to force it to be is to misrepresent reality.

I believe that the inappropriate application of simple rules and models onto complex mechanisms causes damage—to whatever project is at hand and even to the company as a whole. The simple explanation is so desirable that it is often embraced even when it's completely inappropriate.

So what if we oversimplify in order to get through our days? So what if we hold tight to familiar ideas that give us the answers we crave? What does it matter? In my view, it matters a lot. In creative endeavors, we must face the unknown. But if we do so with blinders on—if we shut out reality in the interest of keeping things simple—we will not excel. The mechanisms that keep us safe from unknown threats have been hardwired into us since before our ancestors were fighting off saber-toothed tigers with sticks. But when it comes to creativity, the unknown is not our enemy. If we make room for it instead of shunning it, the unknown can bring inspiration and originality. How, then, do we make friends with the random and unknowable? How do we get more comfortable with our lack of control? It helps to understand just how pervasive randomness is.

One mathematical concept that everybody understands (though they may not know the name for it) is linearity—the idea that things proceed along the same course or repeat themselves in predictable ways. The rhythm of the day or the year is always the same—it's a repetitive cycle. The sun comes up. The sun goes down. Monday is followed by Tuesday. February is cold, August is warm. None of that feels like change—or, at least, it feels like predictable, understandable change. It is linear, and that is comforting.

A slightly less obvious concept is that of the bell curve, although most of us have an intuitive sense of what it means. In school we are sometimes graded on the bell curve—with a few people getting poor grades, a few getting excellent grades, and the rest bunched in the middle. If you plotted these test results on a graph, putting the scores on one axis and the number of people who received them on the other, the result is shaped like a bell. Human height works the same way, with most adults between five feet and six feet tall, and fewer numbers on either extreme. Professionals such as doctors or plumbers also have a similar distribution in their abilities—some are extraordinary, and some you wouldn't trust to tie your shoes. But most exist in the range between excellent and bumbling.

We are quite adept at working with repeatable events and at understanding bell-shaped variance. However, since we aren't good at modeling random events, we tend to use the mental facilities that we are good at and apply them to our view of the world, even when such an application is demonstrably wrong. Randomness, for example, doesn't occur in a linear fashion. For one thing, random processes do not evolve only in one way; by definition, they are indeterminate. So how do we develop ways of understanding randomness? By which I mean: How can we think clearly about unexpected events that are lurking out there that don't fit any of our existing models?

There is a third concept, also from the world of mathematics, that can help: stochastic self-similarity. *Stochastic* simply means random or chance; *self-similarity* describes the phenomenon— found in everything from stock market fluctuations to seismic activity to rainfall—of patterns that look the same when viewed at different degrees of magnification. If you break off a branch of a tree and hold that branch upright, for example, it looks a lot like a little tree. A stretch of coastline has that craggy coastline shape whether it is glimpsed from a hang glider or from outer space. Look at a tiny section of a snowflake under a microscope, and it will resemble a miniature version of the whole. This phenomenon occurs all the time in nature—in cloud formations, in the human circulatory system, in mountain ranges, in the way fern fronds are shaped.

But how does stochastic self-similarity relate to human experience?

We face hundreds of challenges, every day, in our lives. The majority hardly qualify as challenges at all: One of our shoes has disappeared under the couch, the toothpaste tube is empty, the light in the refrigerator burns out. A smaller number are more disruptive but still relatively minor: You sprain your ankle while jogging or the alarm clock fails to go off, making you late for work. An even smaller set causes larger ripples: You are passed over for an expected promotion; you have a heated argument with your spouse. Smaller still: You get into a car accident; a water main breaks in your basement; your toddler breaks his arm. Finally, there are the far rarer major events like wars, diseases, terrorist attacks— importantly, there is no limit to how bad these can get. So it's good that the more impactful an event is, generally speaking, the fewer of them there are. But, just like the tree branch that looks like a miniature tree, these challenges—though of different magnitudes— have more in common than people think.

Remember that while we are quick to assign patterns and causes to an event after it occurs, beforehand we don't even see it coming. In other words, while we may attribute to it a pattern later, random events don't come on time or on schedule. The distribution and nature of problems vary considerably between people—my problems seem to be like your problems, but they're not exactly the same. Moreover, it's not as if randomness happens in a vacuum. It is superimposed on the regular and repeatable patterns in our lives and, as such, is often hidden.

Sometimes a big event happens that changes everything. When it does, it tends to affirm the human tendency to treat big events as fundamentally different from smaller ones. That's a problem, in-side companies. When we put setbacks into two buckets—the "business as usual" bucket and the "holy cow" bucket—and use a different mindset for each, we are signing up for trouble. We be-come so caught up in our big problems that we ignore the little ones, failing to realize that some of our small problems will have long-term consequences—and are, therefore, big problems in the making. What's needed, in my view, is to approach big and small problems with the same set of values and emotions, because they are, in fact, self-similar. In other words, it is important that we don't freak out or start blaming people when some threshold—the "holy cow" bucket I referred to earlier—is reached. We need to be humble enough to recognize that unforeseen things can and do happen that are nobody's fault.

A good example of this occurred during the making of *Toy Story 2*. Earlier, when I described the evolution of that movie, I explained that our decision to overhaul the film so late in the game led to a meltdown of our workforce. This meltdown was the big unexpected event, and our response to it became part of our mythology. But about ten months before the reboot was ordered, in the winter of 1998, we'd been hit with a series of three smaller, random events—the first of which would threaten the future of Pixar.

To understand this first event, you need to know that we rely on Unix and Linux machines to store the thousands of computer files that comprise all the shots of any given film. And on those machines, there is a command—*/bin/rm -r -f **—that removes everything on the file system as fast as it can. Hearing that, you can probably anticipate what's coming: Somehow, by accident, someone used this command on the drives where the *Toy Story 2* files were kept. Not just some of the files, either. *All* of the data that made up the pictures, from objects to backgrounds, from lighting to shading, was dumped out of the system. First, Woody's hat disappeared. Then his boots. Then he disappeared entirely. One by one, the other characters began to vanish, too: Buzz, Mr. Potato Head, Hamm, Rex. Whole sequences—poof!—were deleted from the drive.

Oren Jacobs, one of the lead technical directors on the movie, remembers watching this occur in real time. At first, he couldn't believe what he was seeing. Then, he was frantically dialing the phone to reach systems. "Pull out the plug on the *Toy Story 2* master machine!" he screamed. When the guy on the other end asked, sensibly, why, Oren screamed louder: "Please, God, just pull it out as fast as you can!" The systems guy moved quickly, but still, two years of work—*90 percent of the film*—had been erased in a matter of seconds.

An hour later, Oren and his boss, Galyn Susman, were in my office, trying to figure out what we would do next. "Don't worry," we all reassured each other. "We'll restore the data from the backup system tonight. We'll only lose half a day of work." But then came random event number two: The backup system, we discovered, hadn't been working correctly. The mechanism we had in place specifically to help us recover from data failures had itself failed. *Toy Story 2* was gone and, at this point, the urge to panic was quite real. To reassemble the film would have taken thirty people a solid year.

I remember the meeting when, as this devastating reality began to sink in, the company's leaders gathered in a conference room to discuss our options—of which there seemed to be none. Then, about an hour into our discussion, Galyn Susman, the movie's supervising technical director, remembered something: "Wait," she said. "I might have a backup on my home computer." About six months before, Galyn had had her second baby, which required that she spend more of her time working from home. To make that process more convenient, she'd set up a system that copied the entire film database to her home computer, automatically, once a week. This—our third random event—would be our salvation.

Within a minute of her epiphany, Galyn and Oren were in her Volvo, speeding to her home in San Anselmo. They got her computer, wrapped it in blankets, and placed it carefully in the backseat. Then they drove in the slow lane all the way back to the office, where the machine was, as Oren describes it, "carried into Pixar like an Egyptian pharaoh." Thanks to Galyn's files, Woody was back—along with the rest of the movie.

Here, in rapid succession, we'd had two failures and one success, all of them random, all of them unforeseen. The real lesson of the event, though, was in how we dealt with its aftermath. In short, we didn't waste time playing the blame game. After the loss of the film, our list of priorities, in order, were: (1) Restore the film; (2) Fix our backup systems; (3) Install precautionary restrictions to make it much more difficult to access the deletion command directly.

Notably, one item was not on our list: Find the person responsible who typed the wrong command and punish him or her.

Some people may question that decision, reasoning that as valuable as creating a trusting environment can be, responsibility without accountability can undermine an expectation of excellence. I'm all for accountability. But in this case, my reasoning went like this: Our people have good intentions. To think you can control or prevent random problems by making an example of someone is naïve and wrongheaded. Moreover, if you say it is important to let the people you work with solve their own problems, then you must behave like you mean it. Drill down, certainly, to make sure everyone understands how important it is that we strive to avoid such problems in the future. But always—*always*—walk your talk.

How does this relate to stochastic, or random, self-similarity? In short, when you begin to grasp that big and little problems are structured similarly, then that helps you maintain a calmer perspective. Moreover, it helps you remain open to an important reality: If all our careful planning cannot prevent problems, then our best method of response is to enable employees at every level to own the problems and have the confidence to fix them. We want people to feel like they can take steps to solve problems without asking permission. In this case, Galyn's need to get her work done with a newborn at home led her to improvise and to download a version of the film once a week. Had she not solved that problem that way, Pixar would have missed its deadline on *Toy Story 2,* which would have been catastrophic for a small public company. People who act without an approved plan should not be punished for "going rogue." A culture that allows everyone, no matter their position, to stop the assembly line, both figuratively and literally, maximizes the creative engagement of people who want to help. In other words, we must meet unexpected problems with unexpected responses.

The second takeaway relates to our understanding of the boundary between the big and the small—and, for that matter, between good and bad, important and not important. We tend to think there is delineation—a bright line—between minor, expected problems and massive, unforeseen meltdowns. That encourages us to believe, wrongly, that we should approach these two phenomena—these two buckets, as I referred to them earlier—differently. But there isn't a bright line. Big and small problems are, in key ways, the same.

There is a crucial yet hard-to-understand concept here. Most people grasp the need to set priorities; they put the biggest problems at the top, with smaller problems beneath them. There are simply too many small problems to consider them all. So they draw a horizontal line beneath which they will not tread, directing all their energies to those above the line. I believe there is another approach: If we allow more people to solve problems without permission, and if we tolerate (and don't vilify) their mistakes, then we enable a much larger set of problems to be addressed. When a random problem pops up in this scenario, it causes no panic, because the threat of failure has been defanged. The individual or the organization responds with its best thinking, because the organization is not frozen, fearful, waiting for approval. Mistakes will still be made, but in my experience, they are fewer and farther between and are caught at an earlier stage.

As I've said, you don't always know how big a problem is when you first encounter it. It may seem small, but it also might be the straw that breaks the camel's back. If you have the tendency to put problems in buckets, you may not know which bucket to put it in. The difficulty is that we prioritize problems by size and importance, frequently ignoring small problems because of their abundance. But if you push the ownership of problems down into the ranks of an organization, then everyone feels free (and motivated) to attempt to solve whatever problem they face, big or small. I can't predict everything that our employees will do or how they will respond to problems, and that is a good thing. The key is to create a response structure that matches the problem structure.

The silver lining of a major meltdown is that it gives managers a chance to send clear signals to employees about the company's values, which inform the role each individual should expect to play. When we respond to the flaws of a movie in development by throwing it out and restarting, we are telling people that we value the quality of our movies more than anything else.

So far, I've been talking about randomness in the context of events. But human potential can be unpredictable, too. I've known some geniuses who were such a pain to work with that we had to let them go; then again, some of our most brilliant, delightful, and effective people were let go by previous employers for being none of those things. It would be nice if there were some magic bullet that turned difficult people into success stories, but there isn't. There are just too many unknowns and immeasurable personal characteristics involved for us to pretend that we have figured out how to do that. Everyone says they want to hire excellent people, but in truth we don't *really* know, at first, who will rise up to make a difference. I believe in putting in place a framework for finding potential, then nurturing talent and excellence, believing that many will rise, while knowing that not all will.

When Walt Disney was alive, he was such a singular talent that it was difficult for anyone to conceive of what the company would be like without him. And sure enough, after his death, there wasn't anybody who came close to filling his shoes. For years, Disney employees attempted to keep his spirit alive by constantly asking themselves, "What would Walt do?" Perhaps they thought that if they asked that question they would come up with something original, that they would remain true to Walt's pioneering spirit. In fact, this kind of thinking only accomplished the opposite. Because it looked backward, not forward, it tethered the place to the status quo. A pervasive fear of change took root. Steve Jobs was quite aware of this story and used to repeat it to people at Apple, adding that he never wanted people to ask, "What would Steve do?" No one—not Walt, not Steve, not the people of Pixar—ever achieved creative success by simply clinging to what used to work.

When I look back on Pixar's history, I have to recognize that so many of the good things that happened could easily have gone a different way. Steve could have sold us—he tried more than once. *Toy Story 2* could have been deleted for good, bringing the company down. For years, Disney was trying to steal John back, and they could have succeeded. I am distinctly aware that Disney Animation's success in the 1990s gave Pixar its chance with *Toy Story* and also that their later struggles enabled us to join together and ultimately merge.

I know that a lot of our successes came because we had pure intentions and great talent, and we did a lot of things right, but I also believe that attributing our successes solely to our own intelligence, without acknowledging the role of accidental events, diminishes us. We must acknowledge the random events that went our way, because acknowledging our good fortune—and not telling ourselves that everything we did was some stroke of genius—lets us make more realistic assessments and decisions. The existence of luck also reminds us that our activities are less repeatable. Since change is inevitable, the question is: Do you act to stop it and try to protect yourself from it, or do you become the master of change by accepting it and being open to it? My view, of course, is that working with change is what creativity is about.

CHAPTER 9

THE HIDDEN

In ancient Greek mythology, Apollo, god of poetry and prophecy, falls in love with the beautiful Cassandra, daughter of the king and queen of Troy, whose tangle of red hair and alabaster skin is famed throughout the land. He woos her by giving her a rare and treasured gift—the ability to see the future—and, in response, she agrees to be his consort. But when she later betrays him and breaks that vow, a furious Apollo curses her with a kiss, breathing words into her mouth that forever take away her powers of persuasion. From that day forward, she is doomed to scream into the wind: No one will believe the truths she speaks, and everyone judges her to be insane. Though Cassandra foresees the coming destruction of Troy—she warns that a Greek army will sneak into the city inside a huge wooden horse—she is unable to prevent the tragedy because no one heeds her warning.

The story of Cassandra is traditionally taken as a parable about what happens when valid warnings are ignored. But for me, it raises different issues. Why, I always wonder, do we think of *Cassandra* as the one who's cursed? The real curse, it seems to me, afflicts every-one else—all of those who are unable to perceive the truth she speaks.

I spend a lot of time thinking about the limits of perception. In the management context, particularly, it behooves us to ask our-selves constantly: How much are we able to see? And how much is obscured from view? Is there a Cassandra out there we are failing to listen to? In other words, despite our best intentions, are we cursed, too?

These questions take us to the heart of this book, because the answers are essential to sustaining a creative culture. In the preface, I wondered why the leaders of so many rising Silicon Valley com-panies made bad decisions, decisions that—even at the time—seemed so obviously wrongheaded. They had management and operational skills; they had grand ambitions; they didn't think they were making bad decisions, nor did they think they were being ar-rogant. Yet delusion set in—and as bright as these leaders were, they missed something essential to their continued success. The im-plication, for me, was that we would inevitably be subject to those same delusions at Pixar unless we came to terms with our own limited ability to see. We had to address what I've come to call the Hidden.

In 1995, when Steve Jobs was trying to convince us that we should go public, one of his key arguments was that we would eventually make a film that failed at the box office, and we needed to be prepared, financially, for that day. Going public would give us the capital to fund our own projects and, thus, to have more say about where we were headed, but it would also give us a buffer that could sustain us through failure. Steve's feeling was that Pixar's survival could not depend solely on the performance of each and every movie.

The underlying logic of his reasoning shook me: We were going to screw up, it was inevitable. And we didn't know when or how.

We had to prepare, then, for an unknown problem—a hidden problem. From that day on, I resolved to bring as many hidden problems as possible to light, a process that would require what might seem like an uncommon commitment to self-assessment. Having a financial cushion would help us recover from failure, and Steve was right to secure one. But the more important goal for me was to try to remain vigilant, to always be on the lookout for signs that we were screwing up—without knowing, of course, when that would occur or how it might come to light.

When I mention the mistakes that were made at companies such as Silicon Graphics or Toyota, some people cite hubris as the reason. "They started to believe their own B.S.," they say. "They got complacent." Others argue that companies go off the rails because of unreasonable growth or profitability expectations, which force them into poor short-term decisions. But I believe the deeper issue is that the leaders of these companies were not attuned to the fact that there were problems they could not see. And because they weren't aware of these blind spots, they assumed that the problems didn't exist.

Which brings us to one of my core management beliefs: If you don't try to uncover what is unseen and understand its nature, you will be ill prepared to lead.

We all know people we would describe as not being self-aware. Usually we conclude this because they don't see things about themselves that seem obvious to us—and, just as important, they have no clue that they are missing them. But what about our own awareness? If we accept that what we see and know is inevitably flawed, we must strive to find ways to heighten that awareness—to fill in the gaps, if you will. I, for one, cannot claim a perfectly clear-eyed view, but I do believe that making room in my head for the certainty that, like it or not, some problems will always be hidden from me has made me a better manager.

Most of us are willing to accept that there are fields of expertise we have not mastered. I don't know how to install plumbing, for example. If you asked me to transplant a kidney, replace a transmission, or argue a case before the Supreme Court, I would of course have to admit that I can't. We recognize that there are many topics about which we know very little—physics, math, medicine, law—unless we are trained in those fields. But even if it were possible to learn every discipline and master every profession, we'd still have blind spots. That's because there are other limitations—many of them rooted in the dynamics of human interaction—that keep us from having a clear picture of the world around us.

Imagine a door that, when you swing it open, reveals the universe of all that you do not and cannot know. It's vast, that universe—far larger than we are even conscious of. But ignorance is not necessarily bliss. This universe of unknown stuff will intrude in our lives and activities, so we have no choice but to deal with it. One of the ways to do that is to try to understand the many reasons why something may be difficult or impossible to see. To gain this understanding requires identifying multiple levels of the unknown, from the trivial to the fundamental.

The first level of what's hidden reminds me of when I first became a manager at New York Tech a few months after finishing my graduate studies in 1974. Managing people had never been a goal of mine. If I'm being honest, all I'd wanted, up to that point, was to be one of the guys and do my research. Our group was small and close, bound by a common goal. Since we also socialized with each other, I felt like I had a fairly solid sense of what was going on with each member of the team.

But over time, as I moved on to Lucasfilm and then to Pixar, the number of people who reported to me grew and then grew some more, and it began to dawn on me that our employees were behaving differently around me. They saw me as an "Important Manager" at an "Important Company," whereas the colleagues who'd started out with me at New York Tech just saw me as Ed. As my position changed, people became more careful how they spoke and acted in my presence. I don't think that my actions changed in a way that prompted this; my *position* did. And what this meant was that things I'd once been privy to became increasingly unavailable to me. Gradually, snarky behavior, grousing, and rudeness disappeared from view—from *my* view, anyway. I rarely saw bad behavior because people wouldn't exhibit it in front of me. I was out of a certain loop, and it was essential that I never lose sight of that fact. If I wasn't careful to be vigilant and self-aware, I might well draw the wrong conclusions.

The phenomenon I'm describing, rooted so firmly in that primal human drive for self-preservation, probably doesn't sound surprising: We all know that people bring their best selves to interactions with their bosses and save their lesser moments for their peers, spouses, or therapists. And yet, so many managers aren't aware of it when it's happening (perhaps because they enjoy being deferred to). It simply doesn't occur to them that after they get promoted to a leadership position, no one is going to come out and say, "Now that you are a manager, I can no longer be as candid with you." Instead, many new leaders assume, wrongly, that their access to information is unchanged. But that is just one example of how hidden-ness affects a manager's ability to lead.

Let's go down another layer.

To what extent do hierarchies and structured environments, which have been designed to help large groups of people work together, contribute to the hiding of information? People often shudder when you talk about hierarchy, as if it is inherently bad; they will use *hierarchical* as a pejorative, as shorthand for a workplace that puts too much emphasis on rank. This isn't entirely fair, of course, and I've worked in some highly structured, "hierarchical" environments that inspired top-notch work and a healthy interchange between colleagues.

At the same time, there are some hierarchal environments that are a nightmare.

Here's what turns a successful hierarchy into one that impedes progress: when too many people begin, subconsciously, to equate their own value and that of others with where they fall in the pecking order. Thus, they focus their energies on managing upward while treating people beneath them on the organizational chart poorly. The people I have seen do this seem to be acting on animal instinct, unaware of what they are doing. This problem is not caused by hierarchy itself but by individual or cultural delusions associated with hierarchy, chiefly those that assign personal worth based on rank. By not thinking about how and why we value people, we can fall into this trap almost by default.

Let's pause for a moment and look at it from the point of view of a manager who is having someone manage up *to* them. I'm not talking about brownnosing per se but more subtle forms of flattery. What does that leader see? He or she sees a person who wants to do a good job and who wants to please him or her. What's not to like about that? How does a manager differentiate between a team player and a person who is merely skilled at telling the boss what he or she wants to hear? A manager might rely on other people to alert him or her to a particular employee's lack of authenticity, but many are loath to tattle or to sound envious. The leader's view, then, is obstructed by these people who are skilled at figuring out what the leader wants. When viewed from a single vantage point, a full picture of the dynamics of any group is elusive. While we are all aware of these kinds of behaviors because we see them in others, most of us do not realize that we distort our own view of the world, largely because we think we see more than we actually do.

There is a third layer of hidden-ness—yet another set of things that I can't see. The people in the trenches doing the hard day-to-day work of producing our films are engaged in an incredibly complex set of processes, all of which come with their own attendant problems and idiosyncrasies. There are logistical hurdles that must be cleared, scheduling puzzles to be worked out, interpersonal and management concerns. I am probably capable of understanding each of these issues individually if and when they are brought to my attention and explained to me. But the people who are directly involved have the firmest grasp of the problems because they are in the middle of the action and see things that I don't see. If a crisis is brewing, they will know about it before I do. This would not be a problem if you could always count on people to send up a flare the instant they suspect trouble, but you can't. Even employees with the purest intentions may be too timid to speak up when they sense trouble. They may feel that it's too early to involve upper-level managers, or they may assume that we are aware of the break-downs already. Complex environments are, by definition, too complicated for any one person to grasp fully. Yet many managers, afraid of appearing to not be in control, believe that they have to know everything—or at least act like they do.

So my colleagues know more than I do about what's going on in any given department at any given moment. On the other hand, I know more about issues that people working in production do not: schedule requirements, resource conflicts, market problems, or personnel issues that may be difficult or inappropriate to share with everyone. Each of us, then, draws conclusions based on in-complete pictures. It would be wrong for me to assume that my limited view is necessarily better.

If we can agree that it's hard, if not impossible, to get a complete picture of what is going on at any given time in any given company, it becomes even harder when you are successful. That's because success convinces us that we are doing things the right way. There is nothing quite as effective, when it comes to shutting down alternative viewpoints, as being convinced you are right.

When faced with complexity, it is reassuring to tell ourselves that we can uncover and understand every facet of every problem if we just try hard enough. But that's a fallacy. The better approach, I believe, is to accept that we *can't* understand every facet of a complex environment and to focus, instead, on techniques to deal with combining different viewpoints. If we start with the attitude that different viewpoints are additive rather than competitive, we become more effective because our ideas or decisions are honed and tempered by that discourse. In a healthy, creative culture, the people in the trenches feel free to speak up and bring to light differing views that can help give us clarity.

Or take this example, which occurred at Pixar during what's called an "executive check"—a meeting to approve budgets and schedules—on the production of *Up*. A visual effects producer named Denise Ream was in that meeting, and she spoke up with a fairly radical suggestion: Production would be cheaper and take fewer person-weeks (the measure—the amount of work a single person could accomplish in a week's time—that we use to calculate budgets) if we did something that sounded completely counter to that goal—delay when the animators started on their work. Denise, who had the benefit of a broader perspective because before joining Pixar she'd worked for years at Industrial Light & Magic, was addressing a reality that she saw more clearly than any of us did: The eagerness to get going, which gave the impression of efficiency, was ultimately counterproductive because animators often had to redo their work as changes were made . . . which led to animators sitting around, waiting for assignments . . . which led to increased costs. From her vantage point, it seemed obvious that we would use fewer person-weeks if we gave animators bigger, more fully realized chunks to work on later in the process.

"I believe that animators will work faster than you're giving them credit for," Denise said, "if they have all the pieces they need when they begin." Boy, was she right. Even with all the usual snafus—endless story adjustments and last minute re-rigging of particular characters—*Up* was made in fewer person-weeks than we'd originally thought possible.

Recalling her decision to speak up in that meeting, Denise told me, "They had us delivering the movie at what I felt was an arbitrary early date, and I said, 'I don't understand why we're doing this, because you know we always go to the brick wall. No one *ever* finishes early, so why don't we just call a spade a spade now, two years before our deadline?' To me, it seemed clear that you'd want as much time as possible to get the story working. My goal was to push the back end off as long as I could. And it paid off."

That couldn't have happened if the producer of the movie—and the company's leadership in general—hadn't been open to a new viewpoint that challenged the status quo. That kind of openness is only possible in a culture that acknowledges its own blind spots. It's only possible when managers understand that others see problems they don't—and that they also see solutions.

We know that there are happy accidents, but there is still another level of hidden-ness that relates to the confluence of events that presage any important happening. Often, some of these events are impossible to see, so we don't realize how key a role they played. Consider the children who attend Pixar's day-care program, many of whom are the offspring of couples who met at Pixar. (John and I frequently note with pride the number of Pixar marriages and the many Pixar kids that have come into the world as a result.) Think of all the things that had to happen to make those babies possible. If Pixar had never existed, they would never have been born.

You can turn back the clock a bit more and say that those babies' parents might never have met if John didn't join the production of *The Adventures of André and Wally B.* or if Walt Disney had never existed or if I hadn't been lucky enough to study under Ivan Sutherland at the University of Utah. Or turn back to 1957, when I was twelve years old, returning from vacation in Yellowstone Park with my family. My dad was driving our yellow Ford '57 station wagon, my mom was in the passenger seat and my brothers and sisters and I were piled into the back. We were traveling up a winding canyon road with a steep cliff immediately to our right and no guardrail. Suddenly up ahead, from around a bend, came a car that had drifted into our lane. I remember my mother screaming and my father slamming on the brakes; he couldn't swerve because the cliff was a few feet to the right. I remember time slowing down and a moment of utter quiet before—bang!—the other car slammed into us, crushing the side of our car. When we finally slid to a stop, the adults got out and started yelling at each other, but I just stood there, staring at the damage to our car. If the other car had veered another two inches into our lane, it would have caught our front bumper, instead of the side, and pushed us right over the cliff. Existential threats like this tend to stay with you. Two more inches—no Pixar.

Of course, many people have close calls like this in the course of their lives, but here is the salient point: As I write this, all of those Pixar couples I am so proud to know have no inkling of the two inches that could have kept them from meeting or their children from being conceived.

I have heard people say that Pixar's success was inevitable because of the character of the people who formed it. While character is crucial, I am also certain there were an infinite number of "two-inch" events aside from my own that went our way—events that I have no way of knowing about because they occurred in the lives of other people who were critical to forming Pixar. The full set of possible outcomes at any time is so astonishingly vast that we can't begin to fathom them, so our brains have to simplify in order for us to function. I don't sit around thinking about what would have happened if John hadn't been available to join the production of *The Adventures of André and Wally B.*, for instance, or if Steve had made good on his desire to sell Pixar to Microsoft. But the truth is, the history of Pixar would have been very different if either of these things had happened. When I say that the fate of any group enterprise, and the individuals within it, are interconnected and interdependent, it may sound trite. But it's not. What's more, seeing all of the interdependencies that shape our lives is impossible, no matter how hard or long we look.

If we don't acknowledge how much is hidden, we hurt ourselves in the long run. Acknowledging what you can't see—getting comfortable with the fact that there are a large number of two-inch events occurring right now, out of our sight, that will affect us for better or worse, in myriad ways—helps promote flexibility. You might say I'm an advocate for humility in leaders. But to be truly humble, those leaders must first understand how many of the factors that shape their lives and businesses are—and will always be—out of sight.

In thinking about this chapter and about the limits of our perception, a familiar, oft-repeated phrase kept popping into my head: "Hindsight is 20-20." When we hear it, we normally just nod in agreement—yes, of course—accepting that we can look back on what happened, see it with total clarity, learn from it, and draw the right conclusions.

The problem is, the phrase is dead wrong. Hindsight is not 20-20. Not even close. Our view of the past, in fact, is hardly clearer than our view of the future. While we know more about a past event than a future one, our understanding of the factors that shaped it is severely limited. Not only that, because we *think* we see what happened clearly—hindsight being 20-20 and all—we often aren't open to knowing more. "We should be careful to get out of an experience only the wisdom that is in it—and stop there," as Mark Twain once said, "lest we be like the cat that sits down on a hot stove-lid. She will never sit down on a hot stove-lid again—and that is well; but also she will never sit down on a cold one anymore." The cat's hindsight, in other words, distorts her view. The past should be our teacher, not our master.

There is a kind of symmetry between looking forward and backward, though we seldom think of it that way. We know that in plotting our next move, we are selecting paths into the future, analyzing the best available information and deciding on a route forward. But we are usually not aware that when we look back in time, our penchant for pattern-making leads us to be selective about which memories have meaning. And we do not always make the right selections. We build our story—our model of the past—as best we can. We may seek out other people's memories and examine our own limited records to come up with a better model. Even then, it is still only a model—not reality.

In chapter 5, I took you into a meeting where the Braintrust was discussing *The Untitled Pixar Movie That Takes You Inside the Mind,* Pete Docter's ambitious film that would eventually become known as *Inside Out.* During the intensive research phase of the film, Pete was surprised to hear from a neuroscientist that only about 40 percent of what we think we "see" comes in through our eyes. "The rest is made up from memory or patterns that we recognize from past experience," he told me.

Animators have been trained to be observant—they know that viewers subconsciously register even the most subtle motions and that those, in turn, trigger recognition. If animators want a character to reach for something to their left, they anticipate that a split-second earlier by having the character move ever so subtly to the right. While most people aren't aware of it, this is what the brain expects to see—it's a tell, if you will, that signals what's to come. We can use that tell to guide the audience's eyes wherever we want them to look. Or conversely, if we want to surprise people, we can leave it out, making the unforeseen motion more startling. In *Toy Story 2,* for example, when Jessie talks about her fears, she twists one of her braids around her finger. Seeing this little motion, you sense her state of mind, perhaps without even knowing why. The meaning in that simple action is supplied by the audience, though—by their own experiences and emotional intelligence. Most think of animation as the characters just moving around in funny ways while they deliver their lines, but great animators carefully craft the movements that elicit an emotional response, convincing us that these characters have feelings, emotions, intentions.

This is all based on how we actually function, and it isn't what we normally assume. Our brain has a difficult job: The actual amount of visual detail in front of us is vast, and our eyes are only able to take in a tiny fraction through that little spot at the back of our eyeball, the fovea. Basically, we either don't perceive or have to ignore most of what is outside of us. However, we do have to function, so simultaneously, the brain fills in the details we miss. We fill in or make up a great deal more than we think we do. What I'm really talking about here are our mental models, which play a major role in our perception of the world.

The models in our head operate at awesome speed, allowing us to function in real time, picking out what is good or what is threatening in any given scenario. This process is so fast and automatic, in fact, that we don't notice that it is happening. A snippet of sound or the briefest glance at someone is sufficient to activate these models; a subtle facial twitch can cause us to see that something is troubling a friend; a slight shift in the quality of light tells us that a storm is coming. All we need is a tiny bit of information to make huge leaps of inference based on our models—as I say, we fill it in. We are meaning-making creatures who read other people's subtle clues just as they read ours.

One way to understand the implications of how our mental models work is to consider the magician's sleight of hand. As he or she makes, say, a coin or a playing card disappear, we take delight in being fooled, and our eyes dart about, trying to divine the trick. We can only see a small amount of what is going on as the magician moves his or her hands around, lulling us with distracting patter and extraneous movement. In order for the magic trick to work, two things must occur: First, the magician must divert our eyes from where the hidden action is actually happening; second, our brains must fill in the missing information, combining what we already know with what we are perceiving in that moment. This is a great example of the 40-percent rule that Pete referred to: We aren't aware that the majority of what we think we see is actually our brain filling in the gaps. The illusion that we have a complete picture is extraordinarily persuasive. However, the magician doesn't create the illusion—we do. We firmly believe that we are perceiving reality in its totality rather than a sliver of it. In other words, we are aware of the results of our brain's processing but not the processing itself.

Typically, people imagine consciousness to be something that is achieved *inside* our brains. Alva Noe, a professor of philosophy at the University of California at Berkeley who focuses on theories of perception, has suggested another way of thinking about consciousness—as something we do, or enact, or perform in our dynamic involvement with the world around us. Consciousness, in other words, happens within a context. "We spend all our lives embodied, environmentally situated, with others," he writes. "We are not merely recipients of external influences but are creatures built to receive influences that we ourselves enact; we are dynamically coupled with the world, not separate from it." He describes money, for example, as something that only has value and meaning as part of a vast interconnected system. Even though our day-to-day interactions with money tend to focus on numbers printed on bits of metal and rectangular pieces of sturdy paper, our mental model of money is far more complicated. That model shapes—and is shaped by—our views of our lifestyle, our concerns about our fair share, our feelings about status, and our judgments of other people and ourselves.

The models we have of our relationships at work, with friends, in our families, and in our society are all even more complicated than our visual models. These constructs—call them personal models—shape what we perceive. But they are each unique to us— no one can see relationships quite the way we do. If only we could remember that! Most of us walk around thinking that our view is best—probably because it is the only one we really know. You'd think the fact that we all have major misunderstandings with people at times—squabbles over what was said or what was meant— would clue us in to the reality that so incredibly much is hidden from us. But, no. We have to learn, over and over again, that the perceptions and experiences of others are vastly different than our own. In a creative environment, those differences can be assets. But when we don't acknowledge and honor them, they can erode, rather than enrich, our creative work.

This sounds simple enough—honor the viewpoints of others!—but it can be enormously difficult to put into practice throughout your company. That's because when humans see things that challenge our mental models, we tend not just to resist them but to ignore them. This has been scientifically proven. The concept of "confirmation bias"—the tendency of people to favor information, true or not, that confirms their preexisting beliefs—was introduced in the 1960s by Peter Wason, a British psychologist. Wason did a famous series of experiments that explored how people give lesser weight to data that contradicts what they think is true. (As if we needed more proof that what's hidden can make us draw the wrong conclusions.)

If our mental models are mere approximations of reality, then, the conclusions we draw cannot help but be prone to error. A few words uttered by someone close to us can carry enormous weight, for example, whereas the same words uttered by a stranger won't resonate at all. At our jobs, we may interpret not being invited to a meeting as a threat to us or to our projects, even when no threat is intended. But because we often don't see the flaws in our reasoning —or our biases—it's easy to be deluded while being quite convinced that we are the only sane ones around.

To show you how easily this kind of delusion takes hold in the workplace, I want to share a story of a mistake we made in the early days of Pixar. We had hired outside writers to help with a film, but we weren't happy with the result. So we brought in someone else, another writer who ultimately did a terrific job, but we made the mistake of leaving the original writers' names on the next draft. When the movie came out, we had to give credit to the original, failed writers, due to the rules in the industry that we operate under. Having to give undue credit left a bad taste in the mouths of many at Pixar. We make a big deal out of our belief in giving credit where credit is due.

Somehow, though, this episode led Pixar's directors to decide that, going forward, *they* should write the first drafts of their movies and thus be credited as writers. This belief shaped our model of how we should work as a studio, and this, in turn, affected how several of the directors defined what it meant to be a director. The problem was that these were all wrong conclusions, based on a single bad experience. And that led to more problems. Now, for example, we suddenly found an almost passive-aggressive resistance internally to hiring outside writers at the beginning of our process, even when we declared that we didn't want directors to write the first draft if they hadn't written a movie before. What this meant, in some cases, was a lot of wasted time. Not only is writing time-consuming but writers also bring structural thinking to the development process—input that most directors really need. Several projects stalled because directors were underwater, trying to write scripts themselves when they should have been doing other things.

I think we're out of the woods now, but it took a while. And all because a flawed mental model, constructed in response to a single event, had taken hold. Once a model of how we should work gets in our head, it is difficult to change.

We've all experienced times when other people see the same event we see but remember it differently. (Typically, we think *our* view is the correct one.) The differences arise because of the ways our separate mental models shape what we see. I'll say it again: *Our mental models aren't reality*. They are tools, like the models weather forecasters use to predict the weather. But, as we know all too well, sometimes the forecast says rain and, boom, the sun comes out. The tool is not reality.

The key is knowing the difference.

When we are making a movie, the movie doesn't exist yet. We are not uncovering it or discovering it; it's not as if it resides somewhere and is just waiting to be found. *There is no movie.* We are making decisions, one by one, to create it. In a fundamental way, the movie is hidden from us. (I refer to this concept as the "Unmade Future," and I will devote a subsequent chapter to the central role it plays in creativity.) I know this can feel overwhelming. There is a reason that writers talk about the terror of the blank page and painters shudder at the sight of an empty canvas. It's extremely difficult to create something out of nothing, especially when you consider that much of what you're trying to realize is hidden, at least at first. There is hope, however. There are things we can do to help ourselves open up and see more clearly.

I've talked about my belief that balance is a dynamic activity —by which I mean, one that never ends. I've spelled out my reasons for not defaulting to one or another extreme because it feels safer or more stable. Now I am urging you to attempt a similar balancing act when navigating between the known and the unknown. While the allure of safety and predictability is strong, achieving true balance means engaging in activities whose outcomes and payoffs are not yet apparent. The most creative people are willing to work in the shadow of uncertainty.

Let us return, for a moment, to the metaphor I used earlier in this chapter, that of the door. On one side is everything we see and know—the world as we understand it. On the other side is everything we can't see and don't know—unsolved problems, unexpressed emotions, unrealized possibilities so innumerable that imagining them is inconceivable. This side, then, is not an alternate reality but something even harder to fathom: that which has not yet been created.

The goal is to place one foot on either side of the door—one grounded in what we know, what we are confident about, our areas of expertise, the people and processes we can count on—and the other in the unknown, where things are murky, unseen, or uncreated.

Many fear this side of the door. We crave stability and certainty, so we keep both feet rooted in what we know, believing that if we repeat ourselves or repeat what is known to work, we will be safe. This feels like a rational view. Just as we know that the rule of law leads to healthier, more productive societies or that practice makes perfect or that the planets orbit the sun, we all need things that we can count on. But no matter how intensely we desire certainty, we should understand that whether because of our limits or randomness or future unknowable confluences of events, something will inevitably come, unbidden, through that door. Some of it will be uplifting and inspiring, and some of it will be disastrous.

We all know people who eagerly face the unknown; they engage with the seemingly intractable problems of science, engineering, and society; they embrace the complexities of visual or written expression; they are invigorated by uncertainty. That's because they believe that, through questioning, they can do more than merely look through the door. They can venture across its threshold.

There are others who venture into the unknown with surprising success but with little understanding of what they have done. Believing in their cleverness, they revel in their brilliance, telling others about the importance of taking risks. But having stumbled into greatness once, they are not eager for another trip into the unknown. That's because success makes them warier than ever of failure, so they retreat, content to repeat what they have done before. They stay on the side of the known.

As I discuss the elements of a healthy creative environment, you may have noticed that I have expressly not sought to define the word *creativity*—and that's intentional. I don't do it because it doesn't seem useful. I believe that we all have the potential to solve problems and express ourselves creatively. What stands in our way are these hidden barriers—the misconceptions and assumptions that impede us without our knowing it. The issue of what is hidden, then, is not just an abstraction to be bandied about as an intellectual exercise. The Hidden—and our acknowledgement of it—is an absolutely essential part of rooting out what impedes our progress: clinging to what works, fearing change, and deluding ourselves about our roles in our own success. Candor, safety, research, self-assessment, and protecting the new are all mechanisms we can use to confront the unknown and to keep the chaos and fear to a minimum. These concepts don't necessarily make anything easier, but they can help us uncover hidden problems and, thus, enable us to address them. It is to this we now turn in earnest.

PART III

BUILDING AND SUSTAINING

CHAPTER 10

BROADENING OUR VIEW

In the late 1970s, I took a road trip from New York City to Washington, D.C., with my wife and another couple. We rented one of those giant campers with two rear wheels on each side so that if one wheel blew, the other would still hold the camper up. Navigating this thing was a challenge, to say the least, and was only made more challenging by the fact that the other husband, Dick, had never driven a camper before. Instead of taking the New Jersey Turnpike, which probably would have been the prudent thing to do, we took an alternate route because it didn't have tolls; we were being cheap. The problem was, this alternate route had a roundabout every few miles—one of those circular intersection substitutes that require vehicles to merge, drive part of the way around, and then exit in their chosen direction. Easy enough in a car. Not so easy in a camper.

As we approached one of these roundabouts, Dick clipped the curb, and I heard a rear tire blow out.

"Dick, you popped a tire!" Dick's wife, Anne, said.

"No, I didn't," he shot back.

As we continued down the road, Dick and Anne engaged in a long, heated argument about the tire and his driving. "You need to be more careful," Anne scolded, while Dick fumed ("I didn't pop the tire!") and defended himself ("These campers are hard to drive!"). It was evident to my wife and me that there was history fueling this exchange, but Dick and Anne's backstory—whatever it may have been—wasn't moving them any closer to the obvious and somewhat urgent conclusion that we should pull over and fix our flat. It was as if accumulated tensions about other, unrelated issues had made them blind to reality: We were hurtling along the highway on one less tire than our massive vehicle was designed for. We needed to stop and assess the damage.

After several minutes of listening to their bickering, I felt it necessary to interject and say that, in fact, the tire *had* blown. Because while Dick and Anne seemed to think they were talking about the tire, they clearly weren't, and anyone else could see that our safety was not top of mind for either of them. Their mental models, forged by years of interacting with one another, altered their interpretation of straightforward events—we had dinged a curb and popped a tire—and blinded them to the danger we could be in if we didn't pull over and take care of the problem immediately.

This story—the oversized vehicle, the oblivious couple, the shredded tire, the *Honeymooners*-level sniping that ensued—has an element of dark humor, for sure, but I tell it here because it demonstrates four ideas that inform the way I think about managing. The first, which I discussed in chapter 9, is that our models of the world so distort what we perceive that they can make it hard to see what is right in front of us. (I'm using *model* somewhat generally here to mean the preconceptions we have built up over time that we use to evaluate what we see and hear as well as to reason and anticipate.) The second is that we don't typically see the boundary between new information coming in from the outside and our old, established mental models—we perceive both together, as a unified experience. The third is that when we unknowingly get caught up in our own interpretations, we become inflexible, less able to deal with the problems at hand. And the fourth idea is that people who work or live together—people like Dick and Anne, for example—have, by virtue of proximity and shared history, models of the world that are deeply (sometimes hopelessly) intertwined with one another. If my wife and I had been traveling with just Dick or just Anne, he or she almost certainly would have responded appropriately, but because they were together, their combined model was more complex—and more limiting—than either of their models would have been on its own.

Now, consider this: The tire incident involved the interconnected models of just two people. In business, where dozens if not hundreds of people may work in close proximity, that effect multiplies quickly, and before you know it, these competing and often at-odds models lead to a kind of inertia that makes it difficult to change or respond well to challenges. The intertwining of many views is an unavoidable part of any culture, and unless you are careful, the conflicts that arise can keep groups of people locked into their restrictive viewpoints even if, as is often the case, each member of the group is ordinarily open to better ideas.

As more people are added to any group, there is an inexorable drift toward inflexibility. While we can agree in principle that an organization needs to be flexible in order to solve problems, living up to that principle can be extraordinarily difficult. Rigidity—by which I mean the determination that one's own view is the correct one—can be hard to recognize at first. And just as individuals have biases and jump to conclusions because of the lens through which they view the world, organizations perceive the world through what they already know how to do.

This third section of the book is devoted to some of the specific methods we have employed at Pixar to prevent our disparate views from hindering our collaboration. In each case, we are trying to force ourselves—individually and as a company—to challenge our preconceptions. In this chapter I discuss several of the mechanisms we use to put our collective heads into a different frame of mind.

1. Dailies, or Solving Problems Together
2. Research Trips
3. The Power of Limits
4. Integrating Technology and Art
5. Short Experiments
6. Learning to See
7. Postmortems
8. Continuing to Learn

1. DAILIES, OR SOLVING PROBLEMS TOGETHER

In the fall of 2011, eight months before the release of *Brave*, a dozen or so animators ambled into the dailies meeting in the screening room at the far end of Pixar's atrium and plopped down heavily on oversized couches. It was just after 9 A.M., and more than a few attendees were sipping cups of coffee in an attempt to look alive. The director Mark Andrews, meanwhile, is not the groggy type. By the time he bounded into the room, he'd already spent an hour outside on the lawn, thrusting and parrying—he's an avid fencer—with a thirty-eight-inch longsword.

Mark had stepped in to direct *Brave* midway through production at the request of John and myself, and he was widely seen as an inspiring leader. A proud descendant of Scotland, where *Brave* is set, Mark urged his crew to join him in wearing a kilt to work every Friday (he likes to say that men in skirts boost morale). Many viewed him as nothing short of a force of nature. "Mark talks to you as if he's trying to drown out an F5 class tornado behind him—and winning," is how one animator described him. "I suspect he consumes plutonium pills." This dailies meeting would do nothing to disprove that suspicion.

"Good morning, everybody! Wake up!" Mark yelled, kicking off an hour-long session during which the assembled animators shared glimpses of the scenes they were bringing to life. Mark watched carefully and gave detailed notes on how to improve each scene and encouraged everyone else in the room—a rigging supervisor, the movie's producer, its head of story, and the other animators—to do so as well. The goal of this meeting, as with all dailies meetings, was to see the shots, together, as they really were.

Dailies are a key part of Pixar culture, not just because of what they accomplish—constructive midstream feedback—but because of *how* they accomplish it. Participants have learned to check their egos at the door—they are about to show incomplete work to their director and colleagues. This requires engagement at all levels, and it's our directors' job to foster and create a safe place for that. Mark Andrews did this at the *Brave* meeting by being irrepressible: singing '80s songs, reveling in people's nicknames (Wu-dog! Dr. K!), and mocking his own drawing ability as he hurriedly sketched out suggested tweaks. "Is that all the energy you got for me today?" he teased one sleepy colleague. To another, whose work he deemed flawless, he shouted the words all animators yearn to hear: "Final that! Bang!" Whether or not all the animators would get that same go-ahead, everyone could count on this: When each finished his or her presentation, the room would burst into applause.

This wasn't a pep rally, though. The critiques that were offered were specific and meticulous. Every scene was prosecuted relentlessly, and each animator seemed to welcome the feedback. "Is that stick big enough for everybody?" Mark asked at one point, referring to a flimsy-looking branch that was supposed to keep a heavy door propped open in one scene. Several people didn't think so, and as Mark scribbled with a stylus on a tablet in front of him, a sturdier log appeared on the screen on the front of the room. "Better?" he asked. One by one, each scene that the group reviewed raised new issues. That old man who just ran up a flight of stairs? He should look more winded. The facial expression of a young spy? It could be more devilish. "Chime in!" Mark urged. "Sound off!"

For all the barking and levity, you could feel the focused concentration in the room. What these people were engaged in was the kind of detailed analysis—and openness to constructive criticism— that would determine whether merely good animation would become great. Mark bore down on ten frames in which Queen Elinor, the mom character who has turned into a bear, walks on stones while traversing a creek. "She looks like she's stepping more catlike than heavy-bear-like," he said. "I like the overall speed, but I'm not feeling the *weight*. She's walking like a ninja." Everybody nodded and—note taken—they moved on.

Dailies are master classes in how to see and think more expansively, and their impact can be felt throughout the building. "Some people show their scenes to get critique from others, others come to watch and see what kind of notes are being given—to learn from their peers and from me—my style, what I like and dislike," Mark told me. "The dailies keep everyone in top form. It's an intimidating room to be in because the goal is to create the best animation possible. We go through every single frame with a fine-toothed comb, over and over and over again. Sometimes there are full-on debates because, truly, I don't have all the answers. We work it out together."

I give this glimpse into a dailies session because sharing and analyzing a team's ongoing work every morning is, by definition, a group effort—but it does not come naturally. People join us with a set of expectations about what they think is important. They want to please, impress, and show their worth. They really don't want to embarrass themselves by showing incomplete work or ill-conceived ideas, and they don't want to say something dumb in front of the director. The first step is to teach them that everyone at Pixar shows incomplete work, and everyone is free to make suggestions. When they realize this, the embarrassment goes away—and when the embarrassment goes away, people become more creative. By making the struggles to solve the problems safe to discuss, then everyone learns from—and inspires—one another. The whole activity becomes socially rewarding and productive. To participate fully each morning requires empathy, clarity, generosity, and the ability to listen. Dailies are designed to promote everyone's ability to be open to others, in the recognition that individual creativity is magnified by the people around you. The result: We see more clearly.

2. RESEARCH TRIPS

I was once in a conference room at Disney in which two directors were pitching the latest version of a film they were developing. The walls of the room were covered with large corkboards, which were filled with illustrations of what happens in each act, as well as drawings of characters and collages of inspirational artwork. To give a sense of the overall flavor of the film, the directors had posted dozens of images from well-known movies that they felt were in a similar visual and contextual vein: panoramic shots they hoped to mimic, landscapes they found inspiring, character studies that showed costumes like the ones they planned to use. While they had hoped to convey the sense of their movie idea by displaying examples from other films, every single board was based on these iconic references, with the unintended result that everything presented felt terribly derivative. In one way, this made sense—every director gets into this business because they love movies; it is inevitable that references to other movies often pop up when talking about filmmaking. (At Pixar, we joke that only one mention of *Star Wars* is allowed per meeting.) References to movies, both good and bad, are part of the vocabulary of talking about filmmaking. And yet if you rely too much on the references to what came before, you doom your film to being derivative.

Brad Bird noticed a similar phenomenon when he was studying at the California Institute of the Arts. He remembers a group of students that simply aped the animation of the masters, an approach he dubbed "Frankensteining." "They'd have a character do the kind of walk that animator Milt Kahl did for Medusa in *The Rescuers*," he says. "And then they'd have her wave her hands like Frank Thomas had Fauna do in *Sleeping Beauty*. And so on. . . ."

When filmmakers, industrial designers, software designers, or people in any other creative profession merely cut up and reassemble what has come before, it gives the illusion of creativity, but it is craft without art. Craft is what we are expected to know; art is the unexpected use of our craft.

Even though copying what's come before is a guaranteed path to mediocrity, it *appears* to be a safe choice, and the desire to be safe—to succeed with minimal risk—can infect not just individuals but also entire companies. If we sense that our structures are rigid, inflexible, or bureaucratic, we must bust them open—without destroying ourselves in the process. The question of how to do this must continually be addressed—there is no single answer—because conditions and people are constantly in flux.

Whenever filmmakers make a derivative presentation to John, he will often stop them, urging them to slow down, and look beyond what they think they already know. "You must," he tells them, "go out and do research."

It is impossible to overstate how strongly John believes in the power of research. At his urging, when Pixar was prepping a movie about a Parisian rat who aspires to be a gourmet chef, for example, several members of *Ratatouille*'s team went to France and spent two weeks dining in extraordinary, Michelin-starred restaurants, visiting their kitchens, and interviewing their chefs. (They also trudged through the Paris sewers, where many a rat makes his home.) When it was decided that Carl Fredrickson's balloon-propelled house would sail to the mountains of South America in *Up*, John sent a group of artists to see the tepuis in Venezuela up close; not only that, but an ostrich was brought into Pixar's headquarters to inspire the animators who were modeling the giant bird character. And when a plotline emerged in *Finding Nemo* that required Nemo, who believed that all drains lead to the ocean, to escape from a dentist's office by jumping into a sink, a trip was arranged to the San Francisco sewage treatment plant. (And yes, the filmmakers learned, it *is* possible for a fish to get from the drain to the sea without being killed.) Many of the crew on *Finding Nemo* also became scuba-certified.

These experiences are more than field trips or diversions. Because they take place early in the filmmaking process, they fuel the film's development. Take *Monsters University* as an example. In December 2009, more than three years before the movie premiered in theaters, a dozen people from Pixar—the director, producer, and writers, as well as several people from the art and story departments—flew east to visit MIT, Harvard, and Princeton. "Monsters University was to be one of the most prestigious campuses for scaring, so we wanted to visit big-name, old-world, prestigious schools," recalls Nick Berry, the film's art department manager, who helped arrange that excursion as well as day trips to UC Berkeley and Stanford. They visited dorm rooms, lecture halls, research labs, and frat houses; they hung out on the campus lawns, ate pizza at dives that students frequented, and took a lot of pictures and notes—"documenting everything, right down to the details of how pathways integrated into the quads," Nick says, "and what the graffiti scratches looked like on the wooden desks." The finished film was loaded with these kinds of details—what letter jackets look like up close or those "Roommate Wanted" fliers (complete with rip-off tags) that students post on campus bulletin boards—all of which gave audiences a feeling of reality.

Ultimately, what we're after is authenticity. What feels daunting to the filmmakers when John sends them out on such trips is that they don't yet know what they are looking for, so they're not sure what they will gain. But think about it: You'll never stumble upon the unexpected if you stick only to the familiar. In my experience, when people go out on research trips, they always come back changed.

In any business, it's important to do your homework, but the point I'm making goes beyond merely getting the facts straight. Research trips challenge our preconceived notions and keep clichés at bay. They fuel inspiration. They are, I believe, what keeps us creating rather than copying.

Here's a curious thing about research: The authenticity it fosters in the film always comes through, even if moviegoers know nothing about the reality the film is depicting. Very few moviegoers have actually been inside the kitchen of a high-end French restaurant, for example, so you might think the obsessive specificity of *Ratatouille*'s kitchen scenes—the chefs' clogs clacking on the black-and-white tile floors, the way they hold their arms when they cut up vegetables, or how they organize their work spaces—would be lost on the audience. But what we've found is that when we are accurate, the audiences can tell. It just feels right.

Does this kind of microdetail matter? I believe it does. There's something about knowing your subject and your setting inside and out—a confidence—that seeps into every frame of your film. It's a hidden engine, an unspoken contract with the viewer that says: We are striving to tell you something impactful and true. When attempting to make good on that promise, no detail is too small.

3. THE POWER OF LIMITS

There is a phenomenon that producers at Pixar call "the beautifully shaded penny." It refers to the fact that artists who work on our films care so much about every detail that they will sometimes spend days or weeks crafting what Katherine Sarafian, a Pixar producer, calls "the equivalent of a penny on a nightstand that you'll never see." Katherine, who was the production manager on *Mon-*

sters, Inc., remembers one scene that perfectly illustrates the beautifully shaded penny idea. It occurs when a bewildered Boo first arrives in Mike and Sulley's apartment and begins, as toddlers do, to explore. As the monsters try to contain her, she wanders up to two towering piles of compact discs—more than ninety in all. "Don't touch those!" Mike screams as she grabs a CD case from the bottom, sending the piles crashing to the floor. "Aw, those were *alphabetized*," Mike complains as she waddles away. The moment is over in three seconds, and during it, only a few of the CD cases are at all visible. But for every one of those CDs, Pixar artists created not just a CD cover but a shader—a program that calculates how an object's rendering changes as it moves.

"Can you see all the CD cases?" Sarafian says. "No. Was it fun to design them all? Yes. Maybe it was an in-joke, but there was someone on the crew who believed that each one of those was going to be seen close-up, and so they were lovingly crafted."

I don't want to think about how many person-weeks this consumed.

Clearly, something in our process had broken—the desire for quality had gone well beyond rationality. But because of the way production unfolded, our people had to work on scenes without knowing the context for them—so they overbuilt them just to be safe. To make things worse, our standards of excellence are extremely high, leading them to conclude that more is always more. How, then, do you fix the "beautifully shaded penny" problem without telling people, in effect, to care less or to be less excellent? I knew that none of these people on *Monster's, Inc.* thought that detail was so important that they should waste time to achieve it. And of course they knew that there were limits—they just couldn't see them. This was a failure on management's part; the truth is, we have consistently struggled with how we set useful limits and also how we make them visible.

Many of our limits are imposed not by our internal processes but by external realities—finite resources, deadlines, a shifting economy or business climate. Those things, we can't control. But the limits we impose internally, if deployed correctly, can be a tool to force people to amend the way they are working and, sometimes, to invent another way. The very concept of a limit implies that you can't do everything you want—so we must think of smarter ways to work. Let's be honest: Many of us don't make this kind of adjustment until we are required to. Limits force us to rethink how we are working and push us to new heights of creativity.

Another area where limits are invaluable is what we call "appetite control." In Pixar's case, when we are making a movie the demand for resources is literally bottomless. Unless you impose limits, people will always justify spending more time and more money by saying, "We're just trying to make a better movie." This occurs not because people are greedy or wasteful but because they care about their particular part of the film and don't necessarily have a clear view of how it fits into the whole. They believe that investing more is the only way to succeed.

In any creative endeavor, there is a long list of features and effects that you want to include to nudge it toward greatness—a *very* long list. At some point, though, you realize it is impossible to do everything on the list. So you set a deadline, which then forces a priority-based reordering of the list, followed by the difficult discussion of what, on this list, is absolutely necessary—or if the project is even feasible at all. You don't want to have this discussion too soon, because at the outset, you don't know what you are doing. If you wait too long, however, you run out of time or resources.

Complicating matters is that frequently, neither the film's leaders nor its team members know the true cost of the items on the list. The director may have only the fuzziest sense, for example, of how much extra work a particular tweak to the story will require. Likewise, an artist or technical director may think that the thing they are working on is essential and may pour his or her heart into it while having no sense of its actual value to the film. In my story of the camper and the blown tire, Dick found it difficult to separate the reality of events from what he *wanted* to be true. In a complex process such as making a film, that difficulty of separating out what you want from what you can achieve is exponentially larger. It is all the more important to have tools that enable us to see more clearly.

Brad Bird likes to tell a story about exactly this conundrum. During the making of *The Incredibles,* he became distracted by what he calls "mirages"—scenes or ideas he fell in love with but that, ultimately, didn't serve the film. As an example, for a long time he was obsessed with a vision of some fish in an aquarium that would appear in the background of a scene. He wanted them to move and flicker in a way that evoked flames in a fireplace—he was fixated, in fact, on realizing the vision in his head. But the film's animators were really struggling to make it look right, and after five months—and thousands of hours of work—Brad suddenly realized it didn't improve the movie in any real way. A mirage had led him astray.

Luckily, Brad had a producer, John Walker, who came up with a system (in collaboration with a department manager, Laura Reynolds) that would help the crew see what was possible given the available resources. John's system consisted of popsicle sticks stuck to a wall with Velcro. Each stick represented a person-week, which, as I've said, is the amount of work a single animator could accomplish in a week's time. A bunch of sticks would be lined up next to a particular character for easy reference. A glance at the wall would tell you: If you use that many popsicle sticks on Elastigirl, you'll have less to spend on Jack-Jack. And so on. "Brad would come to me and say: 'We've got to have this done today,'" John recalls. "And I could point to the wall and say, 'Well, you need another stick, then. Where are you going to take the stick from? Because we only have so many.'" I see this as a great example of the positive creative impact of limits.

However, some efforts to impose limits can backfire. When John and I arrived at Disney Animation in 2006, we encountered an interesting conflict. Production of animation is complex and costly, so the previous management thought that the best way to keep everybody operating within agreed-upon limits was to put in an "oversight group" that would, in essence, be the eyes and ears of management. Its sole mandate was to ensure that budget and scheduling goals were met. This group pored over all of the production reports on all of the films to make sure things were going as expected and then communicated what they found to the studio leadership. As a result, those studio bosses felt comfortable they were doing everything they could to avoid costly missteps.

However, from the point of view of those who worked in production on any given film, the oversight group was a hindrance, not a help. They felt they no longer had the flexibility they needed to respond quickly to problems because the oversight group nitpicked every decision—even the tiniest decision—to death. They felt powerless. In this case, the way limits were imposed impeded progress. Not only that, it created political problems: Increasingly, the oversight group was at war with the production group. And, as a result, morale plummeted.

To John and me, the solution was clear: We simply eliminated the oversight group. We believed that the production people were conscientious managers who were trying to bring a complex project in on time and on budget. In our view, the oversight group added nothing to the process but tension. The micromanagement they imposed was of no value, since the production people already had a set of limits that determined their every move—the overall budget and the deadline. Within that, they needed all the flexibility they could get. As soon as we made the change, the war ended and production began running much more smoothly.

The solution we implemented may have been obvious, but here's something that wasn't: It could never have come from the people in the oversight group, because that would have required them to recognize and admit that their group's existence was unnecessary. They were not in a position to challenge the preconception that their group was based on. In addition, the solution could never have been suggested by the leadership we replaced, either, because they believed that the oversight group was performing an important function by creating more transparency and imposing discipline on the process. But here was the irony: Creating this layer to enforce the limits actually made the limits less clear, diminishing their effectiveness.

The oversight group had been put in place without anyone asking a fundamental question: How do we enable our people to solve problems? Instead, they asked: How do we prevent our people from screwing up? That approach never encourages a creative response. My rule of thumb is that any time we impose limits or procedures, we should ask how they will aid in enabling people to respond creatively. If the answer is that they won't, then the proposals are ill suited to the task at hand.

4. INTEGRATING TECHNOLOGY AND ART

One of the best-loved instructors at CalArts in the 1980s was the legendary animator Bob McCrea, who took up teaching after forty years at Disney, where he worked closely with Walt himself. McCrea was as beloved as he was cantankerous—Andrew Stanton would later immortalize him in the character of Captain B. McCrea in *WALL-E*—and he helped shape the creative sensibilities of many of the people who would go on to define Pixar. Andrew remembers that he and his fellow CalArts students saw themselves as "animation purists," determined to emulate masters like Bob from the early days of Disney. They were conflicted, therefore, about using certain newer technologies—VHS videotape, for example—that had not existed in the studio's heyday. If Walt's Nine Old Men didn't use videotape, Andrew remembers telling Bob McCrea one day, maybe he shouldn't either.

"Don't be an idiot," Bob said. "If we'd had those tools then, we would have used them."

As I noted in chapter 2, Walt Disney was unrelenting in his determination to incorporate the cutting edge and to understand all available technologies. He brought sound and color into animation. He developed matting for filmmaking, the multiplane camera, the Xerox room for animation cels. One of the advantages we had at Pixar, from the beginning, was that technology, art, and business were integrated into the leadership, with each of the company's leaders—me, John, and Steve—paying a fair amount of attention to the areas where we weren't considered expert. We have worked assiduously, ever since, to maintain a balance among all three legs of this stool. Our business model, our way of making films, and our technology continually changed, but by integrating them we let them drive each other. The impetus for innovation, in other words, came from the inside rather than the outside.

As John often says, "Art challenges technology, technology inspires art." This is not meant to be some clever catchphrase—it articulates our philosophy of integration. When everything is functioning as it should be, art and technology play off each other and spur each other to new heights. Given how different the two mindsets can be, it can be tough to keep them aligned and engaged with each other. But in my view, the effort is always worth it. Our specialized skills and mental models are challenged when we integrate with people who are different. If we can constantly change and improve our models by using technology in the pursuit of art, we keep ourselves fresh. The whole history of Pixar is a testament to this dynamic interplay.

I have a couple of examples that demonstrate this point. While making *The Incredibles,* Brad Bird was frustrated by the imprecision—and thus the inefficiency—of giving feedback to animators verbally. If you were talking about how to draw a better scene, for example, didn't it make sense to sketch out your thoughts? Wouldn't that be more efficient? Brad asked if there was a way that he could draw on top of a projected image—a scene that was in the process of being animated—to communicate to animators the changes he wanted and to do so more effectively. Our software department went to work. The result: the Review Sketch tool, which gives directors a digital stylus to draw directly on top of an image, then saves those sketches and makes them accessible online to anyone who needs to reference them. In the years since its invention, it

has become an essential tool, used by all of our directors. (This is what Mark Andrews used in the dailies session I described.)

Another key innovation occurred after a frustrated Pete Docter stopped by my office one day in 2002. What he really needed, he said, was the ability to splice together rough storyboards of a scene, time them out precisely, and then narrate over them in a Braintrust meeting, enabling him to convey the same enthusiasm and passion as he did in his initial live pitch and better approximating the desired end result: a film. I went to one of our software leaders, Michael Johnson, to see if he could put something together for Pete. Two weeks later, Michael came back with a prototype that would later become known as "Pitch Docter," in homage to Pete.

The basic problem Pitch Docter sought to solve is one I've mentioned before—that when a director first pitches a movie, he or she is basically acting it out like a piece of performance art. A pitch is dynamic. The director is able to look the audience in the eye, see how the various elements are playing, and adjust on the fly. This performance, though, is not the film, and when the story is put up on reels and forced to stand on its own, it frequently falls flat. Conventional pitching was good theater, in other words, but it didn't begin to simulate a movie. Pitch Docter did that.

Pitch Docter let artists seek criticism earlier, which is always better. It allowed those giving feedback to evaluate the material by simulating its presentation in film. Initially we didn't know if the artists would accept this way of working—they had spent their careers working on paper, and if they were going to adopt this technology, they needed to discover and embrace it on their own. Soon, though, they saw its advantages. Since storyboards are frequently modified, having them on the computer simplified the process; the delivery of new versions to the team was as easy as a push of a button. As more artists adopted the tool, meanwhile, their requests for more features improved the tool itself. The software developers and the artists worked together to move the tools forward, and the model of how the artists did their work changed as the software evolved to meet their needs.

The Luxo Jr. sculpture—Pixar's logo come to life—outside the main building in Emeryville, California. *Copyright © 2008 Pixar. Photo: Deborah Coleman*

Inside the entryway of Pixar's headquarters in the spring of 2012, featuring a painting from the movie *Brave*. *Copyright © 2012 Pixar. Photo: Deborah Coleman*

Ed Catmull as a toddler with his mother, Jean, and as an infant with his father, Earl. *Ed Catmull Collection*

Ed at work in the original Lucasfilm offices, circa 1979. *Ed Catmull Collection*

Members of the Lucasfilm Computer Graphics Group, circa 1985. Front: Alvy Ray Smith. Back, left to right: Loren Carpenter, Bill Reeves, Ed Catmull, Rob Cook, John Lasseter, Eben Ostby, David Salesin, Craig Good, and Sam Leffler. *Copyright © 1985 Pixar*

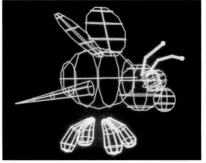

John Lasseter's design sketch of the character Wally B., from the short film *The Adventures of André & Wally B. Copyright © 1984 Pixar*

The "wireframe," or the underlying architecture of the computer model, of the character Wally B. *Copyright © Pixar*

To consult regularly with Disney executives, Joe Ranft, Pete Docter, John Lasseter, and Andrew Stanton logged a lot of Southwest Airlines miles flying between Oakland and Burbank during the making of *Toy Story*, circa 1994. *Copyright © Pixar*

A group of producers in the Presto Theatre on Pixar's campus, 2011. Front row: Jonas Rivera, Jim Morris, Darla K. Anderson. Middle: Lindsey Collins, Denise Ream, Galyn Susman. Back: Kevin Reher, Katherine Sarafian, John Walker, Tom Porter. *Copyright © 2011 Pixar. Photo: Deborah Coleman*

Members of Pixar's development department and the Braintrust—including Andrew Stanton, Lee Unkrich, and Pete Docter—gather for the first script reading of *Toy Story 3*. *Copyright © 2006 Pixar. Photo: Deborah Coleman*

Left to right: Darla K. Anderson, Jason Katz, Dan Scanlon, John Lasseter, Lee Unkrich, and Susan Levin during a *Toy Story 3* story review. *Copyright © 2007 Pixar. Photo: Deborah Coleman*

Ratatouille director Brad Bird working on storyboards for the movie. *Copyright © 2011 Pixar. Photo: Deborah Coleman*

From left: Pixar Executive Vice President of Creative John Lasseter, Pixar CEO Steve Jobs, Disney CEO Bob Iger, and Pixar President Ed Catmull in the Pixar atrium, announcing Disney's decision to buy Pixar, on January 24, 2006. *Copyright © 2006 Pixar. Photo: Deborah Coleman*

Ed, John Lasseter, and Bob Iger rededicate Pixar's main building as The Steve Jobs Building on November 5, 2012, a little over a year after Jobs's death. *Photo: Andrew Tupman*

Producers Kori Rae, Denise Ream, Katherine Sarafian, and Darla K. Anderson in the Brooklyn building at Pixar Animation Studios, 2013.
Photo: Ed Catmull

Up co-director Bob Peterson, production designer Ricky Nierva, and director Pete Docter observe ostriches to help them better animate Kevin, the giant bird in *Up*. *Copyright © 2007 Pixar. Photo: Deborah Coleman*

More research: Three-star Michelin-rated chef Thomas Keller (left) shows *Ratatouille* producer Brad Lewis the art of making ratatouille in the kitchen of his restaurant The French Laundry. *Copyright © 2007 Pixar. Photo: Deborah Coleman*

Pixar Animation Studio crew members for the film *Brave* take an archery class in Golden Gate Park in San Francisco. *Copyright © 2006 Pixar. Photo: Deborah Coleman*

Steve Jobs, John Lasseter, and Ed chat after Pixar University's graduation ceremony in September 1997. *Copyright © 1997 Pixar.*

John Lasseter shares his thoughts about the value of honest feedback at the kickoff to Notes Day in the Pixar atrium. *Copyright © 2013 Pixar. Photo: Deborah Coleman*

The rainbow that appeared over Pixar headquarters shortly after the announcement of Steve Jobs's death on October 5, 2011. *Photo: Angelique Reisch, taken with an iPhone*

This process was driven both by requests from artists and suggestions from programmers—a back and forth that came about because of the integration of technology and art. Michael's team, known as the Moving Pictures Group, meanwhile, has become an example of the mindset we value—a mindset that doesn't fear change. We apply this concept throughout the studio—software people rotate in and out of production. This way of doing things is responsive; it is nimble—and it makes us better.

5. SHORT EXPERIMENTS

In most companies, you have to justify so much of what you do—to prepare for quarterly earnings statements if the company is publicly traded or, if it is not, to build support for your decisions. I believe, however, that you should not be required to justify everything. We must always leave the door open for the unexpected. Scientific research operates in this way—when you embark on an experiment, you don't know if you will achieve a breakthrough. Chances are, you won't. But nevertheless, you may stumble on a piece of the puzzle along the way—a glimpse, if you will, into the unknown.

Our short films are Pixar's way of experimenting, and we produce them in the hopes of getting exactly these kinds of glimpses. Over the years, Pixar has become known for including short films at the beginning of our feature films. These three- to six-minute films, each of which might cost as much as two million dollars to make, certainly don't yield any profits for the company; in the immediate term, then, they're hard to justify. What sustains them is a kind of gut feeling that making shorts is a good thing to do.

Our shorts tradition began in the early 1980s, when John Lasseter joined us at Lucasfilm to work on *The Adventures of André and Wally B.* Our first wave of Pixar shorts—including *Luxo Jr.*, *Red's Dream*, and the Oscar-winning *Tin Toy*—were a way of sharing technological innovations with our colleagues in the scientific community. Then, in 1989, we stopped producing them. For the next seven years, we focused instead on revenue-generating ads and on our first feature film. But in 1996, a year after the release of *Toy Story,* John and I decided it was important to reinvigorate our short film program. Our hope was that making shorts would encourage experimentation and, more important, become a proving ground for fledgling filmmakers we hoped would go on to direct features someday. We justified the expense as R&D. If technical innovations could be honed on our short films, we figured, that alone would make the program worth the money. In the end, the payoffs would be many—but not necessarily the ones we expected.

Geri's Game, which was screened in front of *A Bug's Life* in 1998, was the first of what we came to call our second-generation shorts. It featured an old man sitting outside in the park in autumn and playing a cutthroat game of chess against himself. During the nearly five-minute film—which was written and directed by Jan Pinkava and would go on to win an Oscar—not a word is spoken other than the occasional "Ha!" that the old man utters when slamming down a chess piece with glee. The humor is located in the way the octogenarian's personality changes as he switches from one side of the board

to the other. When his meeker persona beats his gloating alter ego by (literally) turning the tables, you can't help but laugh.

But here was what mattered: In addition to being a delightful film, *Geri's Game* helped us improve technically. Our only directive to Jan before he made it was that it had to include a human character. Why? Because we needed to get better at them. We needed to work on rendering not only the smoothly irregular surfaces of faces and hands but also the clothes that people wear. At this point, remember, because of our inability to render skin and hair and certain curved surfaces to our satisfaction, humans had only been ancillary characters in our movies. That needed to change, and *Geri's Game* was an opportunity to start working that out.

While we'd used R&D to justify the program initially, we soon realized that our feature films were the major drivers of technological innovation—not our shorts. In fact, in the years since *Geri's Game,* not a single short until *Blue Umbrella* in 2013 had been instrumental in our technological innovation. And while we thought at first that directing a short would be superb preparation for directing a feature—a way to grow talent—we have come to believe we were wrong on this front, too. Directing a short is a terrific education, and some of what you learn will come in handy if you ever direct a feature. But the differences between directing a five-minute short and directing an 85-minute feature are many. Doing the former is merely a baby step on the road to the latter, not the intermediate step we thought it was.

And yet, for all our faulty assumptions, the shorts accomplished other things for Pixar. People who work on them, for example, get a broader range of experience than they would on a feature, where the sheer scale and complexity of the project demands more specialization among the crew. Because shorts are staffed with fewer people, each employee has to do more things, developing a variety of skills that come in handy down the line. Moreover, working in small groups forges deeper relationships that can carry forward and, in the long term, benefit the company's future projects.

Our shorts also create a deeper value in two key areas. Externally, they help us forge a bond with moviegoers, who have come to regard them as a kind of bonus—something added solely for their enjoyment. Internally, because everyone knows the shorts have no commercial value, the fact that we continue to make them sends a message that we care about artistry at Pixar; it reinforces and affirms our values. And that creates a feeling of goodwill that we draw on, consciously and unconsciously, all the time.

Finally, we have learned that shorts are a relatively inexpensive way to screw up. (And since I believe that mistakes are not just unavoidable but valuable, this is something to be welcomed.) Many years ago, for example, we met with a children's book author who wanted to direct a feature film for us. We liked his work and sensibility but sensed it would be wise to try him out on a short first to determine not only whether he had filmmaking chops but also if he could work well with others. The first sign of trouble? The film he delivered clocked in at twelve minutes—more of a "medium" than a "short." But length is flexible; the real problem was that although the director was extraordinarily creative, he was unable to settle on a spine for a story. The piece meandered, lacked focus, and thus packed no emotional punch. It wouldn't be the first time we would find someone who was able to invent wildly creative elements but was unable to solve the problems of story—the central and most important creative challenge. So we pulled the plug.

Some might have lost sleep over the two million dollars we expended on this experiment. But we consider it money well spent. As Joe Ranft said at the time, "Better to have train wrecks with miniature trains than with real ones."

6. LEARNING TO SEE

In the year after *Toy Story*'s release, we introduced a ten-week program to teach every new hire how to use our proprietary software.

We called this program Pixar University, and I hired a first-rate technical trainer to run it. At that point, the moniker *university* was a little misleading, though, as this was more of a training seminar than anything resembling an institution of higher learning. It is easy to justify a training program, but I had another agenda, and in trying to accomplish it, we would find surprising bonuses.

While some people at Pixar already knew how to draw—and beautifully—the majority of our employees were not artists. But there was an important principle that underlies the process of learning to draw and we wanted everyone to understand it. So I hired Elyse Klaidman, who had taught drawing workshops inspired by the 1979 book *Drawing on the Right Side of the Brain* by Betty Edwards, to come in and teach us how to heighten our powers of observation. In those days, you'd often hear about the concepts of left- and right-brained thinking, later called L-mode and R-mode. The L-mode was verbal/analytic, R-mode was visual/perceptual. Elyse taught us that while many activities used both L-mode and R-mode, drawing required shutting the L-mode off. This amounted to learning to suppress that part of your brain that jumps to conclusions, seeing an image as only an image and not as an object.

Think about what happens when we try to draw a face. Most of us sketch out the nose, eyes, forehead, ears, and mouth but—unless we've learned to draw formally—they're terribly out of proportion. They don't resemble anybody in particular. That's because, to the brain, all parts of the face are not created equal. For example, since the eyes and mouth—the loci of communication—are more important to us than foreheads, more emphasis is put on recognizing them, and when we draw them, we tend to draw them too large, while the forehead is drawn too small. We don't draw a face as it is; rather, we draw it as our models *say* it is.

The models of three-dimensional objects that we carry in our heads have to be general; they must represent all variations of the given objects. Our mental model of a shoe, for example, must encompass everything from a stiletto heel to a steel-toed boot; it can't be so specific that it excludes those extremes. Our brain's ability to generalize is an essential tool, but some people are able to move from the general to the specific to see more clearly. To stay with our drawing example, some people draw *better* than others. What are they doing that most of us aren't? And if the answer is that they are setting aside their preconceptions, can we all learn to do that?

In most cases, the answer is yes.

Art teachers use a few different tricks to train new artists. They place an object upside down, for example, so that each student can look at it as a pure shape and not as a familiar, recognizable thing (a shoe, say). The brain does not distort this upside-down object because it doesn't automatically impose its model of a shoe upon it. Another trick is to ask students to focus on negative spaces—the areas of space around an object that are not the object itself. For instance, in drawing a chair, the new artist might draw it poorly, because she knows what a chair is supposed to look like (and that chair in her head—her mental model—keeps her from reproducing precisely what she sees in front of her). However, if she is asked to draw what is *not* the chair—the spaces between the chair legs, for example—then the proportions are easier to get right, and the chair itself will look more realistic. The reason is that while the brain recognizes a chair as a chair, it assigns no meaning to the shape of the spaces between the chair's legs (and, thus, doesn't try to "correct" it to make it match the artist's mental model).

The lesson is intended to help students to see shapes as they are—to ignore that part of the brain that wants to turn what is seen into a general notion: a model of the chair. A trained artist who sees a chair, then, is able to capture what the eye perceives (shape, color) before their "recognizer" function tells them what it is *supposed* to be.

The same thing is true with color. When we look at a body of water, our brains think—and thus *see*—blue. If we're asked to paint a picture of a lake, we pick the color blue, and then we're surprised that it doesn't look right on the canvas. But if we look at different points in that same lake through a pinhole (thus divorcing it from the overall idea of "lake"), we see what is actually there: green and yellow and black and flashes of white. We don't let the brain fill in. Instead, we see the color as it really is.

I want to add an important side note: that artists have learned to employ these ways of seeing does not mean they don't also see what we see. They do. They just see *more* because they've learned how to turn off their minds' tendency to jump to conclusions. They've added some observational skills to their toolboxes. (This is why it is so frustrating that funding for arts programs in schools has been decimated. And those cuts stem from a fundamental misconception that art classes are about learning to draw. In fact, they are about learning to see.)

Whether or not you ever pick up a sketchpad or dream of being an animator, I hope you understand how it is possible, with practice, to teach your brain to observe something clearly without letting your preconceptions kick in. It is a fact of life, though a confounding one, that focusing on something can make it more difficult to see. The goal is to learn to suspend, if only temporarily, the habits and impulses that obscure your vision.

I did not introduce this topic to convince you that anyone can learn to draw. The real point is that you can learn to set aside preconceptions. It isn't that you don't have biases, more that there are ways of learning to ignore them while considering a problem. Drawing the "un-chair" can be a sort of metaphor for increasing perceptivity. Just as looking at what is *not* the chair helps bring it into relief, pulling focus away from a particular problem (and, instead, looking at the environment around it) can lead to better solutions. When we give notes on Pixar movies and isolate a scene, say, that isn't working, we have learned that fixing that scene usually requires making changes somewhere else in the film, and that is where our attention should go. Our filmmakers have become skilled at not getting caught up in a problem but instead looking elsewhere in the story for solutions. Likewise at Disney, the conflict between production and the oversight group could have been addressed by insisting that everyone behave better, when in fact, the real solution came from questioning the premise on which the oversight group was formed. It was the setup—the preconceptions that preceded the problem—that needed to be faced.

7. POSTMORTEMS

The phases we go through while making a movie—conception, protection, developmental planning, and production—unfold over a period of years. When the release date finally rolls around, everyone is ready to move on to something new. But we are not done yet. At Pixar, there is one more essential phase of the process: the postmortem. A postmortem is a meeting held shortly after the completion of every movie in which we explore what did and didn't work and attempt to consolidate lessons learned. Companies, like individuals, do not become exceptional by believing they are exceptional but by understanding the ways in which they *aren't* exceptional. Postmortems are one route into that understanding.

Our first postmortem was held in Tiburon, California, in 1998, a few weeks after we'd finished *A Bug's Life*. We had made all of two films at that point and were hyperaware of how much we still had to learn. To keep anyone from going on too long (we had a fifteen-minute limit), someone brought in a kitchen timer in the shape of a rooster. Here we were, talking about some of the most high-tech animation ever done, and we were managing the process with an old kitchen utensil.

This postmortem, which took an entire day, delved into all aspects of the production. There was no "Aha!" moment, no epiphany that would turn our processes inside out. Instead, it's the spirit of the meeting that I remember most. Everyone was so engaged in rethinking the way we did things, so open to challenging long-held ideas and learning from the errors we'd made. No one was defensive. Everyone was proud, not only of the film but of how committed we were to the culture from which the film had sprung. Afterward, we decided we should do this kind of deep analysis after every movie.

Achieving that same level of insight in subsequent postmortems, however, proved elusive. Over the years, some were profound, and others were a complete waste of time. Sometimes people showed up but pulled their punches. I understood that this was human nature—why poke a sleeping bear when you can just as easily move on to another campsite? In truth, to most people postmortems seem a bit like having to swallow some kind of bad-tasting medicine. They know it's necessary, but they don't like it one bit. This was another puzzle for us: What was it that made some postmortems so bad, while others had a great outcome?

Given that we all agree, in principle, that postmortems are good for us, I'm always struck by how much people dread them.

Most feel that they've learned what they could during the execution of the project, so they'd just as soon move on. Problems that arose are frequently personal, so most are eager to avoid revisiting them. Who looks forward to a forum for being second-guessed? People, in general, would rather talk about what went right than what went wrong, using the occasion to give additional kudos to their most deserving team members. Left to our own devices, we avoid unpleasantness.

It isn't just postmortems, though: In general, people are resistant to self-assessment. Companies are bad at it, too. Looking inward, to them, often boils down to this: "We are successful, so what we are doing must be correct." Or the converse: "We failed, so what we did was wrong." This is shallow. Do not be cowed into missing this opportunity. There are five reasons, I believe, to do postmortems. The first two are fairly obvious, the next three less so.

Consolidate What's Been Learned

While it is true that you learn the most in the midst of a project, the lessons are not generally coherent. Any individual can have a great insight but may not have the time to pass it on. A process might be flawed, but you don't have time to fix it under the current schedule. Sitting down afterward is a way of consolidating all that you've learned—before you forget it. Postmortems are a rare opportunity to do analysis that simply wasn't possible in the heat of the project.

Teach Others Who Weren't There

Even if everyone involved in a production understands what it taught them, the postmortem is a great way of passing on the positive and negative lessons to other people who were not on the project. So much of what we do is not obvious—the result of hard-won experience. Then again, some of what we do doesn't really make sense. The postmortem provides a forum for others to learn or challenge the logic behind certain decisions.

Don't Let Resentments Fester

Many things that go wrong are caused by misunderstandings or screw-ups. These lead to resentments that, if left unaddressed, can fester for years. But if people are given a forum in which to express their frustrations about the screw-ups in a respectful manner, then they are better able to let them go and move on. I have seen many cases where hurt feelings lingered far after the project, feelings that would have been worked through much more easily if they had been expressed in a postmortem.

Use the Schedule to Force Reflection

I favor principles that lead you to think. Postmortems—but also other activities such as Braintrust meetings and dailies—are all about getting people to think and evaluate. The time we spend getting ready for a postmortem meeting is as valuable as the meeting itself. In other words, the scheduling of a postmortem forces self-reflection. If a postmortem is a chance to struggle openly with our problems, the "pre-postmortem" sets the stage for a successful struggle. I would even say that 90 percent of the value is derived from the preparation leading up to the postmortem.

Pay It Forward

In a postmortem, you can raise questions that should be asked on the next project. A good postmortem arms people with the right questions to ask going forward. We shouldn't expect to find the right answers, but if we can get people to frame the right questions, then we'll be ahead of the game.

While I think the reasons for postmortems are compelling, I know that most people still resist them. So I want to share some techniques that can help managers get the most out of them. First of all, vary the way you conduct them. By definition, postmortems are supposed to be about lessons learned, so if you repeat the same format, you tend to uncover the same lessons, which isn't much help to anyone. Even if you come up with a format that works well in one instance, people will know what to expect the next time, and they will game the process. I've noticed what might be called a "law of subverting successful approaches," by which I mean once you've hit on something that works, don't expect it to work again, because attendees will know how to manipulate it the second time around. So try "mid-mortems" or narrow the focus of your postmortem to special topics. At Pixar, we have had groups give courses to others on their approaches. We have occasionally formed task forces to address problems that span several films. Our first task force dramatically altered the way we thought about scheduling. The second one was an utter fiasco. The third one led to a profound change at Pixar, which I'll discuss in the final chapter.

Next, remain aware that, no matter how much you urge them otherwise, your people will be afraid to be critical in such an overt manner. One technique I've used to soften the process is to ask everyone in the room to make two lists: the top five things that they would do again and the top five things that they *wouldn't* do again. People find it easier to be candid if they balance the negative with the positive, and a good facilitator can make it easier for that balance to be struck.

Finally, make use of data. Because we're a creative organization, people tend to assume that much of what we do can't be measured or analyzed. That's wrong. Many of our processes involve activities and deliverables that can be quantified. We keep track of the rates at which things happen, how often something has to be reworked, how long something actually took versus how long we estimated it would take, whether a piece of work was completely finished or not when it was sent to another department, and so on. I like data because it is neutral—there are no value judgments, only facts. That allows people to discuss the issues raised by data less emotionally than they might an anecdotal experience.

Lindsey Collins, one of our producers at Pixar, says that data can be nothing less than soothing. "It was such a relief for me, when I began in this job, to be able to look at historical data and see the patterns," she says. "It took what felt like a very nebulous process and allowed me to break it down and start to put a loose structure on it."

Having introduced the subject of data, however, I want to be clear about both its power and its limits. The power lies in the analysis of what we know about the production process—we have data, for example, on the time spent building models and sets, animating and lighting them. This data, of course, only gives a narrow glimpse into what happened while the models and sets were being built and lit. But it gives us something to work with to reveal potential patterns, which can be used to feed discussions that help us improve.

There are limits to data, however, and some people rely on it too heavily. Analyzing it correctly is difficult, and it is dangerous to assume that you always know what it means. It is very easy to find false patterns in data. Instead, I prefer to think of data as one way of seeing, one of many tools we can use to look for what's hidden. If we think data alone provides answers, then we have misapplied the tool. It is important to get this right. Some people swing to the extremes of either having no interest in the data or believing that the facts of measurement alone should drive our management. Either extreme can lead to false conclusions.

"You can't manage what you can't measure" is a maxim that is taught and believed by many in both the business and education sectors. But in fact, the phrase is ridiculous—something said by people who are unaware of how much is hidden. A large portion of what we manage *can't* be measured, and not realizing this has unintended consequences. The problem comes when people think that data paints a full picture, leading them to ignore what they can't see. Here's my approach: Measure what you can, evaluate what you measure, and appreciate that you cannot measure the vast majority of what you do. And at least every once in a while, make time to take a step back and think about what you are doing.

8. CONTINUING TO LEARN

I want to end this list by talking a little more about the founding of Pixar University and Elyse Klaidman's mind-expanding drawing classes in particular. Those first classes were such a success—of the 120 people who worked at Pixar then, 100 enrolled—that we gradually began expanding P.U.'s curriculum. Sculpting, painting, acting, meditation, belly dancing, live-action filmmaking, computer programming, design and color theory, ballet—over the years, we have offered free classes in all of them. This meant spending not only the time to find the best outside teachers but also the real cost of freeing people up during their workday to take the classes.

So what exactly was *Pixar* getting out of all of this?

It wasn't that the class material directly enhanced our employees' job performance. Instead, there was something about an apprentice lighting technician sitting alongside an experienced animator, who in turn was sitting next to someone who worked in legal or accounting or security—that proved immensely valuable. In the classroom setting, people interacted in a way they didn't in the workplace. They felt free to be goofy, relaxed, open, vulnerable. Hierarchy did not apply, and as a result, communication thrived. Simply by providing an excuse for us all to toil side by side, humbled by the challenge of sketching a self-portrait or writing computer code or taming a lump of clay, P.U. changed the culture for the better. It taught everyone at Pixar, no matter their title, to respect the work that their colleagues did. And it made us all beginners again. Creativity involves missteps and imperfections. I wanted our people to get comfortable with that idea—that both the organization and its members should be willing, at times, to operate on the edge.

I can understand that the leaders of many companies might wonder whether or not such classes would truly be useful, worth the expense. And I'll admit that these social interactions I describe were an unexpected benefit. But the purpose of P.U. was never to turn programmers into artists or artists into belly dancers. Instead, it was to send a signal about how important it is for every one of us to keep learning new things. That, too, is a key part of remaining flexible: keeping our brains nimble by pushing ourselves to try things we haven't tried before. That's what P.U. lets our people do, and I believe it makes us stronger.

We begin life, as children, being open to the ideas of others because we *need* to be open to learn. Most of what children encounter, after all, are things they've never seen before. The child has no choice but to embrace the new. If this openness is so wonderful, however, why do we lose it as we grow up? Where, along the way, do we turn from the wide-eyed child into the adult who fears surprises and has all the answers and seeks to control all outcomes?

It puts me in mind of a night, many years ago, when I found myself at an art exhibit at my daughter's elementary school in Marin. As I walked up and down the hallways, looking at the paintings and sketches made by kids in grades K through 5, I noticed that the first- and second-graders' drawings looked better and fresher than those of the fifth-graders. Somewhere along the line, the fifth-graders had realized that their drawings did not look realistic, and they had become self-conscious and tentative. The result? Their drawings became more stilted and staid, less inventive, because they probably thought that others would recognize this "fault." The fear of judgment was hindering creativity.

If fear hinders us even in grade school, no wonder it takes such discipline—some people even call it a practice—to turn off that inner critic in adulthood and return to a place of openness. In Korean Zen, the belief that it is good to branch out beyond what we already know is expressed in a phrase that means, literally, "not know mind." To have a "not know mind" is a goal of creative people. It means you are open to the new, just as children are. Similarly, in Japanese Zen, that idea of not being constrained by what we already know is called "beginner's mind." And people practice for years to recapture and keep ahold of it.

When a new company is formed, its founders must have a startup mentality—a beginner's mind, open to everything because, well, what do they have to lose? (This is often something they later look back upon wistfully.) But when that company becomes successful, its leaders often cast off that startup mentality because, they tell themselves, they have figured out what to do. They don't want to be beginners anymore. That may be human nature, but I believe it is a part of our nature that should be resisted. By resisting the beginner's mind, you make yourself more prone to repeat yourself than to create something new. The attempt to avoid failure, in other words, makes failure more likely.

Paying attention to the present moment without letting your thoughts and ideas about the past and the future get in the way is essential. Why? Because it makes room for the views of others. It allows us to begin to trust them—and, more important, to *hear* them. It makes us willing to experiment, and it makes it safe to try something that may fail. It encourages us to work on our awareness, trying to set up our own feedback loop in which paying attention improves our ability to pay attention. It requires us to understand that to advance creatively, we must let go of something. As the composer Philip Glass once said, "The real issue is not how do you find your voice, but . . . getting rid of the damn thing."

CHAPTER 11

THE UNMADE FUTURE

Many of us have a romantic idea about how creativity happens: A lone visionary conceives of a film or a product in a flash of insight. Then that visionary leads a team of people through hardship to finally deliver on that great promise. The truth is, this isn't my experience at all. I've known many people I consider to be creative geniuses, and not just at Pixar and Disney, yet I can't remember a single one who could articulate exactly what this vision was that they were striving for when they started.

In my experience, creative people discover and realize their visions over time and through dedicated, protracted struggle. In that way, creativity is more like a marathon than a sprint. You have to pace yourself. I'm often asked to predict what the future of computer animation will look like, and I try my best to come up with a thoughtful answer. But the fact is, just as our directors lack a clear picture of what their embryonic movies will grow up to be, I can't envision how our technical future will unfold *because it doesn't exist yet*. As we forge ahead, while we imagine what might be, we

must rely on our guiding principles, our intentions, and our goals—
not on being able to see and react to what's coming before it happens. My old friend from the University of Utah, Alan Kay—Apple's
chief scientist and the man who introduced me to Steve Jobs—
expressed it well when he said, "The best way to predict the future
is to invent it."

This sounds like the kind of slogan you'd see on a bumper
sticker, but it contains hidden depths. Invention, after all, is an active process that results from decisions we make; to change the
world, we must bring new things into being. But how do we go
about creating the unmade future? I believe that all we can do is
foster the optimal conditions in which it—whatever "it" is—can
emerge and flourish. This is where real confidence comes in. Not
the confidence that we know exactly what to do at all times but the
confidence that, together, we will figure it out.

That uncertainty can make us uncomfortable. We humans like
to know where we are headed, but creativity demands that we travel
paths that lead to who-knows-where. That requires us to step up to
the boundary of what we know and what we don't know. While we
all have the potential to be creative, some people hang back, while
others forge ahead. What are the tools they use that lead them
toward the new? Those with superior talent and the ability to marshal the energies of others have learned from experience that there
is a sweet spot between the known and the unknown where originality happens; the key is to be able to linger there without panicking. And that, according to the people who make films at Pixar and
Disney Animation, means developing a mental model that sustains
you. It might sound silly or woo-woo, this kind of visualization,
but I believe it's crucial. Sometimes—especially at the beginning of
a daunting project—our mental models are all we've got.

For example, one of our producers, John Walker, stays calm by
imagining his very taxing job as holding a giant upside-down pyramid in his palm by its pointy tip. "I'm always looking up, trying to

balance it," he says. "Are there too many people on this side or that side? In my job, I do two things, fundamentally: artist management and cost control. Both depend on hundreds of interactions that are happening above me, up in the fat end of the pyramid. And I have to be okay with the fact that I don't understand a freaking thing that's going on half the time—and that that is the magic. The trick, always, is keeping the pyramid in balance."

So far in this section of the book, I've explored some of the mechanisms we use at Pixar to build and protect our creative culture. I've talked about specific techniques and traditions that broaden our viewpoints—from research trips to Pixar University to the Braintrust. I've talked somewhat abstractly about the importance of remaining open, not occasionally but all the time, as a route to self-awareness. Now I want to share some concrete examples of the kinds of mental models I believe are essential to fortify and sustain anyone engaged in the hard work of inventing something new. Let's now examine several of the approaches that my colleagues and I use to keep our doubts at bay as we push toward originality—toward that unmade future.

When Brad Bird was directing *The Incredibles,* he had a recurring anxiety dream. In this dream, he was driving down a winding and precarious stretch of highway in a rickety old station wagon, with no one else in the car. Apparently, it was up to him to pilot the vehicle. "But I was in the backseat!" he says. "For some reason, I still had a steering wheel, but my visibility was terrible because of where I was sitting. Basically, all I could do is say to myself, 'Don't crash! Don't crash! Don't crash!'" The takeaway, as he puts it: "Sometimes, as a director, you're driving. And other times, you're letting the car drive."

Whenever I hear Brad describe this dream, I'm struck by its familiar themes—blindness, fear of the unknown, helplessness, lack of control. These fears came to him in sleep, but during his waking hours, he sought to master them by rejecting the backseat driver analogy in favor of a different mental model: skiing.

Brad has told me that he thinks of directing the way he thinks about skiing. In either pursuit, he says, if he tightens up or thinks too much, he crashes. There are moments, as a director, where there is so much work to do and so little time to do it that he can't help but feel fear. But he also knows that if he lingers too long in that frightened place, he will freak out. "So I tell myself that I have time, even when I don't. As in, 'Okay, I'm going to proceed as if I have time—I'm going to sit back and muse rather than looking at the clock—because if I sit back and muse, I'm more likely to solve the problem.'" This is where directing is a lot like skiing. "I like to go fast," Brad says, before launching into a story about a trip he took to Vail when, "in the course of a week, I cracked the lens of my goggles four times. *Four times* I had to go to the ski store and say, 'I need a new piece of plastic,' because I had shattered it crashing into something. And at some point, I realized that I was crashing because I was trying so hard *not* to crash. So I relaxed and told myself, 'It's going to be scary when I make the turns really fast, but I'm going to push that mountain away and enjoy it.' When I adopted this positive attitude, I stopped crashing. In some ways, it's probably like an Olympic athlete who's spent years training for one moment when they can't make a mistake. If they start thinking too much about that, they'll be unable to do what they know how to do."

Athletes and musicians often refer to being in "the zone"—that mystical place where their inner critic is silenced and they completely inhabit the moment, where the thinking is clear and the motions are precise. Often, mental models help get them there. Just as George Lucas liked to imagine his company as a wagon train headed west—its passengers full of purpose, part of a team, unwavering in their pursuit of their destination—the coping mechanisms used by Pixar and Disney Animation's directors, producers, and writers draw heavily on visualization. By imagining their problems as familiar pictures, they are able to keep their wits about them when the pressures of not knowing shake their confidence.

Byron Howard, one of our directors at Disney, told me that when he was learning to play the guitar, a teacher taught him the phrase, "If you think, you stink." The idea resonated with him—and it informs his work as a director to this day. "The goal is to get so comfortable and relaxed with your instrument, or process, that you can just get Zen with it and let the music flow without thinking," he told me. "I notice the same thing when I storyboard. I do my best work when I'm zipping through the scene, not overthinking, not worrying if every drawing is perfect, but just flowing with and connecting to the scene—sort of doing it by the seat of my pants."

I'm particularly struck by Byron's focus on speed—on "zipping through" complex problems of logic and storytelling—because it reminds me of what Andrew Stanton says about being a director. I've told you about Andrew's belief that we will all be happier and more productive if we hurry up and fail. For him, moving quickly is a plus because it prevents him from getting stuck worrying about whether his chosen course of action is the wrong one. Instead, he favors being decisive, then forgiving yourself if your initial decision proves misguided. Andrew likens the director's job to that of a ship captain, out in the middle of the ocean, with a crew that's depending on him to make land. The director's job is to say, "Land is that way." Maybe land actually *is* that way and maybe it isn't, but Andrew says that if you don't have somebody choosing a course—pointing their finger toward that spot *there,* on the horizon—then the ship goes nowhere. It's not a tragedy if the leader changes her mind later and says, "Okay, it's actually not that way, it's *this* way. I was wrong." As long as you commit to a destination and drive toward it with all your might, people will accept when you correct course.

"People want decisiveness, but they also want honesty about

when you've effed up," as Andrew says. "It's a huge lesson: Include people in your problems, not just your solutions."

This is key to an idea I introduced earlier in the book: The director, or leader, can never lose the confidence of his or her crew. As long as you have been candid and had good reasons for making your (now-flawed-in-retrospect) decisions, your crew will keep rowing. But if you find that the ship is just spinning around—and if you assert that such meaningless activity is, in fact, forward motion—then the crew will balk. They know better than anyone when they are working hard but not going anywhere. People want their leaders to be confident. Andrew doesn't advise being confident merely for confident's sake. He believes that leadership is about making your best guess and hurrying up about it so if it's wrong, there's still time to change course.

There's something else, too. If you're going to undertake a creative project that requires working closely with other people, you must accept that collaboration brings complications. Other people have so much to recommend them: They will help you see outside yourself; they will rally when you are flagging; they will offer ideas that push you to be better. But they will also require constant interaction and communication. Other people are your allies, in other words, but that alliance takes sustained effort to build. And you should be prepared for that, not irritated by it. As Andrew says, continuing his nautical metaphor, "If you're sailing across the ocean and your goal is to avoid weather and waves, then why the hell are you sailing?" he says. "You have to embrace that sailing means that you can't control the elements and that there will be good days and bad days and that, whatever comes, you will deal with it because your goal is to eventually get to the other side. You will not be able to control exactly how you get across. That's the game you've decided to be in. If your goal is to make it easier and simpler, then don't get in the boat."

Andrew's mental model addresses the fear that inevitably comes when your boat is tossed by a storm or stalls for lack of wind. If one looks at creativity as a resource that we continually draw upon to make something from nothing, then our fear stems from the need to make the nonexistent come into being. As we've discussed, people often try to overcome this fear by simply repeating what has worked in the past. That leads nowhere—or, more accurately, it leads in the opposite direction of originality. The trick is to use our skills and knowledge not to duplicate but to invent.

In talking to directors and writers, I'm constantly inspired by the models they keep in their heads—each a unique mechanism they use to keep moving forward, through adversity, in pursuit of their goals. Pete Docter compares directing to running through a long tunnel having no idea how long it will last but trusting that he will eventually come out, intact, at the other end. "There's a really scary point in the middle where it's just dark," he says. "There's no light from where you came in and there's no light at the other end; all you can do is keep going. And then you start to see a little light and then a little more light and then, suddenly, you're out in the bright sun." For Pete, this metaphor is a way of making that moment—the one in which you can't see your own hand in front of your face and you aren't sure you'll ever find your way out—a bit less frightening. Because your rational mind knows that tunnels have two ends, your emotional mind can be kept in check when pitch blackness descends in the confusing middle. Instead of collapsing into a nervous mess, the director who has a clear internal model of what creativity is—and the discomfort it requires—finds it easier to trust that light will shine again. The key is to never stop moving forward.

Rich Moore, who directed *Wreck-It Ralph* for Disney Animation, envisions a slightly different scenario. He imagines himself in a maze while he's making a movie. Instead of running through willy-nilly, frantically searching for his way out, he places the tips of his fingers along one wall as he moves forward, slowing down here and there to assess and using his sense of touch to help him remember the route he's traveled so far. But he keeps moving so as not to panic. "I loved mazes as a kid," Rich says. "But you have to keep your head to find your way out. When I see a movie go south, I think to myself, 'Well, they went nuts in the maze. They freaked out in there, and it fell apart.'"

Bob Peterson, who has helped solve creative problems on almost every Pixar film, credits Andrew with giving him a model that has been invaluable to his career. On *A Bug's Life,* Bob says, Andrew compared making a movie to an archeological dig. This adds yet another element to the picture—the idea that as you progress, your project is revealing itself to you. "You're digging away, and you don't know what dinosaur you're digging for," Bob says. "Then, you reveal a little bit of it. And you may be digging in two different places at once and you think what you have is one thing, but as you go farther and farther, blindly digging, it starts revealing itself. Once you start getting a glimpse of it, you know how better to dig."

Bob and Andrew have heard me voice my objection to this particular metaphor many times. As I've said, I believe that when we work on a movie, we are not uncovering an existing thing that had the bad luck to get buried under eons of sediment; we are creating something new. But they argue that the *idea* the movie is in there somewhere—think of David, trapped in Michelangelo's block of marble—helps them stay on track and not lose hope. So while I started this chapter by insisting that what moviegoers see on the screen does *not* emerge fully formed from some visionary's brain, I have to allow for this idea: Having faith that the elements of a movie are all there for us to find often sustains us during the search.

If this model resonates with you, just recognize that it has its pitfalls. Even Andrew warns that during your excavation, not every bone you unearth will necessarily belong to the skeleton you are trying to assemble. (There may be the bones of several different dinosaurs—or stories—mixed up in your dig site.) The temptation to use everything you find, even if it doesn't fit, is strong. After all, you probably worked hard to dig each element up. But if you are discerning and rigorous in your analysis of each piece—if you compare it to the bits you've found already to see if it's a match— your movie or project will reveal itself to you. "After a while, it starts to tell me what's there," Andrew says. "That's the place you're looking for: when the movie starts to tell *you* what it wants to be."

Michael Arndt, who wrote *Toy Story 3*, and I have had an ongoing dialectic about the way he envisions his job. He compares writing a screenplay to climbing a mountain blindfolded. "The first trick," he likes to say, "is to find the mountain." In other words, you must feel your way, letting the mountain reveal itself to you. And notably, he says, climbing a mountain doesn't necessarily mean ascending. Sometimes you hike up for a while, feeling good, only to be forced back down into a crevasse before clawing your way out again. And there is no way of knowing where the crevasses will be.

I like a lot about this metaphor—except for its implication that the mountain exists. Like Andrew's archeological dig, it suggests that the artist must simply "find" the piece of art, or the idea, that is hidden from sight. It seems to me to contradict one of my central beliefs: that the future is unmade, and we must create it. If writing a screenplay is like climbing a mountain blindfolded, that implies that the goal is to see an existing mountain—while I believe it should be the goal of creative people to build their *own* mountain from scratch.

But as I've talked to my colleagues who perform a variety of different jobs, I've come to respect that the most important thing about a mental model is that it enables whoever relies on it to get their job—whatever it is—done. The uncreated is a vast, empty space. This emptiness is so scary that most hold on to what they know, making minor adjustments to what they understand, unable to move on to something unknown. To enter that place of fear, and to fill that empty space, we need all the help we can get. Michael is a screenwriter, which means he starts with a blank page. That requires charting the path from nothing to something, and imagining himself as a blindfolded mountain climber serves him, he says, because it girds him for the inevitable ups and downs of his job.

I've now described several models, and the thing I believe they have in common is the search for an unseen destination—for land across the ocean (Andrew), for light at the end of the tunnel (Pete), for a way out of the maze (Rich), for the mountain itself (Michael). This makes sense for creative leaders who must guide so many people through the beats of a story or the production of a film. At the beginning, the director's or writer's destination is unclear, but he or she must forge ahead anyway.

Producers, however, have a different, more logistical job. If directors must summon their creative vision, and writers must impose structure and make a story sing, producers are there to keep things real. Their job is to make sure a project stays on track and on budget, so it makes perfect sense that their mental models differ markedly from those of their colleagues. Remember John Walker's upside-down pyramid? His mental model focuses not on climbing a hill or reaching a destination but on balancing a multitude of competing demands. Other producers have their own ways of imagining their jobs, but to a one, they have this in common: Managing a multiplicity of forces, not to mention hundreds of people with minds of their own, requires balance.

Lindsey Collins, a producer who has worked with Andrew on several films, imagines herself as a chameleon who can change her colors depending on which constituency she's dealing with. The goal is not to be fake or curry favor but to be whatever person is needed in the moment. "In my job, sometimes I'm a leader, sometimes I'm a follower; sometimes I run the room and sometimes I say nothing and let the room run itself," she says. Adapting to your environment, like a lizard that blends into whatever background it finds itself in, is Lindsey's way of managing the competing—and potentially crazy-making—forces she encounters in her job. "I'm a firm believer in the chaotic nature of the creative process needing to be chaotic. If we put too much structure on it, we will kill it. So there's a fine balance between providing some structure and safety—financial and emotional—but also letting it get messy and stay messy for a while. To do that, you need to assess each situation to see what's called for. And then you need to *become* what's called for."

How does one make such an assessment? Lindsey jokes that she employs "the Columbo effect"—a reference to Peter Falk's iconic TV detective, who appeared to bumble his way through a case, even as he inevitably zeroed in on the culprit. When mediating between two groups who aren't communicating well, for example, Lindsey feigns confusion. "You say, 'You know, maybe it's just me, but I don't understand. I'm sorry I'm slowing you down here with all my silly questions, but could you just explain to me one more time what that means? Just break it down for me like I'm a two-year-old.'"

Good producers—and good managers—don't dictate from on high. They reach out, they listen, they wrangle, coax, and cajole. And their mental models of their jobs reflect that. Katherine Sarafian, another Pixar producer, credits the clinical psychologist Taibi Kahler with giving her a helpful way of visualizing her role. "One of Kahler's big teachings is about meeting people where they are," Katherine says, referring to what Kahler calls the Process Communication Model, which compares being a manager to taking the elevator from floor to floor in a big building. "It makes sense to look at every personality as a condominium," Katherine says. "People live on different floors and enjoy different views." Those on the upper floors may sit out on their balconies; those on the ground floor may lounge on their patios. Regardless, to communicate effectively with them all, you must meet them where they live. "The most talented members of Pixar's workforce—whether they're directors, producers, production staff, artists, whatever— are able to take the elevator to whatever floor and meet each person based on what they need in the moment and how they like to communicate. One person may need to spew and vent for twenty minutes about why something doesn't look right before we can move in and focus on the details. Another person may be all about, 'I can't make these deadlines unless you give me this particular thing that I need.' I always think of my job as moving between floors, up and down, all day long."

When she's not imagining herself in an elevator, Katherine pretends she's a shepherd guiding a flock of sheep. Like Lindsey, she spends some time assessing the situation, figuring out the best way to guide her flock. "I'm going to lose a few sheep over the hill, and I have to go collect them," she says. "I'm going to have to run to the front at times, and I'm going to have to stay back at times. And somewhere in the middle of the flock, there is going to be a bunch of stuff going on that I can't even see. And while I'm looking for the sheep that are lost, something else is going to happen that I'm not aiming my attention at. Also, I'm not entirely sure where we're going. Over the hill? Back to the barn? Eventually, I know we will get there, but it can be very, very slow. You know, a car crosses the road, and the sheep are all in the way. I'm looking at my watch going, 'Oh, my God, sheep, *move* already!' But the sheep are going to move how they move, and we can try to control them as best we can, but what we really want to do is pay attention to the general direction they're heading and try to steer a little bit."

Notice how each of these models contains so many of the themes we've talked about so far: the need to keep fear in its place, the need for balance, the need to make decisions (but also to admit fallibility), and the need to feel that progress is being made. What's important, I think, as you construct the mental model that works best for you, is to be thoughtful about the problems it is helping you to solve.

I've always been intrigued, for example, by the way that many people use the analogy of a train to describe their companies. Massive and powerful, the train moves inexorably down the track, over mountains and across vast plains, through the densest fog and darkest night. When things go wrong, we talk of getting "derailed" and of experiencing a "train wreck." And I've heard people refer to Pixar's production group as a finely tuned locomotive that they would love the chance to drive. What interests me is the number of people who believe that they have the *ability* to drive the train and who think that this is the power position—that driving the train is the way to shape their companies' futures. The truth is, it's not. Driving the train doesn't set its course. The real job is laying the track.

I am constantly rethinking my own models for how to deal with uncertainty and change and how to enable people. At Lucasfilm, I had the image of riding bareback on a herd of wild horses, some of them faster than others, trying to keep steady. Other times, I've imagined my feet on either side of one of those balance boards that moves atop a cylindrical roller. No matter what image I come up with, questions remain: How do we keep from veering too far to one side or another? How do we follow our carefully laid plans yet remain open to ideas that are not our own? Over time, with new experiences, my model has continued to evolve—and is still evolving, even as I write this book.

One model that has been extremely helpful to me I found completely by accident. It came from the study of mindfulness, which has attracted a lot of attention in recent years, both in academia and in business. Those who write about it focus on how it helps people reduce stress in their lives and direct their attention. But for me, it has also helped clarify my thinking about how groups of creative people work best together.

Several summers ago my wife, Susan, gave me a gift that led to this insight. Sensing that I needed a break, she arranged for me to attend a silent meditation retreat at the Shambhala Mountain Center in Red Feather Lakes, Colorado. The week-long immersion was open to beginners, but of the seventy people there, I was the only one who'd never meditated. For me, the thought of spending several days in silence seemed unimaginable, even weird. I was intrigued and sort of bumbling along, when two days into it, we went into full silence. I wasn't sure what to do. The voice in my head chattered continuously, and I wasn't sure how to process it. On the third day, with my mind abuzz from all the nonspeaking I was doing, I almost bailed out.

Most people have heard of the Eastern teaching that it is important to exist in the moment. It can be hard to train yourself to observe what is right now (and not to bog down in thoughts of what was and what will be), but the philosophical teaching that underlies that idea—the reason that staying in the moment is so vital—is equally important: Everything is changing. All the time. And you can't stop it. And your attempts to stop it actually put you in a bad place. It causes pain, but we don't seem to learn from it. Worse than that, resisting change robs you of your beginner's mind—your openness to the new.

At the Shambhala Mountain Center that summer, I didn't bail. Even though the terminology was alien to me, it resonated with many of the issues I spent so much time thinking about at Pixar: control, change, randomness, trust, consequences. The search for a clear mind is one of the fundamental goals of creative people, but the route each one of us travels to get there is unmarked. For me, a man who has always valued introspection, silence was a path I hadn't tried before. I've gone on a silent retreat every year since, and in addition to benefiting personally, I have done a lot of thinking about the management implications of mindfulness.

If you are mindful, you are able to focus on the problem at hand without getting caught up in plans or processes. Mindfulness helps us accept the fleeting and subjective nature of our thoughts, to make peace with what we cannot control. Most important, it allows us to remain open to new ideas and to deal with our problems squarely. Some people make the mistake of thinking that they are being mindful because they are focusing diligently on problems. But if they are doing so while subconsciously bound up with their worries and expectations, with no awareness that they can't see clearly or that others may know more, they aren't open at all.

Similarly, within organizations groups often hold so tightly to plans and past practices that they are not open to seeing what is changing in front of them.

My thinking about this was enriched further when I happened upon a podcast of a talk given in 2011 at an annual event called the Buddhist Geeks Conference. There, a woman named Kelly McGonigal delivered a talk called "What Science Can Teach Us About Practice." McGonigal, who teaches at Stanford University, discussed how recent studies of the brain's inner workings proved that the practice of meditation can lessen human suffering—not just the existential angst kind of suffering, which is bad enough, but actual physical pain.

First, she talked about a study done at the University of Montreal in 2010, in which two groups—one made up of experienced Zen meditators, the other of non-meditators—were given the exact same type of pain experience: a thermal heat source strapped to one calf. They were hooked up to monitors that tracked which areas of the brain were stimulated. What researchers later discovered by looking at the brain imaging was that even though the experienced meditators weren't actively meditating in the course of the experiment, their threshold for pain was much higher than the non-meditators'. The meditators' brains were paying attention to the pain, McGonigal explained, but because they knew how to turn off the inner chatter—the running commentary our untrained brains, or monkey minds, so happily serve up—they were better able to tolerate pain than those who did not practice meditation.

Next, McGonigal cited a similar study done at Wake Forest University that focused on a group of brand new meditators who'd undergone only four days of training. When they were brought into the laboratory and given the same pain test, some were able to tolerate greater levels of pain than others. Why? The temptation might be to surmise that these people were simply quick studies in the art of meditation, that they were better at it than others. Brain imagery showed, however, that in fact their minds were doing the *opposite* of what experienced meditators' brains do. Instead of paying attention to the moment they were in, McGonigal said, "they were *inhibiting* sensory information—somehow shifting their attention to ignore what was happening in the present moment. And that was giving rise to less suffering: inhibiting awareness rather than carefully attending to it."

I found this fascinating—and analogous to behavior I'd witnessed as a manager. McGonigal was talking about the brain's tendency to suppress problems instead of facing them head-on. What makes this even more difficult is that the people who were suppressing *thought* that they were doing the same thing as the people who were addressing the problem. It is sobering to think that in trying to be mindful, some of us accidentally end up being exactly the opposite. We deflect and ignore. And for a while, at least, this behavior can even yield good results. But in the experiments McGonigal cited, people who'd made a practice of becoming mindful didn't ignore the problem at hand—in this case, the painful heat source strapped to their legs. They saw and felt it for what it was but quieted their reaction to it—the brain's natural tendency to amplify by overthinking—and thus coped much better.

This model of paying attention to what is in front of you, not hanging on too tightly to the past or the future, has proved immensely useful to me as I have tried to sort out organizational issues and to dissuade my colleagues from clinging to processes or plans that have outlived their usefulness. Likewise, the notion of acknowledging problems (rather than putting in place rules that seek to suppress them) has meaning to me.

Ultimately, it doesn't matter if your model is different than mine. Upside-down pyramid or invisible mountain, stampeding horses or meandering sheep, what's essential is that each of us struggles to build a framework to help us be open to making something new. The models in our heads embolden us as we whistle through the dark. Not only that, they enable us to do the exhilarating and difficult work of navigating the unknown.

PART IV

TESTING WHAT WE KNOW

CHAPTER 12

A NEW CHALLENGE

"I'm thinking about selling Pixar to Disney," Steve said. To say that John and I were surprised doesn't really begin to capture it.

"You're what?" we responded in unison.

It was October 2005, and we'd just arrived at Steve's house in Palo Alto, where he lived with his wife and his three youngest kids. He'd invited us over for dinner, but suddenly, neither John nor I had much of an appetite.

Just eighteen months before, after many fruitful years together, Disney and Pixar had had a very public falling out. Steve and Disney's chairman and CEO at the time, Michael Eisner, had abruptly halted discussions to renew our partnership agreement, and there were bad feelings all around. Specifically, we were rankled by Eisner's announcement of a new division within Disney Animation, called Circle 7, which he'd created to exercise the studio's right to make sequels to our films without our input. This was hardball, an attempt to force our hand by wrenching control of our characters away from the people who'd created them. For John, it was almost as if Eisner were trying to kidnap his children. He loved Woody, Buzz, Slinky Dog, Rex, and the rest like he loved his own five sons and was heartbroken at the thought that he couldn't protect them.

Now, Steve was thinking of joining forces with the company that had done this to him?

In retrospect, I should say that I'd had inklings that something major might be afoot. I knew that even when Steve and Michael's relationship was at its worst, Steve still held the rest of Disney in high regard. For example, even when he didn't agree with a proposal from Disney's marketing folks, he would remind us privately that they knew more about that than he did. And Steve felt that Disney's marketing prowess, its mastery of consumer products, and its theme parks had always made it the preferred partner for Pixar, hands down.

By the time Steve floated the idea of selling Pixar with John and me, I also knew that a lot had changed at Disney—Eisner was out, for one thing, having been replaced by Bob Iger. And one of Bob's first acts as CEO had been to reach out to Steve in an effort to mend fences. They'd then struck a deal to make the top shows on ABC available on iTunes, and largely because of this, Steve trusted Bob. To Steve, that deal demonstrated two things: Iger was a man of action, and he was willing to buck the knee-jerk, industry-wide trend to oppose distribution of entertainment content on the Internet. The iTunes deal took about ten days to complete; Iger didn't let entrenched forces get in the way. But the fact remained: Circle 7 was still up and running, and still preparing to put *Toy Story 3* into production without any input from us.

As John and I sat there, trying to get our heads around a merger, Steve began pacing around his living room, laying out the reasons that it made sense. He'd studied all the angles, of course. Number one, Pixar needed a marketing and distribution partner to get its movies into theaters around the world—okay, that we knew already. Number two, Steve felt that a merger would help Pixar have more of a creative impact by allowing it to play on a bigger, sturdier stage. "Right now, Pixar is a yacht," he said. "But a merger will put us on a giant ocean liner, where big waves and poor weather won't affect us as much. We'll be protected." At the end of his pitch, Steve looked us in the eye and assured us that he would not go forward with the sale unless he had both of our blessings. But he asked us to do him a favor before we made any decisions.

"Get to know Bob Iger," he said. "That's all I ask. He's a good man."

A few months later, in January of 2006, the deal went through. But Walt Disney Company's acquisition of Pixar Animation Studios for $7.4 billion was not your typical merger. Steve had made sure of that. He proposed that John and I be put in charge of both Pixar and Disney Animation—I'd be president and John chief creative officer—because he thought, and Bob agreed, that if the leadership of the two studios were separate, an unhealthy competition would emerge that would eventually drag both studios down. (He also thought, frankly, that making us the stewards of both entities would guarantee that Pixar's traditions didn't get overtaken by those of the much larger corporation, the Walt Disney Company.)

The result was that John and I suddenly had the rare opportunity to take the ideas we'd honed over decades at Pixar and test them in another context. Would our theories about the necessity of candor, fearlessness, and self-awareness bear out in this new environment? Or were they peculiar to our own, smaller shop? Figuring out the answers—not to mention how to manage two very different companies in a way that benefited both—would fall largely to John and me.

John has always thought of Pixar as a studio full of pioneers who pride themselves on having invented a new art form while always aspiring to the highest level of storytelling. Disney Animation, by contrast, is a studio with a grand heritage. It's the gold standard of animation excellence; its employees yearn to make movies that are worthy of Walt—as good as those he made but resonant in our time. To be honest, John and I had no idea whether our theories about how to manage creative people would hold up there. The challenge was to keep Pixar healthy while making Disney Animation great again.

This chapter is largely devoted to some of the ways we went about that, and it goes to the heart of one of the main reasons I wrote this book. You'll recall that my new goal after the completion of *Toy Story* was to figure out how to make a sustainable creative environment. Pixar's joining with Disney was our chance to prove—to ourselves, if not anyone else—that what we'd created at Pixar could work outside of Pixar. Both the run-up to the acquisition and its execution provided the ultimate case study, and as such, it was enormously exciting to be a part of. First, I'll talk about how the merger came to pass in the first place, because I believe we did several things in the very early stages that put our partnership on a strong footing.

"Get to know Bob Iger," Steve had said. So a few weeks later, I did.

We met for dinner near the Disney Studios in Burbank, and I liked him immediately. The first thing he did was tell me a story: A month earlier, at the opening of Hong Kong Disneyland, he'd had an epiphany. It happened as he was watching a parade of characters trooping by: Donald Duck, Mickey Mouse, Snow White, Ariel . . . and Buzz Lightyear and Woody. "It occurred to me that the only classic characters that had been created in the past ten years were Pixar characters," Bob said. He told me that while the Walt Disney Company had many interests—from theme parks to cruise ships to consumer products to live-action films—animation would always be its lifeblood, and he was determined to see that part of the business rise again.

One thing that struck me about Bob was that he preferred asking questions to holding forth—and his queries were incisive and straightforward. Something unusual had been built at Pixar, he said, and he wanted to understand it. For the first time in all the years that Pixar and Disney had worked together, someone from Disney was asking what we were doing that made our company different.

Bob had already been through two major acquisitions in his career as an executive—when Capital Cities Communications bought the American Broadcasting Company in 1985 and when Disney bought Cap Cities/ABC in 1996. One, he said, was a good experience and the other a negative one, so he knew firsthand how destructive it could be when one culture was allowed to dominate the other in a merger. Should the Pixar acquisition go forward, he assured me, he was going to work hard not to let that happen. His agenda was clear: reviving Disney Animation while also preserving Pixar's autonomy.

A few days later, John had dinner with Bob, and afterward, we sat down to compare notes. John agreed that Bob seemed to share our core values, but he was worried about the acquisition destroying what we held most dear: a culture of candor and freedom and the kind of constructive self-criticism that allowed our people, and the movies they made, to evolve into their best selves. John often likens the Pixar culture to a living organism—"It's like we found a way," he once told me, "to grow life on a planet that had never supported it before"—and he didn't want anything to threaten its existence. We believed Bob had good intentions but were wary of the larger company's ability—even inadvertently—to roll over us. Still, Bob had reassured John by indicating he wanted to work together to make sure that didn't happen. The deal was going to be expensive, he told us, and in lobbying for it with the Disney board, he was putting his own reputation on the line. Why, Bob asked, would he endanger the value of the asset Disney was buying?

We had come to the fork in the road. A decision had to be made, and there were major factors to consider. What would the relationship between the studios really be? Could Pixar and Disney Animation flourish independent of one another, separate but equal?

In mid-November 2005, John, Steve, and I met for dinner at one of Steve's favorite Japanese restaurants in San Francisco. As we discussed the challenges of the merger, Steve told a story. Twenty years before, in the early 1980s, Apple was developing two personal computers—the Macintosh and the Lisa—and Steve was asked to preside over the Lisa division. It was a job he didn't want, and he admitted that he didn't handle it well: Instead of inspiring the Lisa team, he basically told them that they had already lost out to the Mac team—in other words, that their work was never going to pay off. He'd effectively crushed their spirits, he told us, and that had been wrong. Should this merger happen, he continued, "what we have to do is to not make people at Disney Animation feel like they've lost. We have to make them feel good about themselves."

The fact that John and I had such affection for Disney would certainly help with that. We had both spent our lives trying to live up to Walt Disney's artistic ideals, so the thought of walking through the doors of Disney Animation, entrusted with the mission of reinvigorating its people and helping them return to greatness, felt daunting but also worthy and important. By the end of dinner, the three of us were in agreement. The future of Pixar, of Disney, and of animation itself would be brighter if we joined forces.

John and I understood that this news would come as a shock to our colleagues at Pixar. ("We figured that everybody would feel exactly the same as *we* did when Steve first floated the idea in his living room," John recalls.) Before any official announcement, then, we needed to do everything we could to ensure that people felt safe and that we had taken steps to prevent change being made for the wrong reasons. With Iger's blessing, then, we set about drafting a document that came to be known as "The Five Year Social Compact." This seven-page, single-spaced list was an enumeration of all the things that had to remain the same at Pixar, should the merger go through.

The document's fifty-nine bullet points addressed many topics you might expect: compensation, HR policies, vacation, and benefits. (Item number 1 ensured that Pixar's executive team could still reward employees with bonuses, as Pixar has always done, once a film's box-office receipts reached a certain benchmark.) Others were strictly related to personal expression. (Number 11, for example, stated that Pixar employees must remain free to exercise their creative freedom with their titles and names on their business cards; number 33 ensured that Pixar's people could continue to exert "personal cube/office/space decorating to reflect person's individuality.") Some sought to preserve popular company rituals. (Number 12: "Event parties (holiday, wrap, various events) are prevalent at Pixar. Various holiday parties, end of film parties, the annual car show, the paper airplane contest, Cinco de Mayo festivities and the summer barbecue to name a few.") Some sought to ensure the survival of Pixar's egalitarian ethos. (Number 29: "No assigned parking for any employee, including executives. All spaces are first-come, first served.")

We couldn't say for sure that these items we sought to safeguard were what had propelled us to such success, but we felt strongly about them, and we were going to work hard to prevent them from changing. We were different, and since we believe being different helps us maintain our identity, we wanted to remain that way.

There was one other important factor that shaped the deal that was not reported at the time. It related to the issue of trust. As we were finalizing the merger, Disney's board of directors didn't like the fact that key Pixar talent was not under contract.

If Disney bought us and then John or I or certain other leaders left the company, they felt, it would be a disaster, so they asked that we all sign contracts before the deal went through. We declined. It is a tenet of the Pixar culture that people should work there because they want to, not because a contract requires them to, and as a result, no one at Pixar was under contract. But even though this rejection was based on a core belief, it made the deal feel questionable for Disney. On the Pixar side, meanwhile, there was considerable concern that the Disney bureaucracy would inadvertently destroy what we had built. Both sides, then, felt at considerable risk. The result, though, was that at the heart of this merger was an understanding that both companies had to trust each other. Each side felt a personal obligation to live up to the intent of the agreement—and I believe this was the ideal way to begin our relationship.

On the day of the sale, Bob flew up to Pixar's headquarters in Emeryville, near Oakland, for the announcement, and once the documents were signed and the stock exchanges were notified, Steve, John, and I walked out onto a stage at the far end of Pixar's atrium and greeted all eight hundred of our employees. This was a crucial moment for the company, and we wanted our colleagues to understand its genesis and how the deal would work.

One by one, John, Steve, and I spoke about the thinking behind the deal—how Pixar needed a strong partner, how this was a positive step in our evolution, and how determined we were, despite the changes, to protect our culture. Looking out into the faces of our colleagues, I could see that they were upset—as we knew they would be. We, too, were emotional. We loved our colleagues and the company they'd built, and we knew how big a change we were setting in motion.

We welcomed Bob onto the stage then, and our people greeted him with a warmth that made me proud. Bob told the Pixar staff exactly what he'd told us: that he loved the work we did, first of all, but also that he'd been through one bad merger and one good one in his life—and he was determined to do this right. "Disney Animation needs help, so I have two options," he said. "One, to leave the place in the hands of the people who are already in charge; or two, to go to people who I trust, who have a proven track record of making great stories and characters that people love. That's Pixar. I promise you that the culture of Pixar will be protected."

Later, in an hour-long conference call with analysts, Steve and

Bob moved to make good on that promise: They announced that Circle 7 would be shut down. "We feel very strongly," Steve said, "that if the sequels are going to be made, we want the people who were involved in the original films involved."

It was the end of the day before John, Steve, and I had a chance to take a breath, heading upstairs and ducking into my office. The minute the door shut behind us, Steve put his arms around us and began to cry, tears of pride and relief—and, frankly, love. He had succeeded in providing Pixar, the company he'd helped turn from a struggling hardware supplier into an animation powerhouse, with the two things it needed to endure: a worthy corporate partner in Disney and, in Bob, a genuine advocate.

The next morning, John and I flew to Disney headquarters in Burbank. There were hands to shake and executives to meet, but our main purpose that day was to introduce ourselves to the eight hundred men and women who worked at Disney Animation and to assure them that we came in peace. At three o'clock, we walked over to Soundstage 7 on the Disney back lot, a cavernous space that was packed with animation employees standing shoulder to shoulder.

Bob spoke first. He said that the acquisition of Pixar should not be seen as a sign of disrespect to Disney's ranks but rather as proof of how deeply he loved animation and saw it as Disney's core business. When it was my turn to speak, I kept it brief. I told my new colleagues that a company could only be great if its employees were willing to speak their minds. From that day forward, I said, every Disney Animation employee should feel free to talk to any colleague, regardless of position, and not be afraid of repercussions. This was a central tenet at Pixar, though I was quick to add that this would be one of the few times that I would import an idea from Emeryville without discussing it with them first. "I want you all to know I do *not* want Disney Animation to be a clone of Pixar," I said.

I was eager to turn the microphone over to John, the kindred spirit whom so many of the artists in the room already revered. I sensed that John's presence would reassure them about the transition, and I was right. John gave an impassioned speech about the importance of story and character development and how both got better when artists and filmmakers worked together in a culture of mutual respect. He talked about what it meant to be a director-driven animation company that made movies that sprung from people's hearts and connected in a real way with audiences.

Judging by how the Disney employees were cheering, I gathered that—just as Steve had requested—John and I didn't make them feel like they'd lost the battle. Years later, I would ask the director Nathan Greno—who had been at Disney Animation for a decade when we arrived—what was going through his mind that morning when the merger was announced. "Here's what I thought," he told me. "I thought, 'Maybe now the Disney I wanted to work for when I was a kid will come back.'"

My first day in Burbank, I arrived at Disney Animation before eight in the morning. I wanted to walk the halls before anyone else got there—just to get the lay of the land. I arranged to meet Disney's facilities manager, Chris Hibler, for a tour. We started in the basement, and the first thing I noticed was the strange lack of personal items on employees' desks. At Pixar, people's work areas are virtual shrines to individuality—decorated, adorned, modified in ways that express the quirks and passions of the person who occupies that space. But here, the desks were sterile, cookie-cutter, utterly without personality. When I first mentioned this to Chris, he muttered something evasive and kept moving. It was so stark that I brought it up again a few minutes later—and again, he demurred. As we headed up the stairs into the heart of the building, I turned and asked Chris directly why it was that people in such a creative environment didn't personalize any part of their work areas. Was there a policy against it? The place looked, I said, as if no one spent any time there. At this point, Chris stopped and faced me. In anticipation of my arrival, he confided, everybody had been told to clean off their desks in order to make "a good first impression."

This was an early indication of how much work lay ahead of us. For me, the alarming thing wasn't the lack of tchotchkes. It was the pervasive sense of alienation and fear that the total lack of individuality represented. There seemed to be undue emphasis put on preventing errors; even when it came to something as small as office decor, no one dared to put themselves out there, or to make a mistake.

That sense of alienation was also reflected in the design of the building itself. Its layout seemed to impede the collaboration and exchange of ideas that Steve, John, and I believed was so fundamental to creative work. Employees were spread out over four floors, which made it a chore to drop in on one another. The bottom two floors were dungeon-like, with dreary, dropped ceilings, very few windows, and almost no natural light. Instead of inspiring and fostering creativity, it could hardly have felt more stifling and isolating. Upstairs on the top floor, the "executive suite" was set off by an imposing portal that discouraged entry—creating a sort of gated community kind of vibe. To put it simply, it struck me as a lousy work environment.

One of our most pressing orders of business, then, would be some basic remodeling. First, we turned the off-putting executive suite on the top floor into two spacious story rooms where filmmakers could gather to brainstorm about their films. John and I put our offices on the second floor, right in the middle of things, and removed the secretarial cubicles that had functioned as a sort of obstacle to access (instead, most secretaries got their own offices). John and I made a point of leaving the shades on our office windows open so that people could see us and we could see them. Our goal—in our words and our actions—was to communicate transparency. Instead of a portal separating "us" from "them," we installed a carpet whose brightly colored panels, like lanes of a road, guided people toward our offices, not away from them. We ripped out several walls to create a central gathering place right outside our doors, complete with a new coffee and snack bar.

These may sound like symbolic or even superficial touches, but the messages they sent set the stage for some major organizational changes. And there were many more to come. I told you in chapter 10 how we eliminated the "oversight group" that was charged with poring over production reports to make sure that films were progressing as expected—but really just ended up eroding staff morale. Unfortunately, that group was just one of several hierarchical mechanisms that were impeding creativity at Disney Animation. We tried as best we could to take each of them on, but at first, I'll admit it felt like an uphill climb.

Since we didn't know much of anything about the people, the directors, or the projects at Disney, we had to do a quick audit. John and I asked to be briefed on each film that was under way, and I interviewed every one of the studio's managers and leaders, producers and directors. In truth, I couldn't deduce much from those interviews, but they weren't wasted time—since John and I were perceived as the new sheriffs in town, it was good to prove that I was human just by sitting there talking. Overall, we knew that the studio's way of thinking about films wasn't working, but we didn't know if that was because its leaders lacked ability or if they were just trained poorly. We had to start by assuming that they'd inherited bad practices and that it was our job to reteach them. This led us to look for people who were willing to grow and learn, but this is the kind of thing that you can't ascertain quickly, and there were about eight hundred people to assess.

Nonetheless, we moved forward with a strategy.

We needed to create a version of the Braintrust and teach the studio's people how to work within it. While the directors liked each other, each movie at Disney had been set up to compete for resources, so they were not bonded as a group. In order to create a healthy feedback loop, we'd have to change that.

We had to figure out who the actual leaders within the studio were (that is, not assume the people in the biggest offices were leading).

It was clear that there was internal contention between productions and between technical groups. As far as I could tell, the contentiousness grew out of misconceptions rather than anything substantive. We needed to fix that.

We made the decision early on that we would keep Pixar and Disney Animation completely separate. This was a critical decision that was not obvious to most people. Most people assumed that Pixar would do 3D movies and Disney would do 2D. Or they assumed that we would merge the two studios or mandate that Disney use the Pixar tools. But the key, to us, was separation.

John and I began shuttling back and forth, at least once a week, from Emeryville to Burbank. At first, Pixar's CFO joined us to help think through and implement procedural changes, and one of our technical leaders helped Disney reform its technical group. Other than that, we did not allow either studio to do any production work for the other.

With these strategies in place, we could dive into figuring out what to do.

One top executive at Disney got my attention right away by telling me that he didn't know why Disney had bought Pixar in the first place. Apparently a lover of sports analogies, he told me that Disney Animation was on the one-yard line, ready to score. He felt Disney was on the verge of fixing its own problems—and finally ending its sixteen-year fallow period without a single number one film. I liked this guy's moxie and his willingness to push back, but I told him that if he were to continue at Disney, he needed to figure out why, in fact, Disney was *not* on the one-yard line, *not* about to score, and *not* about to fix its own problems. This executive was smart, but over time I realized that to ask him to help dismantle a culture he had built was too much, so I had to let him go. He was so fixated on existing processes and the notion of being "right" that he couldn't see how flawed his thinking was.

In the end, the person I turned to for leadership was the person many assumed I would let go right off the bat: the head of Circle 7, Andrew Millstein. Most people thought that John and I would automatically view anybody associated with those Pixar "sequels" as tainted, but in truth, that didn't even occur to us. The Circle 7 people had nothing to do with the decision to make sequels to Pixar films; they were just hired to do a job. When I sat down with him, Andrew struck me as thoughtful and eager to understand the new direction we were headed in. "Our filmmakers had lost their voices," he told me, summing up the problem. "It wasn't that they had no desire to express themselves, but there was an imbalance of forces in the organization—not just within it, but between it and the rest of the corporation—that diminished the validity of the creative voice. The balance was gone."

It's easy to see that Andrew spoke my language. This was someone I could work with. Eventually, we'd make him general manager of the studio.

Another lucky break for us was that our head of human resources at Disney Animation was Ann Le Cam. Even though she was steeped in the old ways of doing things, Ann had an intellectual curiosity and a willingness to remake the Animation Studio in a different image. She became my guide to the inner workings of Disney, while I encouraged her to think in new ways about her job. For example, not long after I arrived, she sat down in my office and presented me with a two-year plan that laid out exactly how we should manage various staffing issues going forward. The document was specific about targets we would reach and when we would reach them. It was meticulous—she'd spent two months preparing it—so I was gentle when I told her it wasn't what I wanted. To show her what I wanted, I drew a pyramid on a piece of paper. "What you have done in this report is to assert that in two years we will be here," I said, putting my pencil lead at the top of the pyramid. "Once you assert that, though, it's human nature that you will focus only on making it come true. You will stop thinking about other possibilities. You will narrow your thinking and defend this plan because your name will be on it and you will feel responsible." Then I started drawing lines on the pyramid to show how I'd prefer she approach it.

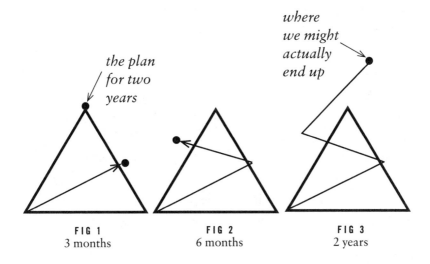

the plan for two years

where we might actually end up

FIG 1
3 months

FIG 2
6 months

FIG 3
2 years

The first line I drew (Fig. 1, above) represented where we would aim to go in three months. The next one (Fig. 2) represented where we might be in three more (and you'll note that it didn't stay within the boundaries of Ann's two year plan). Chances are, I said, we would end up somewhere other than the top of the pyramid she'd imagined. And that (Fig. 3) was as it should be. Instead of setting forth a "perfect" route to achieving future goals (and sticking to it unwaveringly), I wanted Ann to be open to readjusting along the way, to remaining flexible, to accepting that we would be making it up as we go. Not only did she intuitively grasp what I was talking about, she also soon undertook a painful reorganization of her own group to align it with the new way of thinking.

Some things that needed fixing at the studio were glaringly obvious. For example, as we talked to Disney directors, we discovered that they were used to receiving three sets of notes on their films. One came from the studio's development department, another from the head of the studio, and a third from Michael Eisner himself. The notes were not, in fact, "notes." They were mandatory, delivered as a list, with boxes next to each item—boxes that had to be checked as each note was executed. Even worse: None of the people who were giving these notes had ever made a film before, and the three sets of notes often conflicted with one another, creating a sort of schizophrenic quality to the feedback. This concept, completely counter to what we believed and practiced at Pixar, could only result in an inferior product, so we made an announcement: From that day forward, there would be no more mandatory notes.

Disney Animation's directors needed a feedback system that worked, so we immediately set about helping them create their own version of the Braintrust—a safe arena in which to solicit and interpret candid responses to developing projects. (This was made easier by the fact that they already liked and trusted each other. Even before our arrival, we were told, they'd formed their own under-the-radar group called the Story Trust, but the lack of management understanding for that concept had prevented it from evolving into a coherent forum.) As soon as possible, we flew about a dozen Disney directors and story people up to Pixar to observe a Braintrust session about Brad Bird's *Ratatouille*. However, John and I told them they were only allowed to observe, not participate. We wanted them to be flies on the wall—to see how different things could be when people felt free to be candid and when notes were offered in the spirit of helpfulness rather than derision.

The next day, several Pixar directors, writers, and editors accompanied the Disney crew back down to Burbank to observe a Story Trust meeting on a film in the works there called *Meet the Robinsons*. Here, too, we insisted that the Pixar team observe quietly, saying nothing. I thought I noticed a bit more ease in the room that day, as if the Disney people were cautiously feeling for the limits of their new freedom, and the producer of the film later told me it was the most constructive notes session she had ever seen at Disney. Still, both John and I sensed that while everyone embraced the idea of organized candor on an intellectual level and could begin to approximate it when instructed, it would be a while before it came naturally.

A key moment in this evolution came in the fall of 2006, nine months after the merger, at a Story Trust meeting in Burbank. It happened after a fairly awful screening of *American Dog,* a film structured around a famous and pampered canine actor (think Rin Tin Tin) who believed that he was the superhero character he played on TV. When he found himself stranded in the desert, he had to face for the first time how his tidy, scripted life had not prepared him for reality—that he, in fact, had no special powers. That was all well and good, but somewhere along the way, the plot had also come to include a radioactive, cookie-selling Girl Scout zombie serial killer. I'm all for quirky ideas, but this one had metastasized. The movie was still finding its way, to say the least, so John started off the meeting, as he often does, by focusing on the things he liked about it. He also indicated he saw some problems, but he wanted to give the Disney folks the chance to take the lead on those, so instead of digging in and getting too specific, he threw the meeting open to the floor. Throughout the meeting the comments stayed at a superficial level, remaining strangely upbeat—judging by the commentary, you would have never known the film was in disarray. Afterward, one of the Disney directors confided to me that many people in the room had major reservations about the film but didn't say what they thought because John had kicked things off so positively. Taking their cues from him, they didn't want to go against what they thought he liked. Not trusting their own instincts, they held back.

John and I immediately arranged a dinner with the directors—

and told them that if they ever resorted to that kind of thinking again, we'd be finished as a studio.

"Disney Animation was sort of like a dog that had been beaten again and again," Byron Howard, the director, told me when I asked him to describe the mindset back then. "The crew *wanted* to succeed, but they were afraid of pouring their hearts into something that wasn't going to succeed. You could feel that fear. And in notes meetings, everyone was so afraid of hurting someone's feelings that they held back. We had to learn that we weren't attacking the person, we were attacking the project. Only then could we create a crucible that boils away everything that's not working and leaves the strongest framework."

Earning trust takes time; there's no shortcut to understanding that we really do rise and fall together. Without vigilant coaching—pulling people aside who didn't speak their minds in a particular meeting, say, or encouraging those who seem eternally hesitant to jump into the fray—our progress could have easily stalled. Telling the truth isn't easy. But I can say that today, Disney's Story Trust is made up of individuals who understand not only that they must do the difficult work of leveling with one another but how to do it better.

In those first months, we also moved to bolster trust within the studio in another way: Just as we had refused to sign employment contracts, we now moved to eliminate contracts for everyone. At first, many people thought the move was an attempt to wrest power away from the employees and give them less security. In fact, my feeling about employment contracts is that they hurt the employee *and* the employer. The contracts in question were one-sided in favor of the studio, resulting in unexpected negative consequences. First and foremost, there was no longer any effective feedback between bosses and employees. If someone had a problem with the company, there wasn't much point in complaining because they were under contract. If someone didn't perform well, on the other hand, there was no point in confronting them about it; their contract simply wouldn't be renewed, which might be the first time they heard about their need to improve. The whole system discouraged and devalued day-to-day communication and was culturally dysfunctional. But since everybody was used to it, they were blind to the problem.

I wanted to break that cycle. I believed that it was our responsibility to make sure that Disney Animation was a place that people would want to work; if our most talented people could leave, then we would have to be on our toes to keep them happy. When someone had a problem, we wanted it to be brought quickly to the surface, not to fester. Most people know that they don't get their way on everything, but it is very important that they know they are being dealt with straightforwardly and that they, too, will be heard.

As I have said, we decided early on that Pixar and Disney Animation should remain completely separate entities. What this meant was that neither would do any production work for the other, no matter how pressing the deadlines or how dire the situation. No exceptions. Why? Because mixing the two staffs would have been a bureaucratic nightmare. But there was an overarching management principle at work as well. Simply put, we wanted each studio to know that it could stand on its own and solve its own problems. If we made it easy for one studio to borrow people or resources from the other to help solve a problem, the upshot would be that we'd mask the problem. Not allowing such borrowing was a conscious choice on our part to force problems to the surface where we could face them head on.

Almost immediately, we had a crisis on *Ratatouille* that would severely test this policy.

I mentioned earlier that we switched directors on this film midstream—bringing in Brad Bird, fresh off *The Incredibles,* who came in and reworked the story in ways that required a serious technical reboot. Specifically, while in the earlier version all the rats had walked on two feet, Brad felt strongly that (with the exception of Remy, our hero) they should walk on four—like real rats. What that meant was that the rats' "rigging"—a set of complex controls that let animators manipulate the shape and position of the computerized model—had to be changed significantly. Finding themselves way behind schedule, the production team at Pixar felt that it did not have the resources to do the rerigging that Brad's four-footed decision required. The producer said that they couldn't finish the film by the deadline unless they could borrow some people from Disney, which was in a lull between projects, to help out. We said no, not an option. We had already explained the logic to everybody, but I suppose they wanted to see if we really meant it. I can't blame them; getting extra people was easier than having to solve the problems. But in the end, the *Ratatouille* team figured out how to make the film, on time, with what they had.

Not long after, Disney would have a crisis of its own on *American Dog*. I mentioned earlier the emergence of a serial killer storyline, which—while we prided ourselves on always remaining open to new ideas—seemed a tad dark for a family film. Despite our misgivings, though, we decided to give the movie a chance to evolve. Finding a movie's throughline always takes time, we told ourselves. But after ten months of Story Trust meetings—and very little improvement—we concluded that the only option was to restart the project. We asked Chris Williams, a veteran story artist best known for *Mulan* and *The Emperor's New Groove*, and Byron Howard, then a supervising animator on *Lilo and Stitch*, to step in as its directors. Immediately, they began reconceiving the movie. The serial killer was tossed, and the movie was renamed *Bolt*. One of the biggest problems, they felt, was that Bolt himself wasn't appealing enough, visually, to carry the film. "He just wasn't ready," Byron recalled, adding that right before Christmas 2007, "we had a 'This Dog Looks Bad' meeting, where we said, 'What the hell are we going to do about it?' And two of our animators stepped forward and over their Christmas break, worked with our riggers to redo the dog. They spent their whole two-week vacation here, but when we came back, Bolt had gone from 20 percent appealing to 90 percent appealing."

With much to do and little time to do it, *Bolt*'s producer, Clark Spencer, asked if they could borrow some Pixar production people. Again, John and I said no. It was important, we felt, for each studio to know that when they finished a film, nobody had bailed them out—they'd made it themselves.

Chris later told me that to be at the helm of a production whose crew showed this kind of commitment, under such pressure, was energizing. "It was amazing to find myself in the middle of this thing that was so galvanizing for the whole studio," he recalled. "In my fifteen years at Disney, I'd never seen people work so hard and complain so little. They were really invested in this thing—they knew it was the first movie under John—and they wanted it to be great."

Which was good because, as it turned out, yet another crisis was looming.

Very late in the game, problems arose around Rhino the Hamster, our hero's trusty—if deluded—sidekick and the funniest character in the movie. At the beginning of 2008, with only months left to go on the production, the animators reported that Rhino was proving prohibitively time-consuming to animate. The problem was, ironically, sort of the inverse of the one Pixar had on *Ratatouille*. The rebooted script required Rhino to be able to walk on two legs, but he'd originally been designed to walk on four. Which doesn't sound like a big deal, but animating a two-legged character with a four-legged rigging design is extremely difficult to pull off without the character appearing distorted. This was a major setback. Rhino was key to the humor and exposition of the film, but the animators said that he was so hard to animate that it was impossible for them to finish on time. Desperate, we turned for help to the film's technical directors and asked if they could simplify the character's rigging to make it easier to animate. Their answer? Re-rigging would take six months, which was all the time we had left to make the movie. In other words, we were screwed.

John and I called a company-wide meeting. We explained the situation and I gave what some at Disney still call "the Toyota Speech," in which I described the car company's commitment to empowering its employees and letting people on the assembly line make decisions when they encountered problems. In particular, John and I stressed that no one at Disney needed to wait for permission to come up with solutions. What is the point of hiring smart people, we asked, if you don't empower them to fix what's broken? For too long, a culture of fear had stymied those who wanted to step outside of Disney's accepted protocols. That kind of timidity wasn't going to make Disney Animation great, we said. Innovation would, and we knew they had it in them. We challenged them to step up and help us fix this problem.

After this meeting, three members of the crew took it upon themselves, over the weekend, to remodel and rerig Rhino. Within a week, the project was back on track.

Why was a problem that took a few days to solve originally projected to take six months?

The answer, I think, lay in the fact that for too long, the leaders of Disney Animation placed a higher value on error prevention than anything else. Their employees knew there would be repercussions if mistakes were made, so the primary goal was never to make any. To my mind, that institutional fear was behind the *Bolt* re-rigging snafu. With the best intentions, the film's production managers had responded to the crisis with a timetable that would ensure a character that was fully functional *with no errors*. (The irony is that if a solution only takes a few days to find, then you don't care so much if there are errors because you will have plenty of time to fix them.) But seeking to eliminate failure was in this instance—and, I would argue, most instances—precisely the wrong thing to do.

In order for three people to decide to get together offline and dream up solutions, we had to instill an ethos at Disney Animation that made that behavior okay *whether or not they were successful.* That ethos had been at the studio once, but it was sadly absent when we arrived. It was nothing short of exhilarating to see it come back, full force, on *Bolt.* Chris and Byron and their creative team were open and responsive and, most important, able to move the focus away from the notion of the "right" way to fix the problem to actually fixing the problem—a subtle but important distinction.

Even before *Bolt* opened to positive reviews and solid box office, the impact of these internal victories had reinvigorated the ranks of Disney Animation. By pulling together, they'd turned a humdrum, stalled project into a compelling one—and in record time. By early 2009, when the film received an Oscar nomination for Best Animated Feature Film, it felt like a bonus. It's difficult sometimes to tell the difference between what is impossible and what is possible (but requires a big reach). At a creative company, mistaking one for the other can be fatal—but getting it right always elevates. At Disney, *Bolt* was the movie that proved this truth. We were part of the way there.

It's not often talked about, but after the merger, there was some discussion of shutting Disney Animation down altogether. The argument for doing so, expressed by Steve Jobs among others, was that John and I would be spread too thin to do a good job at both places—and that we should focus our energies on keeping Pixar strong. But John and I dearly wanted the opportunity to help revive Disney Animation, and Bob Iger supported us in that goal. We believed, in our souls, that the studio could be golden again.

Still, Steve's worry about our stamina—or, put another way, about our inability to be in two places at once—wasn't unfounded. We had only so many hours in each day, and Pixar would by definition be getting less of them than it once had. From the moment the merger was announced, John and I had attempted to ease our colleagues' fears by hosting several get-togethers for anyone who wanted to hear more about why we thought the merger made sense. Still, as we began to spend more time at Disney, the general feeling at Pixar, which many people articulated to John and me directly, was that our reduced presence in Emeryville, and our focus on Burbank's needs, was a bad sign for the company. One Pixar manager likened the situation to the aftermath of a divorce, when your parents remarry and adopt the kids of their new spouses. "We feel like we're the original kids, and we've been good, but the adopted kids are getting all the attention," he told us. "We're being punished, in a sense, for needing less help."

I didn't want Pixar to feel neglected, but I'll admit I saw an upside to this new reality. Namely, it was an opportunity for other Pixar managers to step forward. Given how long John and I had been there, a dangerous mythology had been constructed around the idea that though we weren't the only ones to recognize problems, we were an essential part of solving them. The truth, though, was that just as other people often recognized problems before we did because they were closer to them, they in turn raised the issues with us and helped us solve them. Our decreased presence in the office was a chance for Pixar's people to see what I already knew: that other leaders at the company had answers, too.

Still, despite the protections we'd put in place, it took a while for the people of Pixar to trust that no one was coming over the hill to change us or that we were abandoning them. Eventually, though, the feeling we had hoped would emerge within Pixar—a sense of strong local ownership combined with a pride in what Disney, the parent company, had accomplished as well—led to a healthier relationship with Disney as a whole. The takeaway for managers is that this didn't happen by accident. This corporate détente, if you will, wouldn't have been possible, I think, without the Five Year Compact.

The document, while providing great comfort to Pixar employees, prompted several complaints from the Disney Studios human resources department. The complaints boiled down to the fact that they didn't care for the exceptionalism that our carefully guarded policies implied. My response to this stemmed less from a loyalty to Pixar than from my commitment to a larger idea: In big organizations there are advantages to consistency, but I strongly believe that smaller groups within the larger whole should be allowed to differentiate themselves and operate according to their own rules, so long as those rules work. This fosters a sense of personal ownership and pride in the company that, to my mind, benefits the larger enterprise.

In a merger of this scope, there are seemingly countless calls to make, every day, on issues big and small. One of the biggest decisions John and I made at Disney was actually to reverse a decision, made in 2004, to shut down the studio's hand-drawn animation efforts. The rise of computer animation—and 3D in particular—had convinced Disney's previous leaders that the era of hand-drawn animation was over. Watching from afar, John and I thought this was tragic. We felt the decline of hand-drawn animation was not attributable to the appeal of 3D but simply to lackluster storytelling. We wanted Disney Animation to return to what had made them great. So when we heard that our predecessors had opted not to renew the contracts of one of the studio's leading directing duos, John Musker and Ron Clements, whose credits included the hand-drawn classics *The Little Mermaid* and *Aladdin,* this particular call seemed like a no-brainer.

As quickly as we could, we brought John and Ron back and told them to start pitching new ideas. Right off, they proposed a twist on a classic fairy tale—*The Frog Prince*—which would take place in New Orleans and feature, as its heroine, Disney's first-ever African-American princess. We green-lighted *The Princess and the Frog* and began reassembling a crew that had been dispersed to the winds. We asked our team at Disney to propose three scenarios for rebuilding the hand-drawn production effort. Their first was to re-establish the old system exactly as it existed before we arrived, which we rejected as too expensive. The second scenario was to farm out the production work—subcontracting it to cheaper animation houses overseas—which we rejected for fear that it would diminish the film's quality. The third scenario, however, felt just right—a combination of hiring key talent inside the studio while outsourcing certain parts of the process that wouldn't affect quality. The number of staffers we'd need to make this happen, I was told, was 192. To which I replied: Done. But they couldn't go over that number.

John and I were excited. Not only were we reviving the art form that the studio was built upon, this was the first movie at Disney that would be made, start to finish, on our watch. We could feel the energy in the building. It was as if everyone working on *The Princess and the Frog* felt that they had something to prove. We set about giving them some of the tools we used at Pixar and teaching them how to use them.

Research trips, for example. We talked our heads off about the value of research while hammering out the storyline of a new film. Frankly, it took a while to get the Disney folks on board with this idea. They seemed to want to lock down the story quickly so they could start making the movie, and they didn't see at first how research would help them; they saw it as a distraction. "It's like a math problem where they say, 'Show your work,'" says Byron Howard, expressing how people at Disney Animation initially viewed John's insistence that people leave the building as they conceived their stories. "John expects that if you have sketched out buildings from your movie, it isn't just bullshit you're throwing up on the screen. The same with characters, costumes, story. John really believes that genuineness come through in every detail."

We persisted: This was something we knew was an essential component of creativity and we weren't kidding about its importance. So during the prepping of *The Princess and the Frog*, the entire creative leadership of the film headed to Louisiana. Attending the Krewe of Bacchus parade on the Sunday before Mardi Gras gave them a vivid frame of reference when they animated a sequence based on that festival; their ride on the riverboat *Natchez* helped them block out a scene set on a similar river-going vessel; a tour of the St. Charles Avenue streetcar line ensured that they captured the distinct clang of the trolley's bell and the sounds and the colors: All of it was right there in front of them. Upon their return, the directors, Ron and John, each told me that research inspired the production in ways they never expected. It was the beginning of a sea change: Today, directors and writers at Disney can't imagine developing an idea for a film without doing research.

Leading up to the release of *The Princess and the Frog,* we'd had many conversations about what to call it. For a while we considered the title "The Frog Princess," but Disney's marketing folks warned us: Having the word *princess* in the title would lead moviegoers to think that the film was for girls only. We pushed back, believing that the quality of the film would trump that association and lure viewers of all ages, male and female. We felt a return to hand-drawn animation, done in the service of a beloved fairy tale, would pack 'em in.

Turns out, it was our own version of a stupid pill.

When *The Princess and the Frog* was released, we believed we had made a good film, the reviews confirmed that belief, and people who saw it loved it. However, we would soon learn that we had made a serious mistake—one that was only compounded by the fact that our movie opened nationwide just five days before James Cameron's science fiction fantasy *Avatar.* This scheduling only encouraged moviegoers to take one look at a film with the word *princess* in the title and think: *That's for little girls only.* To say that we are making a great film but not listen to the input of experienced colleagues within the company imperiled the quality we were so proud of. Quality meant that every aspect—not just the rendering and the storytelling but also the positioning and the marketing—

needed to be done well, which meant being open to reasoned opinions, even when they contradicted our own. The movie had come in under budget, which is the rarest of achievements in the entertainment business. The quality of its animation rivaled the best ever done by the studio. The film was profitable, as we'd kept costs down, but it just didn't make enough to convince anyone at the studio that we should pour more resources into hand-drawn films.

While we'd had high hopes that the film would prove that 2D could rise again, our narrow vision and poor decision-making made it seem like the opposite was true. While we thought then—and still think today—that hand-drawn animation is a wonderfully expressive medium, I realize now that I got carried away by my childhood memories of the Disney Animation I'd once so enjoyed. I'd liked the idea of celebrating, right out of the box, the art form that Walt Disney himself pioneered.

After *The Princess and the Frog*'s somewhat lackluster opening, I knew we had to rethink what we were doing. Around that time, Andrew Millstein pulled me aside and pointed out that our double-barreled approach—reviving 2D while also championing 3D—was confusing the people within the studio we fundamentally wanted to encourage to focus on the future. The issue with 2D was not the validity of the time-honored art form but that Disney's directors needed and wanted to engage with the new.

In the aftermath of the merger, many people had asked me whether we were going to have Disney do 2D and Pixar 3D. They were expecting Disney to do the old stuff and Pixar to do the new. In the wake of *The Princess and the Frog*, I realized how important it was to nip this toxic way of thinking in the bud. The truth was, Disney's directors respected the studio's heritage, but they wanted to build on it—and in order to do that, they had to be free to forge their own path.

Disney Animation's embrace of the new would take on steam, ironically, when it finally figured out how to reframe and rethink something old: the fairy tale *Rapunzel*. This was a project that had languished for years in development hell, kicking around Disney, enduring a few false starts, and finally being left for dead. But now, the studio was becoming creatively healthier, and people were talking to one another. John often said that the problem at Disney Animation was never lack of talent, it was that years of stifling working conditions had made people lose their creative compasses. Now, even with the box-office disappointment of *The Princess and the Frog*, they were dusting those compasses off again.

For years, many at Disney had tried (and failed) to crack the story of Rapunzel—she of the famous mane of hair—in a way that seemed destined to make a terrific movie. The central challenge was that a girl locked in a tower is hardly an active scenario for a feature film. At one point, Michael Eisner himself had proposed updating the tale, calling it *Rapunzel Unbraided,* and setting it in modern-day San Francisco. Then, somehow, our heroine would be transported into the fairy tale world. The director of the film, Glen Keane, one of the greatest animators ever—known for his work on *The Little Mermaid, Aladdin,* and *Beauty and the Beast*—couldn't make this idea work, which left the project at an impasse. The week before John and I arrived, our predecessors shut the project down.

One of our first acts at Disney was to ask Glen to keep *Rapunzel* going. It was a classic story, we reasoned, perfect for the Disney brand. Surely, there was a way to make it work as a film. Right around then Glen had a temporary health scare and was forced to reduce his role in the film to that of an adviser. In October 2008, we brought on directors Byron Howard and Nathan Greno, who were both fresh off their success with *Bolt* (Howard had directed it, with Chris Williams; Greno had been head of story). They took the story in a different direction, teaming up with the writer Dan Fogelman and the composer Alan Menken, who had done the music for the iconic Disney musicals of the 1990s. This Rapunzel was more assertive than the character in the classic tale, and her hair had magical healing powers, which she could activate by singing an incantation. This version of the story was familiar but sassy and modern at the same time.

Determined not to repeat the mistake we'd made with *The Princess and the Frog*, we changed the movie's title from *Rapunzel* to the more gender-neutral *Tangled*. Internally, the decision was controversial, as some people felt we were letting marketing concerns dictate creative decisions, that we were bastardizing a classic property. Nathan and Byron rebutted that charge, saying that because their story focused on a female *and* a male character, a former thief named Flynn Rider, *Tangled* better captured the fact that the movie was about a duo.

"You wouldn't call *Toy Story* 'Buzz Lightyear,'" as Nathan said.

Released in November 2010, *Tangled* was a runaway success, artistically and commercially. A. O. Scott of *The New York Times* wrote, "Its look and spirit convey a modified, updated but nonetheless sincere and unmistakable quality of old-fashioned Disneyness." The movie went on to earn more than $590 million worldwide, becoming the second-highest-grossing film from Disney Animation ever, after *The Lion King*. The studio had its first number one hit in sixteen years, and the reverberations within the building were palpable.

I could stop there, but there is a coda to this story that will resonate with any manager, in any business. It involved John's and my determination to use the success of *Tangled* as a healing moment for the studio, and we felt like we knew just how to do it.

We had learned long ago that while everyone appreciates cash bonuses, they value something else almost as much: being looked in the eye by someone they respect and told, "Thank you." At Pixar, we'd devised a way to give our employees money *and* gratitude. When a movie makes enough money to trigger bonuses, John and I join with the directors and producers and personally distribute checks to every person who worked on the film. This jibes with our belief that each film belongs to *everyone* at the studio (and is related to our "ideas can come from anywhere" credo; everyone is encouraged to give notes and pitch in, and they do). The distribution of bonuses one by one can take a while, but we feel it's essential to take the time to shake each person's hand and tell them how much their contribution mattered.

In the wake of *Tangled*'s success, I asked Ann Le Cam, our vice president of human resources, to help us do something along the same lines at Disney. She printed up personalized letters for each crew member explaining the reason for the bonus, and on a weekday morning in the spring of 2010, Disney Animation's general manager Andrew Millstein, the directors Nathan Greno and Byron Howard, the previous director (and inspiration for the movie) Glen Keane, the producer Roy Conli, and John and I asked everyone who'd worked on *Tangled* to gather in one of the large stages at Disney. As they milled about, they didn't know what was coming—we'd suggested to them that it was a general meeting. But when they saw the envelopes in our hands, they knew something was up. It was Ann's idea to give each crew member a hot-off-the-presses DVD of the movie as well—a small gesture that made our gratitude feel even more genuine. To this day, some *Tangled* veterans still display framed copies of the letter they received that day on their office walls.

Would it have been easier simply to wire bonuses into employees' direct deposit accounts? Yes. But like I always say when talking about making a movie, easy isn't the goal. Quality is the goal.

The ship was beginning to turn—and it would only keep turning.

I mentioned before that Disney's Story Trust has evolved into a strong, supportive group, but in our first years there, it lacked leaders who excelled at storytelling structure. Even though the group was very good, I wasn't sure if any of its members would grow into the kind of facilitators that had emerged at Pixar. This worried me, because I knew how heavily Pixar relied on Andrew Stanton and Brad Bird's ability to chart the beats of a story and to make things better. But all we could do at Disney, I knew, was create a healthy creative environment and see what developed.

I was enormously gratified, then, as the studio was making *Wreck-It Ralph* and *Frozen* (directed by Chris Buck and Jennifer Lee, who also wrote the script), when I noticed something changing from within. The writers at the studio had bonded with each other and, as a group, had begun to play a key role in the Story Trust meetings, especially when it came to structuring the films. This feedback group had become as good as Pixar's Braintrust, but with its own personality. It was an indication of something larger that was happening: The studio as a whole was operating more smoothly. And I want to emphasize that it was still populated by most of the same people John and I had first encountered when we arrived. We had applied our principles to a dysfunctional group and had changed them, unleashing their creative potential. They had become a cohesive team, stocked with standout talents. This brought Disney Animation to a new level. Now we had a creative roster that was as good as the one at Pixar, yet quite different. The studio Walt Disney had built had become worthy of him once again.

CHAPTER 13

NOTES DAY

When I began this book, I hoped to capture some of the thinking that underlies the way we work at Pixar and Disney Animation. I also hoped that by talking with my colleagues, bouncing my theories off of them and reflecting on what we had built, I would clarify my own beliefs about creativity and how it is grown, protected, and sustained. Two years later, I feel like I've managed to do these things, but the clarity didn't come easy. In part, that's because while I was writing this book, I was also working full-time at Disney and Pixar, and the world did not stand still. Partly, too, clarity was elusive because I don't believe in simple, prescriptive formulas for success. I wanted this book to acknowledge the complexity that creativity requires. And that meant wading into some murky areas.

During the period that I worked on this book, Disney continued to evolve rather dramatically, with its Story Trust becoming a candid and supportive feedback system and its production group reaching new levels of technical and storytelling sophistication.

Each of Disney's films had setbacks—which we expected—but we found ways to work our way through them. *Frozen* opened on the day before Thanksgiving 2013 and, like *Tangled,* became a world-wide box-office success—a victory made even sweeter because it came on the heels of the studio's 2012 triumph *Wreck-It Ralph.* The creative culture at Disney Animation, I believe, is fundamentally different than when John and I arrived in 2006.

As all this was taking place, Pixar released *Monsters University,* which you may remember underwent a change of directors during its journey to the multiplex. The film—our fourteenth number one movie in a row—grossed $82 million on its opening weekend (making it the second biggest Pixar opening ever) and went on to make more than $740 million worldwide. The mood inside Pixar was jubilant. But as always, my focus was on the challenges ahead and on staying true to our goal of recognizing problems early and engaging them fully.

I have noted that there are forces at work in any company that are hard to see. At Pixar, those forces—among them the impact of growth and the reverberations of success—had sparked several problems. For example, as we'd grown, we had taken in quite a mixture of people. So in addition to the colleagues who had been with us from the beginning and who understood the principles that guided the company since they'd lived through the events that had forged those principles, we now had more recent arrivals. While some of these people learned quickly, absorbing the ideas that made our company work and becoming new leaders, others were in awe of the place—respectful of our history to the point that they could be hindered by it. Many brought good new ideas with them, but some were reluctant to suggest them. After all, this was the great and mighty Pixar, they thought—who were *they* to call for change? Some were grateful for the supportive environment—the subsidized cafeteria, the top-of-the-line tools—but others took them for granted, figuring that such perks came with the territory. There were many who loved how successful we'd been, but some didn't understand the struggle and risk that success had entailed. Why couldn't we just make things simpler, these people wanted to know?

In short, Pixar had the kind of diverse problems that any successful company has. But chief among them, to my mind, was that more and more people had begun to feel that it was either not safe or not welcome to offer differing ideas. This hesitancy was difficult to see at first, but when we paid attention, we saw many clues that people were holding back. To me, that meant one thing: We, as leaders, were allowing some faulty ideas to take hold, and that was bad for our culture.

There is nothing like a crisis, though, to bring what ails a company to the surface. And now, we had three crises brewing at once: (1) Our production costs were rising and we needed to rein them in; (2) External economic forces were putting pressure on our business; and (3) One of the central tenets of our culture—good ideas can come from anywhere, so everyone must feel empowered to speak up—was faltering. Too many of our people—and to my mind, "too many" is the same as "any"—were self-censoring. That needed to change.

These three challenges—and our belief that there was no single big idea that would solve them—led us to try something that we hoped would break the logjam and reinvigorate the studio. We called it Notes Day, and I see it as a stellar example of how to set the table for creativity. Managers of creative companies must never forget to ask themselves: "How do we tap the brainpower of our people?" From its genesis to its execution, from the goodwill it engendered to the company-wide changes it set in motion, Notes Day was a success in part because it was based on the idea that fixing things is an ongoing, incremental process. Creative people must accept that challenges never cease, failure can't be avoided, and "vision" is often an illusion. But they must also feel safe—always—to speak their minds. Notes Day was a reminder that collaboration, determination, and candor never fail to lift us up.

I am often asked which Pixar movie makes me the proudest. My answer is that, while I take pride in all our movies, what makes me most proud is how our people respond to crisis. When we have a problem, the leaders of the company don't say, "What the hell are you guys going to do about it?" Instead there is talk of "our" problem and of what "we" can do to solve it together. My colleagues see themselves as part owners of the company and of the culture, because they are. They are very protective of Pixar. And it was this protective and participatory spirit that led to Notes Day.

In January 2013, Pixar's leadership—about thirty-five of us, including our producers and directors—gathered for a two-day offsite at Cavallo Point, a former army base–turned–conference center in Sausalito, just across the Golden Gate Bridge from San Francisco. On the agenda were two pressing issues. The first was the rising cost of making our films; the second was an unfortunate shift in the culture that all of Pixar's leaders had noticed. As Pixar had grown, it had changed. No surprise there—change happens, and a 1,200-person company (Pixar now) is going to operate differently than one that employs forty-five (Pixar then). But many of us were concerned that with that growth had come an erosion of some of the principles that had made us successful in the past. The situation wasn't dire—far from it, in fact, as we had some very exciting projects in the works. But as we gathered at Cavallo Point, there was an urgency in the room: Each of the thirty-five men and women there was engaged by the desire to keep Pixar on the right track.

Tom Porter—our head of production, who also happens to be a pioneer in computer graphics and one of the founders of Pixar—led off the day with an extended analysis of our costs. Distribution methods were changing rapidly, he noted, and so too were the economics of our business. That we were doing well as a company didn't make us immune to these greater forces, and we all agreed that we needed to stay ahead of trouble by keeping our costs down. At the same time, we did not want to stop taking risks. We wanted always to be a company that would gamble on unusual films such as *Up*, *Ratatouille*, and *WALL-E*. Not every film had to tackle unconventional stories, of course, but we wanted every filmmaker to feel free to propose them.

These two issues were interconnected. When costs are low, it's easier to justify taking a risk. Thus, unless we lowered our costs, we would effectively limit the kinds of films that we would be able to make. Moreover, there was another benefit of lowering costs. Cheaper films are made with smaller crews, and everyone agrees that the smaller the crew, the better the working experience. It's not just that a leaner crew is closer and more collegial; it's that on a smaller production it's easier for people to feel that they've made an impact. Our first film, *Toy Story*, was made with our smallest crew, but as each successive film became more visually complex, the head count started to creep up. At the time of the off-site at Cavallo Point, making a Pixar film required, on average, about 22,000 person-weeks, the unit of measurement we commonly use in our budget. We needed to reduce that number by about 10 percent.

But we needed something else, as well, something that was harder to quantify. Increasingly, we sensed that our people, having enjoyed years of success, were under a great deal of pressure not to fail. Nobody wanted to have worked on the first movie that didn't open at number one. And the result was a growing temptation to pour too much visual detail into each film—to make it "perfect." That honorable-sounding desire—we call it "plussing"—was accompanied by a kind of paralyzing anxiety. What if we couldn't achieve the expected level of excellence? What if we couldn't break new ground, visually? As a company, our determination to avoid disappointments was also causing us to shy away from risk. The specter of past excellence was sapping us of some of the energy that we'd once used to pursue excellence. In addition to this, many new people had come into the company, people who had not experienced the ups and downs of our previous films. Thus, they had preconceived notions of what it was like to work at a successful company. As at many companies, one of the consequences of wild success is the pernicious distortion of reality. Increasingly we would hear that people had opinions about things they thought were wrong but were unwilling to express them. One of our greatest values—that solutions could come from anyone and that everyone should feel free to weigh in—was slowly being subverted under our watchful eyes. And only we could correct it.

"Sometimes I think people have gotten too comfortable," John said when we gathered in a renovated chapel on the resort grounds. "They need to feel excited—to feel like we once did: on fire and buzzing with possibility!"

This wasn't the first time John and I had wondered about how Pixar's people were affected by being at the front of the pack for so long. Would they gradually begin to take success for granted? "There's a lightness and a speed at Disney that I want to see more of at Pixar," John said.

How, we all wondered, could we maintain Pixar's sense of intensity and playfulness, beating back the creeping conservatism that often accompanies success while also getting leaner and more nimble?

That's when Guido Quaroni spoke up. Guido is vice president of our Tools Department, and he spends a lot of time thinking about how to keep his 120 engineers happy. His challenge on that front is real: His department develops technology, but Pixar doesn't sell technology. It sells stories *enabled* by technology. Which means that when a Pixar engineer develops a piece of software, it is deemed successful only insomuch as it helps our movies get made. I've talked about the problem at Pixar of people questioning how much of each movie's success can be attributed to them personally. For engineers, that uncertainty can be particularly acute. Guido knows that if he's not careful, that disconnect can lead to low morale. So to retain the best engineers, he works extra hard to make sure they enjoy their jobs.

When Guido had the floor, he told a story about something

he'd instituted in his department called "personal project days." Two days a month, he allowed his engineers to work on anything they wanted, using Pixar's resources to engage with whatever problem or question they found interesting. It didn't have to be directly applicable to any particular film or address any of production's needs. If an engineer wanted to see what it was like to light a shot in *Brave,* for example, he or she could. If a group of engineers wanted to build a prototype using Kinect, Microsoft's motion-sensing input device, to help animators capture characters' movements, they could do that, too. Any idea that sparked their curiosity, they were free to pursue.

"You just give people the time, and they come up with the ideas," Guido told us. "That's the beauty of it: It comes from them."

Guido had already told me about how, in just four months, personal project days had reenergized his staff. Privately, we'd even begun to brainstorm ideas about how similar efforts could be implemented company-wide. At one point, he'd suggested shutting down Pixar for a week at the end of a movie's production cycle to talk about what went right, what went wrong, and how to reboot for the next project—a sort of super-postmortem. The idea wasn't practical, in the end, but it was thought-provoking. Now, as we contemplated how to achieve our goal of cutting costs by 10 percent, Guido had a simple suggestion.

"Let's ask Pixar's people—all of them—for ideas about how to do it," he said.

Looking at John, I could see his gears begin turning. "Okay, now *that's* interesting," he said. "What if we closed Pixar for the day? Everybody will come to work but all we'll talk about is how to solve this problem. We dedicate an entire day to it."

The room was instantly abuzz. "This is so Pixar," Andrew said. "Totally unexpected. Yes! You want people to get excited? That's going to do it."

When I asked who in the room would be willing to help organize it, everyone's hands shot up.

I believe that no creative company should ever stop evolving, and this would be our latest attempt to avoid stagnation. We wanted to explore issues big and small—to give candid notes to ourselves about the workings of the company, much like we would give notes on a movie in a Braintrust meeting. So it made sense, as we began to make Guido's idea a reality, to invoke our shorthand term for candid feedback: *notes*. At some point, we decided that Monday, March 11, 2013, would be called "Notes Day."

The exercise would be fruitless without the buy-in of our people, so we scheduled three town hall–style meetings to explain the idea to more than 300 employees at a time. Tom Porter presented an abbreviated version of his off-site talk to set up the problem, and then John and I laid out the plan. "It'll be a day in which you tell us how to make Pixar better," John said. "We'll do no work that day. No visitors will be allowed. Everyone must attend."

"We have a problem," I said, "and we believe the only people who know what to do about it are you."

We appointed Tom to preside over Notes Day and make sure that it was more than merely a feel-good exercise. From the start, he made clear what Notes Day was—and wasn't. "This is not a call for working faster or doing more overtime or making do with fewer people," he said in one town hall forum. "This is about making three films every two years with roughly the same number of people we've got today. We hope to rely on improvements in technology. We hope that productions can share resources and avoid reinventing the wheel each time. We hope that artists can benefit from greater clarity from the directors." But to make good on these hopes—and to realize other areas in which we could improve—Pixar's leaders needed everyone to speak up.

Tom got together with Guido, Lori McAdams, the vice president of human resources, and producers Katherine Sarafian and Galyn Susman to form the core of the Notes Day Working Group.

That group would soon expand, drafting dozens of volunteers for specific assignments. First, it created an electronic suggestion box where Pixar people could submit discussion topics they thought would help us become more innovative and more efficient. Immediately, topic ideas began flooding in, along with suggestions about how to run Notes Day itself.

The suggestion box, in turn, prompted something that none of us had expected. Many departments, without any prodding, created their own wiki pages and blogs to hash out what they believed the core issues at Pixar really were. Weeks before Notes Day, people were talking among themselves in ways they hadn't before about how, specifically, to improve workflow and enact positive change. When people asked for guidance on how to be involved, Tom nudged them along, sending this hypothetical prompt to anyone who asked: "The year is 2017. Both of this year's films were completed in well under 18,500 person-weeks . . . . What innovations helped these productions meet their budget goals? What are some specific things that we did differently?"

In the end, four thousand emails poured into the Notes Day suggestion box—containing one thousand separate ideas in all. As Tom and his team read and evaluated them, they were careful not to dismiss the unexpected. "While we discarded the ones that felt like general grumbling, we also made room for interesting ideas that might, but might not, lead somewhere," he told me. "I am sure we were biased toward ideas that would clearly help us get to 18,500 person-weeks, but there were many topics we picked with only a loose or non-obvious connection to that goal. I'd say our major criterion was, 'Can you imagine twenty people talking about this topic for an hour?'"

Putting like with like, Tom's team distilled the thousand ideas down to 293 discussion topics. That was still way too many for a single day's agenda, so a group of senior managers then met and whittled those down to 120 topics, organized into several broad categories such as Training, Environment and Culture; Cross-Show Resource Pooling (we often call our movies "shows"); Tools and Technology; and Workflow.

The winnowing process was difficult, and it was made even more so by the diversity of the questions posed. Some were valid but highly technical in nature, such as, "Out-of-memory errors related to inadequately pruned sets consume a significant amount of computer and human time. What can be done to improve pruning?" Others were more sociological, as in, "How can we return to a 'good ideas come from anywhere' culture?" And then there was my favorite: "How can we get to a *12,000* person-week movie?" That's right: 12,000. This was a discussion topic prompted by emails from several people whose reaction to the call for a 10 percent budget cut was, naturally, to ask whether a more drastic cut might be possible as well.

"Eighteen Five, Smaiteen Five," said the header on one email received by the Notes Day Working Group. What, this writer asked, if of the three films Pixar made every two years, one of them was produced for a "reduced scope" of 15,000 person-weeks? Or even 12,500? "No skimping on story, just simplifying the rest?"

Another person emailed: "I, for one, would like to work on a '10,000 person-week film.' I feel that the measures you'd design to enable it would inform efforts to make the 18,500 person-week film."

Still another asked: "What kind of film would Pixar make with 12,000 person-weeks? Is there a creative idea that could live up to our reputation but be done for that little? Where would the cuts be? What would be different about the process?" The subject line for that email, by the way, was "GET RADICAL."

Once the whittling process was complete, Tom needed to find out roughly how many people were interested in each discussion topic so that he could plan the day accordingly. To that end, the Notes Day Working Group circulated a survey, and what he learned was striking: The number one topic—the one that the most people wanted to talk about—was how to achieve a 12,000 person-week movie. In the end, Tom and his team would arrange seven separate 90-minute sessions on this topic alone. The people who signed up for these sessions weren't martyrs. The problem of doing more with less was interesting to them, and they wanted to engage with it. (Think about that—the topic that captured my Pixar colleagues' imagination more than any other was an attempt to be even more aggressive in trying to reduce the budget! They truly understood the problem and its implications. Can you see why I have so much pride in this place?)

The nitty-gritty of how all this was organized may seem a bit micro to describe here, but it couldn't have been more vital to the way the day played out. It's all well and good to gather people to discuss workplace challenges, but it was extremely important that we find a way to turn all that talk into something tangible, usable, valuable.

How the day was designed, we felt, would be the deciding factor in accomplishing that.

Tom and his team decided early on that people would determine their own schedules, signing up for only the sessions that interested them. Each of the Notes Day discussion groups would be led by a facilitator recruited from among the company's production managers. The week before Notes Day, all facilitators attended a training session to help them keep each meeting on track and make sure that everyone—the outgoing, the laid-back, and everyone in between—was heard from. Then, to make sure something concrete emerged, the Working Group designed a set of "exit forms" to be filled out by each session's participants.

Red forms were for proposals, blue forms were for brainstorms, and yellow forms were for something we called "best practices"— ideas that were not action items per se but principles about how we should behave as a company. The forms were simple and specific: Each session got its own set, tailored specifically to the topic at hand, that asked a specific question. For example, the session called

"Returning to a 'Good Ideas Come from Anywhere' Culture," had blue exit forms topped with this header: *Imagine it's 2017. We've broken down barriers so that people feel safe to speak up. Senior employees are open to new processes. What did we do to achieve this success?* Underneath that question were boxes in which attendees could pencil in three answers. Then, after they wrote a general description of each idea, they were asked to go a few steps further. What "Benefits to Pixar" would these ideas bring? And what should be the "Next Steps" to make them a reality? Finally, there was space provided to specify "Who is the best audience for this idea?" and "Who should pitch this idea?"

The goal was meaningful engagement that would lead to action. And while Tom and his team had made room for a variety of topics, there was a consistency to the way they were framed. A best practices session called "Lessons from the Outside" had a yellow exit form that posed the question, "What can we learn from best practices at other companies?" Underneath, it had space for three lessons, each with the same "Benefits to Pixar/Next Steps" follow-up.

The red exit form for a proposals session called "Helping Directors Understand Costs in Story" gave the session's attendees a jumping-off point: *Introduce the concept of cost early in the story process. Build in scope discussions in the idea-generation phase. Story plays a role in the budget process when building reels.* Then, in a space marked "Revised Proposal?" this form encouraged participants to improve on the stated approach. "How does this benefit the studio?" the form asked, and "What are the drawbacks?" At the bottom was another question, "Is This Idea Worth Pursuing?" with two boxes underneath: "YES! & Next Steps" or "NO, because . . . ." The yes option asked: "Who's the best audience for this proposal? (Be specific)." And again there was this: "Who should pitch this proposal?"

I think you're getting a sense of how hard our team worked to make sure Notes Day took us where we needed to go. As Tom put it, "We didn't just want to make lists of cool things we could do. The goal was to identify passionate people who would take ideas forward. We wanted to put people with clever insights in front of Pixar's executive team."

On the Friday before Notes Day, I got an email telling me that 1,059 people had signed up—nearly everyone in the company, given that some employees were on leave or away. The following Monday, we would discuss 106 topics in 171 sessions managed by 138 facilitators in 66 meeting spaces across our three buildings—from offices to conference rooms to common spaces like the Poodle Lounge, which has a painting of George Washington on the wall, a bean bag toss game on the floor, and a disco ball hanging overhead.

We were as ready as we were ever going to be to let this experiment unfold.

At 9 A.M. on March 11, everyone gathered in the atrium of the Steve Jobs Building. If the navy blue Pixar sweatshirt I was wearing didn't make it obvious enough, the look on my face gave it away: I was enormously proud of how our people had already shown their commitment to making Notes Day a historic day for us. I told them as much as I welcomed them, and then I handed the mike to John.

John often plays the role of inspirer-in-chief, and the people at Disney and Pixar alike rely on his energy and optimism. But this was no rah-rah call to action. Ambling to the front of the stage, John proceeded to deliver the most heartfelt and emotional speech I had ever heard him give. He started by talking about candor, and how we spend a lot of time at Pixar talking about its importance. But candor is hard, both to deliver and to receive. He knew this firsthand, he said, because in preparation for Notes Day, the organizers had shared something else that had come in to the electronic suggestion box: A fair amount of feedback had focused on John himself, and not all of it was positive. In particular, people were upset that—because he was now splitting his time between two studios—they were seeing less of him. The bottom line was that they missed him, but they also felt that there were ways that John could better handle the inordinate pressure he was under.

John admitted that this hurt; still, he wanted to hear all of the specific criticisms. "So they prepared a list," he said. "I thought it would be a page. Instead, I got two-and-a-half pages." Among the things he learned: John was so tightly scheduled, and meetings with him were so precious, that people tended to overprepare to see him, which served no one. In fact, John said, "there were a *lot* of notes about my time management, and how I carry the emotion of one meeting into the next, making some people ask, 'Why is he upset at us?' I didn't know I was doing any of this, and those two-and-a-half pages were really tough to read. But it was so valuable for me to hear, and I'm already working to correct those things."

The atrium was quiet, despite the crowd.

"So, today, please be honest," John continued. "And those of you in management positions, be aware that some of this is going to feel like it's directed at you personally. I'm not kidding. It's going to happen. But put your tough skin on, and for the sake of Pixar, speak up, and don't stop the honesty. Trust me. That's what today is about. It's about making Pixar better forever, for all of you and for the next generations of Pixarians. This is going to fundamentally change the company for the better. But it starts with you."

It was time to go to class.

For the first hour of Notes Day, everyone at the company headed to their own departmental meeting—Story, Lighting, Shading, Accounting, what have you—where they shared ideas with their closest colleagues about how to be more efficient. These departmental meetings, we felt, would serve as a sort of warm-up for the day; it's always easier to be candid with people you know than with strangers. But as John had urged, Pixar's people needed to put their thickest skins and bravest faces on. Because beginning at 10:45 A.M., when everybody headed to their first session, chances were good that for the rest of the day, no Pixar employee was going to find him- or herself sitting next to any of the people they knew best.

Why? Because the sessions weren't organized by job or by department. They were organized by individual interest. During the lead-up to Notes Day, each person had been asked what they wanted to discuss, and Tom's team had created enough sessions to accommodate everyone. While some topics were so specialized that interest was limited to a narrow subset of employees (for example, to take just one: "What range of solutions do we have for improving Lighting productivity?"), curiosity being what it is, many topics attracted all kinds of people from across the company.

If you showed up, for instance, to a brainstorming session called "Developing and Appreciating a Great Workplace"—*It's 2017. Nobody at the studio behaves as if they are entitled. How did we accomplish that?*—you would have found Pixar's executive chef, a woman who worked in Legal, a woman from Finance, a veteran animator, a man from Systems, and more than a dozen others. What had attracted such a cross-section? For that particular session, everyone said they picked it because of the word *entitled* in the descriptor. They'd all encountered people who acted entitled at Pixar—people who insisted on having their own piece of equipment, even if it could be shared, or who groused that they couldn't bring their dogs to work. "This is a job," one animator said. "A *great* job. We are well paid. These people need to wake up."

What was most striking to those in attendance at the "Great Workplace" session was how much they had in common. The Systems guy told a story about answering a frantic call for tech support. He rushed over to assess the problem, only to be told by the aggrieved artist that the machine should be fixed during lunch— because that's when it would be most convenient for her. "I need to eat lunch, too," he told the group, as everyone nodded their heads. The chef told a similar story about a last-minute request to cater a working lunch that came without any acknowledgement of the hassle (and hustle) it would require of her staff. A character animator lamented that he didn't know more about what people in other departments, like lighting and shading, did. "It makes it easy to vilify and resent each other," he said.

One by one, the people in this session hit on the same themes. "We need to make people behave more like peers," one person said. "I wish more people knew about the whole production pipeline— by which I mean, that they appreciated and understood what other people do," said another. "We need to heighten people's awareness of what they do not know."

Among the ideas this group put on their exit forms: fostering more empathy between departments through a job-swapping program, establishing a lunch lottery that would match people at random to encourage new connections and friendships, and holding cross-departmental mixers designed to let far-flung colleagues get to know each other over a few beers.

I chose to describe that session in part because it's broadly relatable—no matter what business you're in, you've run across the scourge of entitlement. (Were I to describe some other Notes Day sessions—one on centralized rendering, say—I think I'd risk losing a few people.) But regardless of the topic that was being discussed, no matter where you were on campus, you could feel a frisson of energy. If you stepped into a Pixar restroom or stepped outside for some air, you couldn't avoid overhearing people chatting about how exciting Notes Day was. The feeling was that we were engaged in something that would make a difference.

Midway through the day, Tom gathered the facilitators to check, briefly, how things were going and to encourage them to share their experiences thus far. At one point, he asked, "How many of you had suggestions in your sessions that could be implemented immediately?" Everybody raised their hands.

We'd made a decision to separate out Pixar's executives, directors, and producers from the Notes Day sessions. Partly this was because it was vital that people speak freely, and we weren't sure they would if we were there. Partly, too, we peeled off because there were particular topics that we needed to consider among ourselves: creative oversight (Are Braintrust sessions as useful as they were ten years ago?), leadership tone and temperament (How can we better foster a culture of inclusiveness in which anyone can suggest a labor-saving idea?), the need to spend money where it can do the most good (We have a system that is vulnerable to excess, that rewards perfectionists and pleasers. How do we manage perfectionism and the desire to innovate?).

I knew things were going well from the looks on our colleagues' faces as they hurried from session to session. They were beaming. At day's end, as the entire company gathered outside for beer, hot dogs, and some instant analysis, I noticed people from different departments continuing the discussions they'd begun inside. The energy on the whole campus was electric. This was the Pixar that they wanted, that we wanted. I made a point of stopping by several bulletin boards we'd erected to encourage people to share their impressions. Among those posted under a variety of categories were:

Favorite moment from Notes Day: "John Lasseter's candor."

Something new I learned today: "People care; people can change."

How many new people did you meet today? "23."

And then there was this: "Notes Day is the proof that Pixar cares about people as much as about finances." And: "Do this again next year."

The next morning, I received emails from hundreds of employees. One, from a storyboard artist, perfectly captured the feeling expressed by many. "Hello Ed," it read. "I just wanted to say a post–Notes Day thank you. The day was truly amazing, inspirational, informative and as I heard many times throughout the day, from many people, cathartic. If there was any cynicism anywhere, I didn't see it. Coming away from it, I felt as though the company shrank a little. I met new people, got completely new points of view, and learned what other departments struggle with, and succeed with. I don't know if a metric exists to measure the impact of

Notes Day, but from where I was standing, it was huge. In the end, I think we all walked away with a sense of ownership over this amazing place, and its future. A 'we're all in this together' feel. If nothing else, this is a huge victory. John's openness, and courage to speak about his feedback, set an unbelievable bar. His admission put the entire company firmly behind him, and was one of the finest instances of 'leading by example' I can think of. I think we can all learn from that and accept our own introspection/feedback with a similar grace and humility. Thank you so much for creating an environment where this kind of discussion can happen."

You'll remember that the exit forms filled out by Notes Day participants weren't shy about asking, "Who should pitch this proposal?" That was by design—we wanted the best ideas to be pushed forward, not to languish. So in the weeks after Notes Day, all those who'd volunteered to be "idea advocates" were called in to work with Tom and his team to hone their pitches. Then, they began making them to me, John, and our general manager, Jim Morris—and together, we immediately began moving to implement the ones that made sense.

The ideas that emerged on Notes Day, in other words, were not gathering dust in a drawer. They were changing Pixar—meaningfully and for the better. The specific procedural changes will sound mundane to anyone who doesn't work in animation—we implemented a faster, more secure way, to cite a tiny example, of delivering the latest cuts of films to directors—but when you add them all up, they mattered. In the weeks after Notes Day, we implemented four good ideas, committed to five more, and earmarked still a dozen more for continued development. All of them stood to improve either our processes, our culture, or the way Pixar is managed.

Most importantly, though, we broke the logjam that was getting in the way of candor and making it feel dangerous. Some people might measure the day's success by charting the concrete results that resulted from it, and in fact, we have paid attention to that too. But real improvement comes from consistent rigor and participation. For this reason, I believe the biggest payoff of Notes Day was that we made it safer for people to say what they thought. Notes Day made it okay to disagree. That and the feeling our people had that they were part of the solution were its biggest contributions.

What made Notes Day work? To me, it boils down to three factors. First, there was a clear and focused goal. This wasn't a free-for-all but a wide-ranging discussion (organized around topics suggested not by Human Resources or by Pixar's executives, but by the company's employees) aimed at addressing a *specific reality:* the need to cut our costs by 10 percent. While the discussion topics were allowed—even encouraged—to stray into areas that might seem only vaguely related to this goal, the fact that it was there was key. It provided a framework—and it kept us from falling into confusion.

Second, this was an idea championed by those at the highest levels of the company. Had the enormous task of making Notes Day a reality been shunted off on someone who didn't have the clout to throw muscle behind it—and not entrusted to Tom, who in turn recruited the most organized people in the company to help him—it would have been an entirely different experience. Employees wouldn't have bought into the idea because they'd sense that management hadn't, either. And that would have rendered Notes Day moot.

Third, and relatedly, Notes Day was led from within. Many companies hire outside consulting firms to organize their all-staff retreats, and I understand why: Doing them well is a monumental, enormously time-consuming undertaking. But that our own people made Notes Day happen was, I believe, key to its success. Not only did they drive the discussion in meaningful ways, but their involvement also paid its own dividends. Seeing themselves engage and cooperate, steering the agenda toward something that could make a real difference, they remembered why they worked at Pixar. Their commitment was contagious. Notes Day wasn't an end point but a beginning—a way of making room for our employees to step forward and think about their role in our company's future. I said before that problems are easy to identify, but finding the source of those problems is extraordinarily difficult. Notes brought problems to the surface—but we still had the hard work in front of us. Notes Day didn't solve anything all by itself. But it shifted our culture—repaired it, even—in ways that will make us better as we go forward.

I've said it before, but it bears repeating: Things change, constantly, as they should. And with change comes the need for adaptation, for fresh thinking, and, sometimes, for even a total reboot—of your project, your department, your division, or your company as a whole. In times of change, we need support—from our families and from our colleagues. I'm reminded here of a letter written by one of our animators, Austin Madison, which I found particularly uplifting.

"To Whom it May Inspire," Austin wrote. "I, like many of you artists out there, constantly shift between two states. The first (and far more preferable of the two) is white-hot, 'in the zone' seat-of-the-pants, firing on all cylinders creative mode. This is when you lay your pen down and the ideas pour out like wine from a royal chalice! This happens about 3% of the time. The other 97% of the time I am in the frustrated, struggling, office-corner-full-of-crumpled-up-paper mode. The important thing is to slog diligently through this quagmire of discouragement and despair. Put on some audio commentary and listen to the stories of professionals who have been making films for decades going through the same slings and arrows of outrageous production problems. In a word: PERSIST. PERSIST on telling your story. PERSIST on reaching your audience. PERSIST on staying true to your vision . . . ."

I couldn't have put it any better. My goal has never been to tell people how Pixar and Disney figured it all out but rather to show

how we continue to figure it out, every hour of every day. How we persist. The future is not a destination—it is a direction. It is our job, then, to work each day to chart the right course and make corrections when, inevitably, we stray. I already can sense the next crisis coming around the corner. To keep a creative culture vibrant, we must not be afraid of constant uncertainty. We must accept it, just as we accept the weather. Uncertainty and change are life's constants. And that's the fun part.

The truth is, as challenges emerge, mistakes will always be made, and our work is never done. We will always have problems, many of which are hidden from our view; we must work to uncover them and assess our own role in them, even if doing so means making ourselves uncomfortable; when we then come across a problem, we must marshal all our energies to solve it. If those assertions sound familiar, that's because I used them to kick off this book. There's something else that bears repeating here: Unleashing creativity requires that we loosen the controls, accept risk, trust our colleagues, work to clear the path for them, and pay attention to anything that creates fear. Doing all these things won't necessarily make the job of managing a creative culture easier. But ease isn't the goal; excellence is.

THE STEVE WE KNEW

It was the end of 1985, and the computer division I ran at Lucas-film was short on suitors and, it seemed, out of options. Our tires had been kicked by anyone with even the slightest interest in computer-generated imaging. We'd made a promising match with General Motors, only to be left at the altar. Then Steve Jobs swooped in. As I related earlier, it was around this time that one of his attorneys pulled us aside during a meeting and jokingly—I think—said that we were about to climb aboard the Steve Jobs roller coaster. Get on, we did, and what a ride it would prove to be—with all of the attendant ups and downs.

I worked closely with Steve Jobs for twenty-six years. To this day, for all that has been written about him, I don't believe that any of it comes close to capturing the man I knew. I've been frustrated that the stories about him tend to focus so narrowly on his extreme traits and the negative, difficult aspects of his personality. Inevitably, profiles of Steve describe him as stubborn and imperious, a man who held steadfastly and unwaveringly to his own ideals, refusing to budge or change, and who often tried to browbeat others into doing things his way. While many of the anecdotes people repeat about his behavior as a young executive are probably accurate, the overall portrait is way off the mark. The reality is, Steve changed profoundly in the years that I knew him.

The word *genius* is used a lot these days—too much, I think—but with Steve, I actually think it was warranted. Still, when I first came to know him, he was frequently dismissive and brusque. This is the part of Steve that people love to write about. I realize that it is difficult to understand people who deviate so radically from the norm, like Steve did, and I suspect that those who focus on his more extreme traits do so because those traits are entertaining and revealing in some way. To let them drive Steve's narrative, however, is to miss the more important story. In the time I worked with Steve, he didn't just gain the kind of practical experience you would expect to acquire while running two dynamic, successful businesses; he also got smarter about when to stop pushing people and how to keep pushing them, if necessary, without breaking them. He became fairer and wiser, and his understanding of partnership deepened—in large part because of his marriage to Laurene and his relationships with the children he loved so much. This shift didn't lead him to abandon his famous commitment to innovation; it solidified it. At the same time, he developed into a kinder, more self-aware leader. And I think Pixar played a role in that development.

Remember, in the late 1980s, when Pixar was founded, Steve was spending most of his time building NeXT, the computer company he'd started after being forced out of Apple. At Pixar, none of us, including Steve, knew what we were doing. Steve would overreach in early negotiations with customers, which sometimes worked but sometimes backfired. At NeXT, for instance, he struck a $100 million deal that allowed IBM to use the NeXT software. The huge dollar amount, combined with the fact that Steve didn't give IBM rights to subsequent versions of the software, seemed like a home run deal for NeXT. In fact, Steve had overreached—his behavior created ill will, and he later told me he learned from that.

In those early days, Steve sensed that there was something quite special going on at Pixar, but it frustrated him that he couldn't figure it out—and kept losing money in the meantime. He had an expensive group that was ahead of its time. Could he hang on long enough for that potential to flower, especially if he didn't know if it ever *would* flower? What kind of person signs on for that? Would you?

We tend to think of emotion and logic as two distinct, mutually exclusive domains. Not Steve. From the beginning, when making decisions, passion was a key part of his calculus. At first, he often elicited it in a ham-handed way, by making extreme or outrageous statements and challenging people to respond. But at Pixar, even when we were a long way from being in the black, that aggressiveness was tempered by his acknowledgment that we knew things about graphics and storytelling that he did not. He respected our determination to be the first to make a computer-animated feature film. He didn't tell us how to do our work or come in and impose his will. Even when we were unsure how to reach our goal, our passion was something Steve recognized and valued. That's what Steve, John, and I ultimately bonded over: passion for excellence—a passion so ardent we were willing to argue and struggle and stay together, even when things got extremely uncomfortable.

I remember being struck by Steve's response to passion when we were working on our second film, *A Bug's Life*. There was an internal disagreement about the aspect ratio of the film—the proportional relationship between its width and its height. In a movie theater, films are displayed in widescreen format, where the width of the picture is more than twice the height; on the TVs of that time, by contrast, the width of the picture was only one and one-third times the height, more of a boxy shape. When you make a video version of a widescreen film that will be viewed on a TV monitor, then, you either end up with black bars at the top and bottom of the screen, or you clip off the sides of the picture completely, neither of which is a good representation of the original film.

On *A Bug's Life,* the marketing people were in conflict with the filmmakers. The filmmakers wanted the widescreen format because it led to a better panoramic experience in the theater, which they believed to be more important than the home viewing experience. The marketers, believing that consumers were less likely to buy a video with black bars on the top and bottom, argued that the widescreen format would mean a reduction in our DVD sales. Steve—no film buff—agreed with the marketing people that we would be hurting ourselves financially if we released the movie in widescreen. The debate about this was still unresolved when, one afternoon, I took Steve around the offices so he could see some of Pixar's departments in action, and we ended up in a room full of people who were working on lighting a scene from *A Bug's Life.* The production designer on the film, Bill Cone, was showing some images on monitors that happened to be in widescreen format.

Seeing this, Steve interjected, in his way, that it was "nuts" for us to be making a widescreen movie. Bill, to his credit, came right back at him, explaining why the widescreen format was absolutely crucial from an *artistic* standpoint. An intense back-and-forth followed. I wouldn't call it an argument, but it was definitely heated. The discussion seemed to end inconclusively, and Steve and I continued on our rounds.

Later, Bill came to see me, looking rattled. "Oh, my God," he said. "I was just arguing with Steve Jobs. Did I blow it?"

"On the contrary," I told him. "You won."

I could see something that Bill couldn't: Steve had responded to Bill's passion about the issue. The fact that Bill was willing to stand up so forcefully and articulately for what he believed showed Steve that Bill's ideas were worthy of respect. Steve never raised the format issue with us again.

It wasn't that passion trumped logic in Steve's mind. He was well aware that decisions must never be based on emotions alone. But he also saw that creativity wasn't linear, that art was not commerce, and that to insist upon applying dollars-and-cents logic was to risk disrupting the thing that set us apart. Steve put a premium on both sides of this equation, logic and emotion, and the way he maintained that balance was key to understanding him.

In the mid-1990s, it became clear that Pixar, long housed in a few cramped, tilt-up buildings in Point Richmond, California, was going to need a new home. The time had come to establish a proper headquarters—a place of our own, suited to our needs. Steve threw himself into designing it, and the magnificent main building that we occupy today is the outgrowth of all that work. But it didn't come easily.

Steve's first pass at a design was based on some peculiar ideas he had about how to force interaction among people. At an off-site staff meeting to discuss these plans in 1998, several people rose to complain about his intent to build a single women's and a single men's restroom. Steve relented, but he was clearly frustrated that people didn't understand what he was trying to do: Bring people together out of necessity. At first, Steve struggled to find the best way to enable that mutual experience.

Next, he envisioned a separate building for each movie under production—the idea being that each crew would benefit from having its own contained space, free of distraction. I wasn't so sure about that, so I asked him to go on a road trip.

Showing, not telling, worked best with Steve, which is why I coaxed him south to Burbank for a tour of the four-story glazed-glass-and-aluminum building on Thornton Avenue known as Northside. Disney Animation had taken it over in 1997, using it to house the crew for its first 3D animated movie, *Dinosaur,* among other projects.

But the building was more famous for what it had housed in the

1940s: Lockheed's top-secret Skunk Works division, which de-signed jet fighters, spy planes, and at least one stealth fighter. I loved that bit of history—and the fact that the name Skunk Works itself had been borrowed from Al Capp's newspaper comic strip *Li'l Abner*. In that strip, there was a running joke about a mysteri-ous and malodorous place deep in the forest called the "Skonk Works" where a strong beverage was brewed from skunks, old shoes, and other strange ingredients.

Steve knew that my purpose that day wasn't to discuss comic strips or aviation history but to show him the building—a welcom-ing space where several hundred animators worked on multiple projects simultaneously, under a single roof. I liked the feel of the wide-open hallways. I recall Steve being critical of numerous facets of the building's layout, but after an hour or so wandering around the place, I could tell he was getting the message: Creating separate buildings for each film would be isolating. He saw firsthand the way that the Disney people took advantage of the open floor plan, sharing information and brainstorming. Steve was a big believer in the power of accidental mingling; he knew that creativity was not a solitary endeavor. But our trip to Northside helped clarify that thinking. In a creative company, separating your people into dis-tinct silos—Project A over here, Project B over there—can be coun-terproductive.

After that trip, he met again with his architects and laid out the principles for a single building. He took the creation of a new Pixar headquarters as a personal responsibility.

You've heard the saying "Your employees are your most impor-tant asset." For most executives, these are just words you trot out to make people feel good—while they may be accepted as true, few leaders alter their behavior or make decisions based upon them. But Steve did, taking that principle and building our headquarters around it. Everything about the place was designed to encourage people to mingle, meet, and communicate, to support our film-making by enhancing our ability to work together.

In the end, Steve presided over every detail of our new building's construction, from the arched steel bridges that straddle the
central atrium to the type of chairs in our screening rooms. He
didn't want perceived barriers, so the stairs were open and inviting.
He wanted a single entrance to the building so that we saw each
other as we entered. We had meeting rooms, restrooms, a mail-
room, three theaters, a game area, and an eating area all at the
center in our atrium (where to this day, everyone gathers to eat,
play ping pong, or be briefed by Pixar's leaders on the company's
goings on). This all resulted in cross-traffic—people encountered
each other all day long, inadvertently, which meant a better flow of
communication and increased the possibility of chance encounters.
You felt the energy in the building. Steve had thought all this
through with the metalogic of a philosopher and the meticulous-
ness of a craftsman. He believed in simple materials, masterfully
constructed. He wanted all the steel exposed, not painted. He
wanted glass doors to be flush with the walls. No wonder that when
it opened in the fall of 2000, after four years of planning and construction, Pixar's people—who typically worked for four years on
each film—took to calling the building "Steve's movie."

I admit that there were moments when I worried that Pixar
would fall prey to the "edifice complex," wherein companies build
shiny headquarters that are mere extensions of executive ego. But
that worry proved unfounded. From the day we moved in, on
Thanksgiving weekend of 2000, the building became an extraordinary and fertile home. Moreover, in our employees' minds, it trans-
formed Steve—always our external defender—into an integral part
of our internal culture. The environment was so exemplary and so
clearly attributed to Steve that everyone could appreciate his singular contribution to—and understanding of—the way we worked.

That appreciation was a positive development because, as I've
said before, upon meeting Steve, people typically had to become
accustomed to his style. Brad Bird remembers a meeting during the
making of *The Incredibles,* soon after he joined the studio, when

Steve hurt his feelings by saying that some of the *Incredibles* art-work looked "kind of Saturday morning"—a reference to the low-budget cartoons that Hanna-Barbera and others produced. "In my world, that's kind of like saying, 'Your mama sleeps around,'" Brad recalls. "I was seething. When the meeting ended, I went over to Andrew and said, 'Man, Steve just said something that really pissed me off.' And Andrew, without even asking what it was, said, 'Only *one* thing?'" Brad came to understand that Steve was speaking not as a critic but as the ultimate advocate. Too often, animated superheroes had been made on the cheap and looked that way, too—on that Steve and Brad could agree. *The Incredibles,* he was implying, had to reach higher. "He was just saying that we have to show this is something bigger," Brad says. "And that epitomized Steve."

Though no one outside Pixar knew it, Steve developed a lasting bond with our directors. At first I thought this was just because he appreciated their creative and leadership abilities and they, in turn, appreciated the support and insight he gave them. But as I paid closer attention, I recognized there was something very important that they shared. When directors pitch an idea, for example, they invest totally, even though a part of them knows that in the end, it may not work at all. Pitching is a way of testing material, taking its measure—and, importantly, strengthening it—by observing how it plays to an audience. But if the idea doesn't fly, they are extremely adept at dropping it and moving on. This is a rare skill, one that Steve had too.

Steve had a remarkable knack for letting go of things that didn't work. If you were in an argument with him, and you convinced him that you were right, he would instantly change his mind. He didn't hold on to an idea because he had once believed it to be brilliant. His ego didn't attach to the suggestions he made, even as he threw his full weight behind them. When Steve saw Pixar's directors do the same, he recognized them as kindred spirits.

One of the dangers of this approach can be that if you are

pitching intently, your very exuberance can make others reluctant to respond candidly. When someone has a strong personality, others can wilt in the face of their intensity. How do you prevent this from happening? The trick is to shift the emphasis in any meeting away from the source of an idea and onto the idea itself. People often place too much significance on the source of an idea, accepting it (or not criticizing it) because it comes from Steve or a respected director. But Steve had no interest in that kind of affirmation. Countless times, I remember watching him toss ideas—pretty far-out ideas—into the air, just to see how they played. And if they didn't play well, he would move on. This is, in effect, a form of storytelling—searching for the best way to frame and communicate an idea. If people didn't understand Steve, they would misinterpret his floating of ideas as advocacy. And they would wrongly perceive his enthusiasm or insistence as intransigence or bullheadedness. Instead, he was gauging reactions to his ideas to see whether or not he *should* become their advocate.

Steve is not commonly described as a storyteller, and he was always careful to say he didn't know the first thing about filmmaking. Yet part of his bond with our directors stemmed from the fact that he knew how important it was to construct a story that connected with people. This was a skill he used in his presentations at Apple. When he got up in front of an audience to introduce a new product, he understood that he would communicate more effectively if he put forward a narrative, and anyone who ever saw him do it could tell you that he gave extraordinary and carefully crafted performances.

At Pixar, Steve was able to participate in *other* people's crafting of *their* stories, and I believe this process helped him understand more about human dynamics. There was something about applying his intellect to the emotion of a film—Was it landing? Did it ring true?—that freed him up, and he came to see that Pixar's success was reliant on its movies connecting deeply with an audience. Given the way his behavior has been described in the past, you might think that giving constructive feedback to a vulnerable director on a not-baked-yet film would not be something that Steve could do gracefully, if at all. But in fact, over time, he became quite skilled at it. Pete Docter remembers Steve telling him once that he hoped in his next life he would come back as a Pixar director. I have no doubt that if he did, he'd be one of the best.

As summer gave way to fall in 2003, Steve became increasingly hard to get ahold of. He was known for responding to emails, at all times of day and night, within minutes. But now, I would call or email and not hear back. In October, he dropped by Pixar, which was unusual—unless there was a board meeting, we usually briefed each other by phone. When John and I sat down with him, Steve closed the door and told us that he'd been having this aching in his back that wouldn't go away. His doctor had recently sent him for a CAT scan, which revealed pancreatic cancer. Ninety-five percent of people with this diagnosis are not alive five years later, he told us. Steve was determined to fight, but he knew he might not win.

Over the next eight years, Steve underwent a seemingly endless variety of treatments, both traditional and experimental. As his energy waned, our interactions became less frequent, though he still called weekly to check in, offer advice, and voice concerns. At one point during this period, John and I drove down to Apple to have lunch with him. Afterward, Steve took us into a secure room where Apple kept the supersecret products and showed us an early prototype of something he called the iPhone. It had a touch screen that engaged the user, making navigation not just easy but fun. We could instantly see that it made the phones we were carrying in our pockets look like ancient artifacts. He was particularly jazzed about it, he said, because it was his goal not just to create a phone people used but to design a phone people *loved*—one that made their lives better, both functionally and aesthetically. He thought Apple had succeeded in creating such a device.

As we walked out of the vault, Steve stopped in the hallway and said he had been working on a list of three things he wanted to do—and I remember the words precisely—"before I sail away." One goal that mattered enormously to him was to roll out the product he'd just shown us, along with a few others that he believed would ensure Apple's future. The second was to safeguard Pixar's continued success. And the third and most important was to set his three youngest children on a good path. I remember him saying that he hoped he would be around to watch his son Reed, then in 8th grade, graduate from high school. To hear this once-unstoppable man scaling back his hopes and ambitions to a handful of last wishes was heartbreaking, of course, but I remember thinking that when Steve said it, it sounded natural. It felt like he had come to terms with the inevitability of not being here.

In the end, he would achieve all three of his goals.

On a Sunday afternoon in February 2007, my daughter Jeannie and I stepped out of a town car, onto a long, red carpet . . . and ran smack into Steve Jobs. It was a few hours before the 79th Annual Academy Awards, and to get to our seats, the three of us had to plow through the crush of people outside the Kodak Theatre in the heart of Hollywood. *Cars* was nominated for Best Animated Feature Film, and, like all award hopefuls, we had a few preshow jitters. But as the three of us jostled along, Steve looked around at the circus—the elegantly turned-out men and women, the scrum of television interviewers, the throngs of paparazzi and screaming onlookers, the line of limousines pulling up at the curb—and said, "What this scene really needs is a Buddhist monk lighting himself on fire."

Perspective is so hard to capture. I worked with Steve for more than a quarter-century—longer, I believe, than anyone else—and I saw an arc to his life that does not accord with the one-note portraits of relentless perfectionism I've read in magazines, newspapers, and even his own authorized biography. Relentless Steve—the boorish, brilliant, but emotionally tone-deaf guy that we first came to know—changed into a different man during the last two decades of his life. All of us who knew Steve well noticed the transformation. He became more sensitive not only to other people's feelings but also to their value as contributors to the creative process.

His experience with Pixar was part of this change. Steve aspired to create utilitarian things that also brought joy; it was his way of making the world a better place. That was part of why Pixar made him so proud—because he felt the world *was* better for the films we made. He used to say regularly that as brilliant as Apple products were, eventually they all ended up in landfills. Pixar movies, on the other hand, would live forever. He believed, as I do, that because they dig for deeper truths, our movies will endure, and he found beauty in that idea. John talks about "the nobility of entertaining people." Steve understood this mission to his core, particularly toward the end of his life, and—knowing that entertaining wasn't his primary skill set—he felt lucky to have been involved in it.

Pixar occupied a special place in Steve's world, and his role evolved during our time together. In the early years, he was our benefactor, the one who paid the bills to keep the lights on. Later, he became our protector—a constructive critic internally but our fiercest defender to the outside. We had some trying times together, to be sure, but through those difficulties, we forged a rare bond. I've always thought that Pixar was like a well-loved stepchild for Steve—conceived before he entered our lives, maybe, but still nurtured by him in our formative years. In the decade before his death, I watched Steve change Pixar even as Pixar changed him. I say this while acknowledging that no segment of one's life can be divorced from the rest; Steve was, of course, always learning from his family and from his colleagues at Apple. But there was something special about the time he spent with us—enhanced, counterintuitively, by the fact that Pixar was his sideline. His wife and children, of course, were paramount, and Apple was his first and most heralded professional achievement; Pixar was a place he could relax a little and play. While he never lost his intensity, we watched him develop the ability to listen. More and more, he could express empathy and caring and patience. He became truly wise. The change in him was real, and it was deep.

In chapter 5, I mentioned that, at my insistence, Steve didn't attend Braintrust meetings. But he would often give notes after movies were screened for Pixar's board of directors. Once or twice per movie, when a crisis loomed, he would inevitably come in and say something that helped alter our perceptions and improve the film. Whenever offering a note, he always began the same way: "I'm not really a filmmaker, so you can ignore everything I say. . . ." Then he would proceed, with startling efficiency, to diagnose the problem precisely. Steve focused on the problem itself, not the filmmakers, which made his critiques all the more powerful. If you sense a criticism is being leveled for personal reasons, it is easy to dismiss. You couldn't dismiss Steve. Every film he commented on benefited from his insight.

But while in the early days his opinions would swing wildly and his delivery could be abrupt, he became more articulate and observant of people's feelings as time went on. He learned to read the room, demonstrating skills that, years earlier, I didn't think he had. Some people have said that he got mellower with age, but I don't think that's an adequate description of what happened; it sounds too passive, as if he just was letting more go. Steve's transformation was an active one. He continued to engage; he just changed the way he went about it.

There is a phrase that many have used to describe Steve's knack for accomplishing the impossible. Steve, they say, employed a "reality distortion field." In his biography of Steve, Walter Isaacson devoted an entire chapter to it, quoting Andy Hertzfeld, a member of the original Mac team at Apple, saying, "The reality distortion field was a confounding mélange of a charismatic rhetorical style, indomitable will, and eagerness to bend any fact to fit the purpose at hand." I heard the phrase used fairly often around Pixar, too. Some people, after listening to Steve, would feel that they had reached a new level of insight, only to find afterward that they could not reconstruct the steps in his reasoning; then the insight would evaporate, leaving them scratching their heads, feeling they had been led down the garden path. Thus, reality distortion.

I disliked the phrase because it carried a whiff of negativity—implying that Steve would try to will a fantasy world into being on a whim, without regard to how his refusal to face facts meant that everybody around him had to pull all-nighters and upend their lives in the hopes of meeting his unmeetable expectations. Much has been made of Steve's refusal to follow rules—realities—that applied to others; famously, for example, he did not put a license plate on his car. But to focus too much on this is to miss something important. He recognized that many rules were in fact arbitrary. Yes, he tested boundaries and crossed the line at times. As a behavioral trait, that can be seen as antisocial—or if it happens to change the world, it can earn you the label "visionary." We frequently support the idea of pushing boundaries in theory, ignoring the trouble it can cause in practice.

Before Pixar was called Pixar, it was devoted to accomplishing something that had never been done before. For me, this had been a lifelong goal, and my colleagues at Pixar—Steve among them—were willing to make that leap, too, before computers had enough speed or memory to make it a reality. A characteristic of creative people is that they imagine making the impossible possible. That imagining—dreaming, noodling, audaciously rejecting what is (for the moment) true—is the way we discover what is new or important. Steve understood the value of science and law, but he also understood that complex systems respond in nonlinear, unpredictable ways. And that creativity, at its best, surprises us all.

There is another, different meaning of reality distortion for me. It stems from my belief that our decisions and actions have consequences and that those consequences shape our future. Our actions change our reality. Our intentions matter. Most people believe that their actions have consequences but don't think through the implications of that belief. But Steve did. He believed, as I do, that it is precisely by acting on our intentions and staying true to our values that we change the world.

On August 24, 2011, Steve resigned as Apple's CEO, as he was no longer able to keep pace with the rigors of the job he loved. Shortly thereafter, I was exercising at home early in the morning when the phone rang. It was Steve. To be honest, I can't remember exactly what was said, because I knew he was nearing the end, and that was an incredibly difficult reality to deal with. But I recall that his voice was strong—stronger than it should have been, given what he'd been through—as he talked about how many years we'd worked together and how grateful he was to have had that experience. I remember him saying that he felt honored to have been a part of Pixar's success. I told him I felt honored, too, and was thankful for his friendship, his example, and his loyalty. When we hung up, I said to myself, "That was the goodbye call." I was right: He would live six more weeks, but I would never hear his voice again.

On a Monday morning five days after his death, the entire Pixar workforce gathered in the atrium of the building Steve had built to mourn and remember. By 11 A.M., the atrium was full of people, and it was time to begin. I stood off to the side, thinking about the man who'd been Pixar's fiercest champion and a close friend. It fell on me to speak first.

There were so many things I could say about Steve—how he bought the division that would become Pixar from George Lucas in 1986, saving us from extinction; how he encouraged us to embark on our first feature film, Toy Story, three years later, when the idea of a computer-animated film still seemed beyond our reach; how he'd solidified our future by selling us to Disney and then ensured

our autonomy by orchestrating a merger that created a true partnership; how he helped take us from forty-three employees to the
1,100 men and women who stood in front of me now. Looking
back, I could recall the earliest moments of our relationship—him
probing and poking, me honing and fortifying my ideas. He had
made me more focused, more resilient, smarter, better. Over time,
I had come to rely on his demanding specificity, which never failed
to help me clarify my own thinking. I could already feel the weight
of his absence.

"I remember twenty-five years ago in February, the day that
Pixar was formed," I began, recalling how we gathered in a conference room at Lucasfilm to sign the papers transferring majority
ownership to Steve. We were exhausted, having spent months looking for potential suitors before Steve stepped forward. For those
who weren't at Pixar in the beginning, I recalled how Steve had
pulled Alvy Ray Smith and me aside, put his arms around us, and
said, "As we're going through this, there's one thing I dearly ask.
And that is that we be loyal to each other." I told my colleagues
that Steve had always made good on that promise. "Over the years,
Pixar and Steve went through a lot of changes and a lot of hard-
ships," I said. "These were very hard times. Pixar came close to
collapsing. Any other investor or venture capitalist would have
given up." But not Steve. He demanded of himself what he'd asked
of us: loyalty.

"I don't know what happens in the future," I concluded as the
sun streamed through the skylights above us. "But I do believe that
Steve's focus on passion and quality will take us places that we cannot yet perceive. And for that I am truly grateful." At that moment,
I was more aware than ever of how important it was to understand
and protect what had made Steve so proud. It had always been my
goal to create a culture at Pixar that would outlast its leaders—
Steve, John, and me. Now one of us had taken his leave too soon,
and the job of fortifying that culture—ensuring that it would be
self-sustaining—was left to John and me.

When I was done, I offered the microphone to others who'd had a close relationship with Steve and, one by one, they stepped onto the podium. Andrew Stanton described Steve as "the creative firewall." With Steve around, the people of Pixar "were like free-range chickens," he said, getting a laugh. "Steve would do anything to keep us creatively safe."

The ever-observant Pete Docter got up next and recalled one of the most endearing images he had of Steve. During a meeting one day years ago, Pete noticed that Steve had two small, identical holes in one of the legs of his Levis 501s. Steve shifted in his seat, and Pete noticed the same two holes on the other leg, too, in the same spot, right above the ankle. As Pete was trying—and failing—to imagine a reason for these symmetrical holes, Steve reached down to pull up his socks by grabbing them through his pants—putting his fingers right where the holes were! "Here Steve was worth millions, but apparently getting a new pair of pants was not important to him," Pete said. "Or maybe he needed new socks with better elastic. Either way, it was a humanizing aspect to this larger-than-life guy."

Brad Bird recalled that when he first started talking to Pixar about doing *The Incredibles,* he wasn't sure if he would take the offer: He was still considering staying with Warner Bros., which had released his earlier movie, *The Iron Giant.* "But it took me a month to get a meeting with the administration of the studio I'd just made a movie for," Brad said. "And in the meantime, Steve knew the name of my wife, asked how my kids were by name—he did his homework. I thought, 'What the hell am I doing talking to Warner Bros.?' It cinched the deal."

"Steve held the bar for quality," Brad continued. "He was always about the long run. He was into Buddhism, but I see him more as just a spiritual guy. I have to believe that he believed in something beyond this"—he hesitated, overcome for a moment—"and that's where we'll see him again. Where cream rises to the top. So here's to you, Steve, and to the long run."

It was John's turn now. The room fell silent, but you could feel the current of emotion around us all. Stepping to the podium, he described what an honor it had been to be Steve's friend as he changed—like we all aspire to do—for the better.

"When Steve first bought us," John said, "there was a confidence he had. Some people call it arrogance; I call it confidence. But it was basically a belief that he could do anybody's job better than they could. That's why people hated getting into an elevator at Apple with Steve because they felt by the time they got to the top floor, they'd probably be fired." Again, the room broke out in laughter. "But as Pixar evolved into an animation studio, he started to look at all the work that we were doing, and he was amazed. He realized he couldn't even come close to doing what we could do. I like to think that when he was building Pixar, when he and Laurene got married and he had his kids, that that realization of how brilliant the people here at Pixar were—that all this helped make him the amazing leader he was."

Three weeks before, John had visited Steve for the last time. "We sat for about an hour talking about coming projects he was so interested in," John said, his voice catching. "I looked at him and I realized this man had given me—given us—everything that we could ever want. I gave him a big hug. I kissed him on the cheek and for all of you"—John was crying now—"I said, 'Thank you. I love you, Steve.'"

The room erupted in applause, which only ebbed when one of the Pixar Singers took the stage. In a quiet voice, he announced that just as our resident a capella group had sung at every Pixar wrap party in our company's history, it would now sing for Steve, too. Standing in the building that we all called "Steve's movie," I couldn't help but think that he would have loved this—a fitting wrap to the production that was Steve Jobs.

The roller coaster came to a stop and a good friend got off, but what a ride we'd taken together. It had been one hell of a trip.

STARTING POINTS

THOUGHTS FOR MANAGING A CREATIVE CULTURE

Here are some of the principles we've developed over the years to enable and protect a healthy creative culture. I know that when you distill a complex idea into a T-shirt slogan, you risk giving the illusion of understanding—and, in the process, of sapping the idea of its power. An adage worth repeating is also halfway to being irrelevant. You end up with something that is easy to say but not connected to behavior. But while I have been dismissive of reductive truths throughout this book, I do have a point of view, and I thought it might be helpful to share some of the principles that I hold most dear here with you. The trick is to think of each statement as a starting point, as a prompt toward deeper inquiry, and not as a conclusion.

- Give a good idea to a mediocre team, and they will screw it up. Give a mediocre idea to a great team, and they will either fix it or come up with something better. If you get the team right, chances are that they'll get the ideas right.

- When looking to hire people, give their potential to grow more weight than their current skill level. What they will be capable of tomorrow is more important than what they can do today.

- Always try to hire people who are smarter than you. Always take a chance on better, even if it seems like a potential threat.

- If there are people in your organization who feel they are not free to suggest ideas, you lose. Do not discount ideas from unexpected sources. Inspiration can, and does, come from anywhere.

- It isn't enough merely to be open to ideas from others. Engaging the collective brainpower of the people you work with is an active, ongoing process. As a manager, you must coax ideas out of your staff and constantly push them to contribute.

- There are many valid reasons why people aren't candid with one another in a work environment. Your job is to search for those reasons and then address them.

- Likewise, if someone disagrees with you, there is a reason. Our first job is to understand the reasoning behind their conclusions.

- Further, if there is fear in an organization, there is a reason for it—our job is (a) to find what's causing it, (b) to understand it, and (c) to try to root it out.

- There is nothing quite as effective, when it comes to shutting down alternative viewpoints, as being convinced you are right.

- In general, people are hesitant to say things that might rock the boat. Braintrust meetings, dailies, postmortems, and Notes Day are all efforts to reinforce the idea that it is okay to express yourself. All are mechanisms of self-assessment that seek to uncover what's real.

- If there is more truth in the hallways than in meetings, you have a problem.

- Many managers feel that if they are not notified about problems before others are or if they are surprised in a meeting, then that is a sign of disrespect. Get over it.

- Careful "messaging" to downplay problems makes you appear to be lying, deluded, ignorant, or uncaring. Sharing problems is an act of inclusion that makes employees feel invested in the larger enterprise.

- The first conclusions we draw from our successes and failures are typically wrong. Measuring the outcome without evaluating the process is deceiving.

- Do not fall for the illusion that by preventing errors, you won't have errors to fix. The truth is, the cost of preventing errors is often far greater than the cost of fixing them.

- Change and uncertainty are part of life. Our job is not to resist them but to build the capability to recover when unexpected events occur. If you don't always try to uncover what is unseen and understand its nature, you will be ill prepared to lead.

- Similarly, it is not the manager's job to prevent risks. It is the manager's job to make it safe to take them.

- Failure isn't a necessary evil. In fact, it isn't evil at all. It is a necessary consequence of doing something new.

- Trust doesn't mean that you trust that someone won't screw up— it means you trust them even when they do screw up.

- The people ultimately responsible for implementing a plan must be empowered to make decisions when things go wrong, even before getting approval. Finding and fixing problems is everybody's job. Anyone should be able to stop the production line.

- The desire for everything to run smoothly is a false goal—it leads to measuring people by the mistakes they make rather than by their ability to solve problems.

- Don't wait for things to be perfect before you share them with others. Show early and show often. It'll be pretty when we get there, but it won't be pretty along the way. And that's as it should be.

- A company's communication structure should not mirror its organizational structure. Everybody should be able to talk to anybody.

- Be wary of making too many rules. Rules can simplify life for managers, but they can be demeaning to the 95 percent who behave well. Don't create rules to rein in the other 5 percent— address abuses of common sense individually. This is more work but ultimately healthier.

- Imposing limits can encourage a creative response. Excellent work can emerge from uncomfortable or seemingly untenable circumstances.

- Engaging with exceptionally hard problems forces us to think differently.

- An organization, as a whole, is more conservative and resistant to change than the individuals who comprise it. Do not assume that general agreement will lead to change—it takes substantial energy to move a group, even when all are on board.

- The healthiest organizations are made up of departments whose agendas differ but whose goals are interdependent. If one agenda wins, we all lose.

- Our job as managers in creative environments is to protect new ideas from those who don't understand that in order for greatness to emerge, there must be phases of not-so-greatness. Protect the future, not the past.

- New crises are not always lamentable—they test and demonstrate a company's values. The process of problem-solving often bonds people together and keeps the culture in the present.

- *Excellence, quality,* and *good* should be earned words, attributed by others to us, not proclaimed by us about ourselves.

- Do not accidentally make stability a goal. Balance is more important than stability.

- Don't confuse the process with the goal. Working on our processes to make them better, easier, and more efficient is an indispensable activity and something we should continually work on—but it is not the goal. Making the product great is the goal.

ACKNOWLEDGMENTS

ED CATMULL

Writing a book like this one, which draws on so many years of learning and experience, would not be possible without the input of countless people. I'm going to call out several of them by name, but in truth this book benefited from the work of all of my colleagues and friends at Pixar and Disney. I am grateful to each and every one of them.

First, I must thank John Lasseter, chief creative officer of Pixar and Disney Animation and my longtime friend. John is open and generous to his core. He contributed many memories and insights. Bob Iger, the chairman and chief executive of the Walt Disney Company, supported this project from the beginning and his feedback made it immeasurably better. Alan Horn and Alan Bergman, the chairman and president, respectively, of Walt Disney Studios, have been wise leaders who have worked with me as we have gone through many changes.

I am lucky to have an incredible team of managers whom I work with every day: at Pixar, general manager Jim Morris and Lori McAdams, vice president of human resources; at Disney Animation, general manager Andrew Millstein and Ann Le Cam, the vice president of both production and human resources. All four are excellent partners who make me smarter.

This book never would have happened without my agent, Christy Fletcher, and my editor at Random House, Andy Ward. Andy has truly shepherded this project from its inception to its completion. He's a great editor who made every page more readable, more compelling, and simply better. I must also thank Wendy Tanzillo, my assistant of thirteen years, without whose care and attention my life would veer toward chaos.

I've had many, many discussions over the years that have helped me wrestle with some of the more difficult concepts in this book. Among those whose willingness to engage aided me immeasurably are Michael Arndt, Brad Bird, and Bob Peterson. I also benefitted from particularly deep conversations with Phillip Moffitt, president of the Life Balance Institute.

I asked many people to read this book as it took shape. I approached that process much as we do screenings of our films, figuring that the more notes I got, from the most varied group of people, the better and clearer the book would become. Given the length of this book, I know this was no small favor I was asking, and yet each of these people gave me their time without hesitation. For that, I thank: Jennifer Aaker, Darla Anderson, Brad Bird, Jeannie Catmull, Lindsey Collins, Pete Docter, Bob Friese, Marc Greenberg, Casey Hawkins, Byron Howard, Michael Jennings, Michael Johnson, Jim Kennedy, John Lasseter, Ann Le Cam, Jason Levy, Lawrence Levy, Emily Loose, Lenny Mendonca, Andrew Millstein, Jim Morris, Donna Newbold, Karen Paik, Tom Porter, Kori Rae, Jonas Rivera, Ali Rowghani, Peter Sims, Andy Smith, Andrew Stanton, Galyn Susman, Bob Sutton, Karen Tenkoff, Lee Unkrich, and Jamie Woolf. Robert Baird, Dan Gerson, and Nathan Greno arrived in my office one day with an enormous white board; they were particularly helpful in structuring the book. Moreover, Christine Freeman, Pixar's archivist, provided enormous research help, Elyse

Klaidman and Cory Knox kept many of the pieces moving when I'd lost track of them, and Oren Jacob helped fill in important gaps.

I should also note that the ideas in this book were developed over a period of forty-five years, and innumerable characters participated in this journey. This is not a history book. While I do provide some chronological narrative to support the concepts I present, I am aware that some people—especially those who do technical work—are underrepresented, largely because describing what they do is complex and less accessible. For the record, then, Bill Reeves, Eben Ostby, and Alvy Ray Smith were essential to what I deem Pixar's greatest triumph—the integration of art and technology—and this book owes them a debt of gratitude.

Finally, to my wife, Susan, and the seven children circling our lives—Ben, David, Jeannie, Matt, Michael, Miles, and Sean— I thank you for your patience, support, and love. Thanks also go to my ninety-two-year-old father, Earl Catmull, whose memory of my childhood remains clearer than mine, and whose descriptions of my earliest years were invaluable.

AMY WALLACE

Thanks go to my agent, Elyse Cheney, for bringing me this project. To Andy Ward, at Random House, for his all-around brilliance. To my son, Jack Newton, for being his insightful, funny, and inspiring self. To Mary Melton and Jim Nelson, my enormously supportive editors at *Los Angeles* magazine and *GQ*, for making it possible for me to take this book on. To everyone at Pixar and Disney Animation who helped nail down key moments, but particularly to Brad Bird, Pete Docter, Christine Freeman, Elyse Klaidman, John Lasseter, Jim Morris, Tom Porter, Andrew Stanton, and Wendy Tanzillo. To the historians and biographers whose books helped me ask better questions: Walter Isaacson (*Steve Jobs*), Karen Paik (*To Infinity and Beyond! The Story of Pixar Animation Studios*),

David A. Price (*The Pixar Touch: The Making of a Company*), Michael Rubin (*Droidmaker: George Lucas and the Digital Revolution*), and James B. Stewart (*Disney War*). To my parents, for teaching me that "If you want to write, read," and to my dear friends who never stop giving good counsel: Julie Buckner, Karla Clement, Sacha Feinman, Ben Goldhirsh, Carla Hall, Gary Harris, Nancy Hass, Jon Herbst, Claire Hoffman, Beth Hubbard, Justin McLeod, J. R. Moehringer, Bob Roe, Julia St. Pierre, Minna Towbin Pinger, Valerie Van Galder, Brendan Vaughan, and Sherri Wolf. Finally, to Ed Catmull, for giving me a chance and for inviting me inside.

INDEX

Page numbers in *italics* refer to illustrations.

ABOUT THE AUTHORS

ED CATMULL is co-founder of Pixar Animation Studios and president of Pixar Animation and Disney Animation. He has been honored with five Academy Awards, including the Gordon E. Sawyer Award for lifetime achievement in the field of computer graphics. He received his Ph.D. in computer science from the University of Utah. He lives in San Francisco with his wife and children.

AMY WALLACE is a journalist whose work has appeared in *GQ*, *Wired*, *The New Yorker*, and *The New York Times Magazine*. She currently serves as editor-at-large at *Los Angeles* magazine. Previously, she worked as a reporter and editor at the *Los Angeles Times* and wrote a monthly column for *The New York Times* Sunday Business section.

ABOUT THE TYPE

This book was set in Sabon, a typeface designed by the well-known German typographer Jan Tschichold (1902–74). Sabon's design is based upon the original letter forms of sixteenth-century French type designer Claude Garamond and was created specifically to be used for three sources: foundry type for hand composition, Linotype, and Monotype. Tschichold named his typeface for the famous Frankfurt typefounder Jacques Sabon (c. 1520–80).